BRITISH PARAMOUNTCY IN KASHMIR

1876-1894

Madhavi Yasin

PUBLISHERS & DISTRIBUTORS (P) LTD

7/22, Ansari Road, Darya Ganj, New Delhi
Tel.: +91-11-4077 5252, 2327 3880
E-mail: orders@atlanticbooks.com
Web: www.atlanticbooks.com

Published by Atlantic Publishers & Distributors (P) Ltd 2024

Printed & bound in India by Atlantic Print Services

Foreword

In order to maintain their political hegemony over India the British colonialists allowed minimum operational freedom to the rulers of the Princely States. They engineered intrigues against the ruling prince, and always made him feel insecure and consequently dependent on the paramount power for retaining control and authority. These states could, therefore, not emerge as well-knit efficiently administered, politically stable entities. This political strategy of the British colonial ruler was at its climax in the strategically important frontier state of Kashmir and has been highlighted by Mrs. Madhavi Yasin in this fascinating account of British Paramountcy in Kashmir. In a state which bordered Russia, Afghanistan and China, the British rulers of India could not tolerate a ruler who would not toe in their line of thought and action. This is abundantly clear from the role they played in installing Pratap Singh as the Maharaja of Kashmir on the death of Maharaja Ranbir Singh. Because of the strong personality of the late Maharaja the British rulers could not re-establish their Agency in the border area of Gilgit which they promptly did after his death by destabilising the state through engineering court intrigues between Pratap Singh and Amar Singh for succession to the throne. Their strangle-hold over Kashmir was complete by 1889 when they managed to depose Pratap Singh and install Amar Singh as the President of the Council which ostensibly was working under the dictates of President through fraud and forgery.

Mrs. Madhavi Yasin has brought to light through her thorough research the machinations employed by the British rulers of India in maintaining their paramountcy over the Princely States. This work therefore constitutes a valuable addition to the history of the British Rule in India.

Prof. S. Manzoor Alam
Vice Chancellor
Kashmir University, Srinagar

30th September, 1984

Preface

Maxmuller once said, "If I were to look over the whole world to find the country most richly endowed with all the wealth, power and beauty that nature can bestow—in some places a very paradise on earth—I should point to India." Obviously by paradise he meant Kashmir. Apart from its verdant beauty, resplendent lakes and sparkling springs; Kashmir also occupies a strategic position in Central Asia. The Punjab conquest took the Anglo-Indian Empire to the doors of Afghanistan, on whose North-west frontiers the galloping Russian empire had firmly entrenched itself. Another tide of the Russian expansion would have engulfed the northern India. India was the precious jewel in the British Crown, which they could ill-afford to lose. The British imperialists realised their folly in selling Kashmir to Maharaja Gulab Singh in 1848 and tried to bring it under their sphere of influence by fair or foul means. The immortal words of Kalhan, the illustrious historian of Ancient Kashmir, though far removed from the actual scene, amply illustrate the crisis in Kashmir. "This land after having been a virtuous woman, has fallen like a prostitute into the arms of the insolent. Henceforth, whoever knows how to succeed by mere intrigue will aspire to that Kingdom, whose power has gone?" The death of powerful Maharaja Ranbir Singh was a windfall to them. The British found a convenient tool in his son and successor, Maharaja Pratap Singh, though a virtuous man but no match to the British machinations.

The present work is an exercise in the re-enactment of the happenings during the years 1876-1894 A.D. The whole episode is a saga of torture and suffering.

I am very thankful for the ready assistance of the staff of National Archives of India; State Archives at Lucknow and Srinagar; The National Library and its Esplanade Reading Room, Calcutta; the Indian Council of World Affairs, New Delhi;

the Nehru Memorial Library, New Delhi; the ICHR Library, New Delhi; and S.P. Library, Lalmandi, Srinagar. The staff of the Iqbal Library, Kashmir University, Srinagar has always given me their ungrudging help.

My heartfelt gratitude is due to late Baba-i-Qaum, Shaikh Mohammad Abdullah, former Chief Minister of J & K, for his kind consideration towards me.

I acknowledge my grateful obligations to Prof. Shah Manzur Alam, Vice-Chancellor, Kashmir University for his pains in writing the Foreword to the book in spite of his pressing pre-occupations. I am also thankful to Prof. G.N. Siddiqui, the Registrar; the faculty members and administrative staff for their help and co-operation.

My thanks are due to Prof. B.R. Grover, Director of ICHR, New Delhi and his staff. Also I am grateful to Dr. Suren Agarwal, the Director of Social Sciences Documentation Centre, ICSSR, New Delhi and his staff; Prof. G.S. Dikshit Ex-Head of the Department of History, Dharwad University for his inspiring guidance.

I am also thankful to the staff of the Cultural Academy and Information Department of the State of Jammu and Kashmir for their valuable co-operation.

I gratefully acknowledge my debt of gratitude to my parents Shri Radha Krishna Tewari and Smt. Lalita Tewari for their encouragement and inspiration. I am much beholden to my brother-in-law, Prof. B.D. Misra, an eminent Sociologist for his help. My younger brother Shri Ashok Tewari has been a great help to me. Without his unsolicited sincerity and devotion, I would not have been able to weather the storms of my life. At the moment I cannot restrain my feelings and have to remember my younger brothers-in-law late Shri Chandra Mohan Pandey and Manni Lal Pandey, who were a tower of strength to me.

I thank Dr. V.K. Misri and his wife Smt. Vinita Misri for their valuable help. I thank Shri Shabbir Ahmad, Regional Director, Workers Education Centre, my Rakhi brother and Shri Arif Halim a son to me for their affection towards me.

I thank my students, wherever they may be, for they are a great source of strength to me. I thank Shri Nazir Ahmad, for typing the manuscript.

Credit goes to Prof. K.R. Gupta, Managing Director, Atlantic Publishers and Distributors for expeditiously bringing out the book. His dynamism is simply praiseworthy.

Madhavi Yasin
Srinagar

September, 23, 1984

Contents

Abbreviations

Add Mss	Additional Manuscripts
B.M.	British Museum
B.P.I.R.	British Paramountcy and Indian Renaissance
CIPD	Collections to India Political Despatches
CHI	Cambridge History of India
Cons	Consultation
Corres.	Correspondence
Confi.	Confidential
D.P.	Dufferin Papers
Ext.	External
For. Dept. Pol. Progs.	Foreign Department Political Proceedings
GOI	Government of India
H.H.P.R.	His Highness Private Records
IFP	India Foreign Proceedings
K.W.	Keep-withs
K.G.R.	Kashmir Government Records
MH	*The Marquess of Hastings* by Major Ross of Bladensburg
MINWF	Memorandum of Information regarding the North-West Frontier
PAR	Punjab Administrative Reports
PCD	Peshawar Confidential Diary
PFP	Punjab Foreign Proceedings
PP or Par. P.	Parliamentary Papers
PSDI	Political and Secret Despatches to India

PSDOC	Political and Secret Demi-Official Correspondence
PSHC	Political and Secret Home Correspondence
PSLEI	Political and Secret Letters and Enclosures from India
R.P.	Ripon Papers
Sec.	Secret
SLEI	Secret Letters and Enclosures from India
SOS	Secretary of State for India
Selections	Selections from the Vernacular News Papers
THG	*Rise and Fulfilment of British Rule* in *India* by Thompson, Edward Garrat.

Prologue

Kashmir, the 'Sentry State'[1] of the British Indian Empire, the meeting place of the three empires in the east—the British, the Russian and the Chinese was allegorically gifted away to Gulab Singh by the British.[1A] The first reference of the transfer of Jammu, Kashmir, Ladakh and Hazara occurs in the clause 12 of the treaty of Lahore, signed on March 9, 1846, after the termination of the first Anglo-Sikh war. The clause 12 stated that this territory shall be transferred by the British to Maharaja Gulab Singh, ironically, for the "loyalty of the Raja towards the Lahore Darbar", through a separate treaty.[2] This clause was inserted against the clear wishes of Rani Jindan and her advisers, which is evident from the fact that she protested vigorously against it. The separate treaty condemned as the "Sale-deed" of Kashmir, signed at Amritsar on March 16, 1846, by Mr. F. Currie and Brevet—Major Henry Montgomery Lawrence on behalf of Lord Hardinge and Gulab Singh in person.[3] After the treaty had been signed, Maharaja Gulab Singh stood up and, with joined hands, expressed his gratitude to the British Viceroy in the words that he was indeed his 'Zur *Khureed*' or 'gold-boughton slave'.[4] Lord Hardinge justified his policy as a masterstroke—in weakening the Sikh power, and creating a friendly and subordinate power on the most important frontier of India. Both would also resist the attempts on the part of any Muslim power to establish an independent State 'on this side of Indus', or even to occupy Peshawar.[5] The treaty in reality was a diplomatic move. The Punjab was still outside the British empire in India, and Russia also was far away from the Indian borders.

TIMES sometimes move faster than expected. The Second Anglo-Afghan War brought the Punjab under the domination of the British Government, and Russia advanced rapidly towards the Central Asia,[6] making the Government of India and Britain to devise a scientific frontier for India against the

Russian attack. Meanwhile, Gulab Singh, a man of foresight and vision had embarked upon the 'leap forward' policy. Gilgit was occupied by Gulab Singh in 1846. His son and successor Ranbir Singh carried on the policy of his father with the result that by the end of 1870 the Dogra rulers had acquired varied degree of control over Chilas, Ponial, Yasin, Darel, Hunza and Nagar.[7] He had an avid interest in the Central Asian trade and commerce. He established a Russian language school at Srinagar, the first of its kind in India, where Russian, and other languages were taught.[8] He despatched his agents to the Central Asian Khanates to ascertain the current political atmosphere.[9] Ranbir Singh concluded a commercial treaty with Yarkand in 1867 and apprised the Government of India of the whole affair after the Yarkandi Envoy arrived in Kashmir.[10]

At this time the British had come to know Kashmir, its beauty, and its strategic position and began to lament over the sale.[11] "No Englishman can leave Kashmir without a sigh of regret that a province so full of promise should ever have been allowed to slip through our fingers.[12] There began an active propaganda against Ranbir Singh's bona fides. The drawbacks of his administration were highlighted to convince the Government that the only panacea was annexation.[13] "The key to India is as much Kabul as Cashmere and whilst we should render the rulers of the former country subservient to our interests, we ought, without any delay, annex the latter. Expediency, the Maharaja's misgovernment, and his flagrant breach of treaty justify and, in the interests of humanity and statesmanship, demand such an annexation."[14] Maharaja's foreign policy also came under fire. They (the British) rebutted the plea forwarded by Ranbir Singh that when Gilgit, Chilas and Astore were annexed by his father, Gulab Singh, no notice was taken at that time, it was ungracious and uncharitable on the part of the British Government to make such infringement of the Treaty a ground for interference. They also attacked the capture of Shahdullah fort,[14A] on the plea that it would involve the Government of India into a war; as by the Article IX of the Treaty the British Government was to protect the

Maharaja against all external enemies, it was obvious that such little encroachments as that of Shahdullah might plunge "us into a war with Turkistan, or Bokhara, or with Russia herself."[15] A section of the press raised the point that the acquisition of Gilgit and Yasin by the Maharaja was in contravention of the article 4 of the treaty of 1846.[16] It advised the Government that the Maharaja's annexationist policy should be stalled and the Maharaja should be asked to discharge his feudatory duties so long exempted. This could be accomplished by appointing "a Political Resident with full powers" at the Kashmir Darbar, and to fix the Maharaja's boundaries at the Indus.[17]

Lord Lawrence, the Governor-General of India, did not take seriously the adverse press criticisms.[18] When Charles Aitchison, the Commissioner of Lahore, towards the close of 1867, urged the Governor-General to establish direct control over the diplomatic intercourse of the Maharaja, Lawrence ruled it out on the plea that such a requisition, "would be distasteful to the Maharaja, and any attempt to enforce it would be found nugatory."[19] Lord Mayo, while sharing the opinion of his predecessor that the press criticisms were a fig of imagination, fell in line with Aitchinson that safeguarding the interests of Kashmir required a "constant watchfulness over all (its) diplomatic proceedings."[20] Ranbir Singh had sent, with the knowledge of the Government of India, his secret agents to Tashkent in 1868.[21] But as the concerned officials were subsequently changed, the Maharaja's action was interpreted as his manipulations, "to open up direct relations with Russia."[22] Mayo administered a strong warning in 1870 to the Maharaja that he should "commit no aggression on his neighbours and make no attempt to extent his authority beyond the limits which had been conferred on his father."[23]

The interference in the Kashmir affairs dates back to 1848 *i.e.*, soon after the formation of the State, as the Government of India was receiving complaints about the oppressive rule of the Maharaja. Though on the verification it was found out that there was no truth in the allegations, nevertheless Lawrence issued a various warning to the Maharaja Gulab Singh: "The

British Government will not permit tyranny in Kashmir and the country under your rule, and that if you will not act for yourself, some other arrangement will be made for the protection of the Hill people."[24] Gradually, the grip of the Government of India was tightening over Kashmir. The succeeding Governor-General, Lord Hardinge informed the Maharaja on January 7, 1848 that an experienced officer would be sent for a few months next year in spring to know the real state of things.[25] He further added that, "If the aversion of the people to a Prince's rule should by his injustice become so miserable as to cause the people to seek his downfall, the British Government are bound by no obligation to force the people to submit to a Ruler, who has deprived himself of their allegiance by his misconduct."[26] The officiating Resident at Lahore, John Lawrence had the guts to admit that he had not heard of the Maharaja's, "having perpetrated any act of cruelty or even single oppression."[27]

Soon a windfall came into the hands of the Government of India. The European visitors in Kashmir were allowed with permission only. Lately, the Government of India had received several complaints against them.[28] The Governor-General thought that if a British Officer was posted to look after the conduct of offending Europeans he would also be able to give effect to his communication of January 7, 1948 to report about the administration of Kashmir. The Governor-General, therefore, instructed his Agent at Lahore, John Lawrence to take action accordingly. Gulab Singh after some protests accepted the proposed arrangement. The new officer came to be known as "Officer on Special Duty."[29] In the beginning the new officer had to look after only the European visitors to Kashmir during the six months of summer season. Nevertheless it was an important constitutional gain to the Government, as it was the recognition of the right of the Government of India to post their officers in the State. Gradually, the office attained the status of *genius loci*.

The British, primarily a commercial people, could not resist the lure of Central Asian trade. So far the Maharaja had imposed restrictions upon British trade through his country. It was alleged that the Maharaja's Government not only collected customs on the State borders, but also charged exorbitant rates on imports. At Leh, the State Agent was said to oppress the traders and imposed transit duties on goods passing in either direction.[30] The Anglo-Indian Press had started a vigorous propaganda against it. Kashmir was called the Cuba of the East, as it had prohibited them to trade in the region and nicknamed Maharaja's restrictive commercial policy as a close copy of Napoleon's famous 'continental system'.[31]

The Government of India approached and persuaded Ranbir Singh in 1863 to reduce duties on trade. Three years later, in January 1867, a British Agent at Leh was appointed "as an experimental measure for one season" only. Ostensibly appointed as a trade Agent, he was to collect information about the Chinese Turkistan.[32] The Maharaja was assured that the Agent at Leh in no way would interfere either directly or indirectly with his sovereign rights.[33] When the tenure of the Agent was going to expire, Ranbir Singh fervently appealed to the Governor-General through his ex-Diwan Jwala Sahai that the appointment should not be renewed, as it was derogatory to the self-respect of the Ruler and it created misgivings in the minds of his people, who regarded it, as a pledge, even a menace, of further and more direct interference in the affairs of a Kingdom which we have agreed generally to consider and treat as independent".[34]

Lord Lawrence, the Governor-General, who had not forgotten the services of the Maharaja, and the important position Kashmir held as a buffer state between Central Asia and British India, wanted to oblige him.[35] But his colleagues and the Secretary of State for India did not support him on the question of the withdrawal of the Leh Agent. The result was that the Leh Agent became a permanent feature in 1869. In 1870, as a result of a commercial agreement between the State and Government of India, the Agent was replaced by the British Commissioner at Leh[36]. The agreement was a clear case of breach of faith. The two British Officers, stationed at Srinagar and Leh, "secured for them a very strong foot-hold in the State which they effectively used, shortly afterwards, to extend their influence further."[37]

As already stated that the Maharaja had opened commercial relations with Yarkand with the knowledge of the Government of India. A Kashmiri, named Khaliq Dar, who after his return from Yarkand reported in the middle of 1873 that at Yarkand he had met a member of the Russian Mission, who suggested that there should be a direct correspondence between the Government of Russia and Kashmir Darbar. The Maharaja informed at once the Government of Punjab.[38] The Lt. Governor though appreciated the stand of the Maharaja, yet he held that the intercommunication with Russia was an imperial charge.[39] Though the Government of India did not believe in Khaliq Dar's statement, but it served their purpose, to accelerate their plan for the posting of a Resident in Kashmir. The Government despatched a commercial mission in 1873 to Yarkand headed by Sir Thomas Douglas Forsyth. The Captains Biddulph and Trotter were other members of the mission.[40] The mission was a success. Their policy of commercial penetration with the aim of subsequent domination in Central Asia was materialised. A trade mission was established at Kashgar and George Macartney was appointed as the First British Assistant for the Chinese affairs.[41]

The Government of India exploited floating rumours about Ranbir Singh's clandestine correspondence with Russia.[42] They did not believe them,[43] but the thinking gained ground that the imperial interests demanded that a British Resident in Kashmir was the need of hour to apprise them about the happenings beyond the Kashmir frontier. Lord Northbrook, the New Governor-General fully appreciated it, "The appointment .... is one of great and increasing importance. If properly filled the advantage to Government both in respect to the control of political doings of Cashmere and the information to be obtained from Central Asia will be very great."[44] Accordingly the Maharaja was informed about the Resident in Kashmir. The Maharaja was assured that the measure was only to get correct reporting about the Central Asian Affairs, "and the Viceroy has no intention of interfering more than heretofore in the internal affairs of Kashmere."[45] The Maharaja grew apprehensive, and he expressed his misgivings to the Officer on Special Duty.

On the Maharaja's request the Lt. Governor of the Punjab, R.H. Davies, met the Maharaja at Jammu in two successive interviews on December 5, 6, 1873, and explained to him that the intention of the Governor-General was in no way, "intended to indicate a change of policy, or to place him in a different position than he occupied before, and which is defined by treaty." At the second interview, the Maharaja handed over to the Lt. Governor a memorandum, which most ably defended his case. He reminded of his services to the Government of India during the revolt of Sardar Chuttur Singh in alliance with the Amir Dost Mohammad of Kabul and subsequently during the mutiny of 1857. He, unlike other Princes, did not accept any reward for his services during the crisis of 1857, instead requested the Government that, "in dealing with me (it) should keep its eyes upon my services." He received letters from Lord Canning and afterwards from Sir J. Lawrence, "that the British Government would forever keep in view the important services rendered on the occasion."[46] He cited two cases, when interference was actually made in his internal affairs.[47] He also referred Khaliq Dar's case, which he transmitted to the Government of India forthwith. In the memorandum, while he forcefully objected to the stationing of the Resident, he made two very important concessions...........that the British Officer at Leh now could remain them throughout the year, instead of only the summer season under the previous arrangement, and that the Officer on Special Duty in Kashmir could remain for eight months instead of six months.

Northbrook, having met to some extent his point, did not push the matter further,[48] but did not close the matter,[49] either. The powers of the Officer on Special Duty were increased bit by bit with each New Viceroy. In 1852, he was appointed by Lord Dalhousie merely to look after the interests of the Europeans visiting the Kashmir valley, with a stay in the State for not more than six months. During the Viceroyalty of Northbrook his stay in 1874 was extended to eight months and he was further allowed to deal with the affairs of Central Asia. Lord

Lytton in 1877 declared him to be one of the recognised channels of communication between the Maharaja and the Government of India setting aside the Government of the Punjab and Maharaja's *Mautmed*. The Punjab Government which hitherto carried out the communication with the Kashmir State, persisted its old right, which was cleared in 1881. The Punjab Government was directed that in matters of political importance, and upon business exclusively of local or political interest, the correspondence should be conducted by the Officer on Special Duty, acting in subordination to the Government of India.[51] The Maharaja's protests were also of no avail. The Officer on Special Duty gradually had gathered more powers to the detriment of the Maharaja. Lytton would have forced a Resident upon the Maharaja as is evident from his letter to Cranbrook, "Sher Ali's case is a sufficient illustration of the certainty with which 'Don't Care' brings Tommy to a bad end'.[52] The defeat of the Conservative party at the elections terminated Lytton's career in India, but his successor Ripon pursued his policy of posting a Resident in Kashmir after the death of Ranbir Singh.[53] The book brings into focus the machinations of the British Residents in Kashmir to subvert the Maharaja's authority for re-establishing the Gilgit Agency to check the Russian expansion on the frontiers of Kashmir.

References

1. Sinha, Sachchidanand, *Kashmir—The Play-ground of Asia*, 1943, p. 18.

1A. *The Calcutta Review,* Vol. VI, 1846, p. 300. "Gulab Singh has as undoubted a right to purchase, as they (the British) to sell it. In exchange for a crore of rupees they took it; and in exchange for a crore of rupees they parted with it again"; Charak, Sukhdev Singh, *History and Culture of Himalayan States,* II, pp. 307-313.

2. Saraf, Mohammad Yosuf, *Kashmiris Fight—For Freedom,* i, p. 188, Lahore, Pakistan.

3. See Appendix 1.

4. Cunningham, *History of the Sikhs*, n. 1, p. 289.

5. For. Sec. Despatch No. 8, March 19, 1846; Bal, S.S., *British Policy Towards the Punjab*, p. 80; Diver, Mand, *Royal India*, 1943, p. 251;

Pannikar, K.M., *Gulab Singh,* 1930, pp. 106-7. Lord Hardinge wrote to a near relative, "It was necessary last March to weaken the Sikhs by depriving them of Kashmir. The distance from Kashmir to Sutlej is 300 miles of very difficult mountainous country quite impracticable for six months. To keep a British force 300 miles from any possibility to support would have been an undertaking strait waistcoat and not a peerage."

6. Pal, Dharam, *Administration of Sir John Lawrence,* p. 154; Rawlinson, *England and Russia in the Far East,* pp. 370-377; Wright, *Asiatic Russia,* Vol. 1, p. 249.
7. Pannikar, K.M., *op. cit.,* pp. 141-48; Sufi, G.M.D., *Kashmir,* p. 495.
8. K.G.R., File No. 243 of 1851 (P.R.).
9. *Ibid.,* File No. 313-C & 313 & of 1865; *Ibid.,* File No. 330-A. (P.R.); *Ibid.,* File No. 329-D (P.R.).
10. For. Pol. A, No. 76, Progs., January 1868, December 25, 1867.
11. Letters from India and Kashmir, p. 163; Ansley Murray, J.C., *Our Visit to Hindostan, Kashmir and Ladak,* p. 202; Wakefield, W., *The Happy Vale,* p. 86.
12. Torrens, quoted in Saraf, M.Y., *op. cit.,* p. 201.
13. Brinckman, Arthur, *The Wrongs of Cashmere,* the book in its appendix published notices from various newspapers and other media, pp. 27-46, vide *Kashmir Papers,* (ed.) by S.N. Gadru.
14. *Ibid., Indian Public Opinion,* p. 41.

14-A. "Shah'dula is about three days journey beyond the Kara-Koram pass. The fort was provisioned and occupied by the Jamoo troops during the summer of 1865 and 1866............."

"It is true that a Government map has recently been published, which shows the boundary line of the Maharaja's territory in this direction to lie along the Kara-Kash River, and which consequently includes Shah'dula within the Jamoo dominions....." vide *Kashmir Papers,* pp. 89-90;

Gazetteer of Kashmir and Ladak, 1890, The name is given as Shahidula Khoja—Lat. 36° 24′ 57″. Long. 78° 0′. Elev. 11,780′. A camping ground on the left bank of the Karakash river, at the junction of the streams flowing down from the Kirghiz and Suget passes. It lies on the frontiers of Ladak and Yarkand territory, and is passed on the summer route from Leh by the Karakoram pass, and is also a halting-place on the Changchenmo route.

Distance from Leh by summer Karakoram route, 241 miles or sixteen marches.

Distance from Leh by Changchenmo route (western) 312¾ miles or twenty-four marches.

There are three routes from here to Yarkand, *viz.,* by the Kilik, Kilian, and Sanju Passes. The latter is most frequented route, Yarkand being by it 202½ miles or twelve marches. The Kilik route is closed to traders, though it is said to be the shortest and easiest of the three.

A road also branches off here to the west up the ravine and over the; Kirghiz pass to Kirghiz jungle, where the Kugiar (winter) route is joined. This route is very easy, and can be traversed by laden camels. It is, however, not much used, being infested by robbers. The Karakash at Shahidula takes a bend to the north-east and flows towards Khotan, winding through the Kuenlun range. The Sanju route follows its course for about 20 miles, and occasionally crosses it. The passage in summer is very difficult.

15. *Ibid.,* Thorpe, Robert, *Kashmir Misgovernment,* pp. 91-92.
16. *Ibid., Friend of India,* December 31, 1863, p. 1482; *Pioneer,* May 9, 1870, p. 3.
17. *Pioneer,* May 9, 1870, p. 3.
18. Wood Papers, Box 7B, Lawrence to Wood, October 21, 1865.
19. CIPD/96. No. 63, encls. in Political letter No. 15 Dated January 28, 1868.
20. Mayo Papers/39, No. 126, Mayo to Argyll, May 16, 1870; To the S.O.S., May 17, 1870; and enclosures, SLEI/6.
21. For. Sec. Progs., No. 82, April 1873; For. Sec. Progs., No. 131 (K.W.), August 1877.
22. For. Sec, Progs., No. 82, April 1873; For. Sec. Nos. 19-29 (K.W.), Progs., March 1875.
23. For. Sec. Progs., Nos. 34-60B, July 1877.
24. For. Sec. Progs., No. 35, January 28, 1848.
25. For. Sec. Progs., No. 44, January 28, 1848.
26. *Ibid.*, No. 43-A.
27. Lawrence to Foreign Secretary, February 28,1848, For. Sec. Progs., No. 66-70, March 31, 1848.
28. For. Pol. Progs., No. 149, February 13, 1852.
29. For. Dept., Genl. A, No. 1A-1B, April 1868; For. Dept., Pol., Nos. 82-83, December 14, 1852, John Lawrence letter to Jawala Sahai, the Diwan of Gulab Singh, January 14, 1852.
30. For. Pol., A. Progs., No. 82, November 1868.
31. Gadru, *op. cit.*, pp. 27-28, *Friend of India,* "If the British public were told of a country whence their trade is barred by prohibitory imposts, and themselves excluded...., their first thought would be China or Japan. But China and Japan have now been opened to English enterprise. If it were further explained that the country in question not only kept its own trade from us, but cut us off from the commerce of a continent, a rich mart for

our produce and a fertile land for the supply of our wanted, no one would doubt that such a land must be under the rule of a sovereign, formidable by his arms or influence, thus to kept the great British nation at bay. Such things could scarcely be believed of a feudatory of our own, lately the petty chieftain of Jammu, now through our liberality, the Maharaja of Cashmere."

32. For. Dept. Progs., Pol. A, Nos. 6-9, March 1868.
33. For. Secretary to Secretary, Punjab, February 14, 1868, No. 8, *Ibid.*
34. For. Pol. A. Progs., No. 82, November 1868, Foreign Secretary, Punjab, November 9, 1868.
35. *Ibid.*
36. The Commercial Treaty 1870, Treaties & Documents Relating to Jammu & Kashmir State, K.G.R., Srinagar.
37. Kapoor, M.L., *Kashmir Sold and Snatched*, p. 30.
38. For. Pol. Progs., Sec., Nos. 19-29, March 1875.
39. *Ibid.*, Henery Davies to Maharaja Ranbir Singh, September 26, 1873.
40. K.G.R., File No. 569 of 1873 (P.R.).
41. Hasnain, F.M., *British Policy Towards Kashmir*, p. 52.
42. For. Dept., Progs., Sec., Nos. 19-29, March 1875, No. 20. In 1872 the special correspondents of the Punjab Government in Kabul and Yarkand reported that the Maharaja Ranbir Singh had addressed a letter to the Russians saying that they should look upon his country, "as their own" and if they desired to wage a war against the Government of India, "they should avoid the Afghanistan route" and "first take Sar-Kol from the Yarkand Ruler." After that the country would be their own".
43. *Ibid.*, No. 19.
44. *Ibid.*
45. *Ibid.*
46. *Ibid.*
47. *Ibid.*, "..........Dr. Caley.........appointed in 1867 as Agent at Leh........... actually interfered in the internal affairs of the State in contravention of the settled terms of his appointment." Kapoor, M.L., *op. cit.*, p. 48, "Dr. Caley revised the Maharajas' orders about the Shawl wool without the latters' permission and hung up on the gate of the bazar a proclamation written and duly signed by him." For. Dept., Sec., Progs., Nos. 19-29, March 1875. "That in 1866 Mr. Cooper was the Officer on Special Duty in Cashmere, he remitted to the cultivators of the Valley twenty-three lakhs of arrears of land revenue standing in their names from the time of the late Maharaja, but he received a letter from Sir Donald Macleod on the subject expressing gratification at his having remitted so large an amount with the advice of and in consultation with Mr. Cooper".

48. *Ibid.*
49. Northbrook Papers, 11, pp. 12-18, Northbrook to Salisbury, March 27, 1874.
50. For. Dept., Progs., Pol. A, Nos. 269-274, No. 273.
51. For. Dept., Progs., Sec., Nos. 518-525 (K.W.), No. 524, December 1881.
52. Lytton Papers, 518/6, pp. 139-44, Letter to the S.O.S., February 25, 1880.
53. Ghose, D.K., *Kashmir in Transition,* p. 23.

1

A Brief Resume of the Constitutional Position of the Indian States

The Indian States prior to their liquidation in 1947 either with India or Pakistan presented a colourful spectacle. They boasted of domed palaces of exquisite beauty and elegance, which reposited an ancient heritage and culture. The court etiquette manifested a composite culture developed during the Muslim rule in India. The princes attired in brocade robes, wearing strings of pearls and diamonds, and fastening jewel bedecked swords, presented a sight worth capturing. Their *wazirs* (ministers) and courtiers also dressed like them and appeared as if belonging to a Mughal Age.

The Indian states during the British rule were variously called as 'Native States of India', 'Protected States of India' or 'the Feudatory States of India'. They covered nearly 45 per cent of the territory and about 24 per cent of the population before 1947.[1] These 600 odd states were different from each other in size and revenue.[2]

The origin of a majority of the Indian States lies in the disintegration of the Mughal empire after the death of Aurangzeb in 1707.[3] The provincial governors assumed independence to all intent and purposes, paying only nominal allegiance to the ghost of the Mughal Emperor.[4] The European trading companies naturally tried to take advantage of the void created in the decline of the Mughal empire. The East India Company measured swords in which the latter came out victorious. The seeds of the British Empire were planted in the battles of Plassey and Baksar.[5] The superiority of the British arms against the Indians, coupled with the consummate diplomatic skill, lifted the Company from *"primus inter pares"* to a commanding position.[6]

SECTION I: EAST INDIA COMPANY— THE PARAMOUNT POWER

The British Empire in India was built in successive stages. The first stage was the ring fence system. The system maintained buffer states on their vulnerable frontiers, *e.g.*, Oudh was made a buffer state to the British province of Bengal, to absorb the concussions resulting from the invasions of the Marathas or Abdalis. Lord Clive initiated this system in 1965, which was developed by Warren Hastings so as to enable the Company to intervene in the internal affairs of the allied states without the permission of the Ruler.[7] Warren Hastings intervened in Benares to punish the Raja for not obeying his high-handed and arbitrary demands for money. Similarly, in 1782, the Begums of Oudh were tortured and fleeced for money.[8] Lord Wellesley gave a twist to the 'ring-fence' system. The new policy or system is known as 'subsidiary alliance'. Under this system the Indian States lost their independence in matters of defence and foreign affairs. Their armies were disbanded, instead the British army was permanently stationed at strategic spots. The ring fence was converted into an iron-ring for the defence of the Indian States. The Residents were stationed in the capitals of the allied States.[9] The Directors of the Company in England were seriously perplexed and displeased with the expansionist policy of their Governor-General. They recalled him. Wellesley had to return without completing his mission.[10]

It was the Earl of Moira, better known as Marquess of Hastings, who completed the work of Wellesley. He converted 'subsidiary alliance' into 'subsidiary co-operation'. The Indian States under this system lost a large measure of internal sovereignty through the agency of the Residents. It is interesting to note that the treaties[11] under this system had recognised the internal sovereignty of the allied States; but he made the Company 'Paramount Power' in India. In his words: "Our object ought to be to render the British Government paramount in effect, if not declaredly so. We should hold the other states as vassals, in substance though not in name." He made it obligatory on the part of the allied states to fulfil two feudal duties. First, they should support the Company with all their forces at any call. Second, they should submit their mutual differences to the head of the Confederacy (East India Company).[12] The Residents in these states meddled in every conceivable matter in a bid to flaunt their authority over the rulers. They flagrantly violated the Islamic Law of succession in the vulnerable Muslim States. The Rulers' nominee, invariably was set aside against the Resident's own choice.[13]

The assertion of Company's paramountcy was more in evidence in Lord Hastings's attitude towards the Mughal Emperor. The Company until then was treating itself as the *Dewan* of the Emperor, a title bestowed upon it by the Emperor Shah Alam in 1765.[14] The British Resident at Delhi, on certain occasions, presented him the usual *nazar* in the name of the Governor-General. The money coined by the Government of India still bore the effigy of the Mughal Emperor, which was "issued in the nineteenth regnal year of Shah Alam." The Company's seals bore the phrase, which meant the recognition of the fact that the Governor-General was a servant of the Mughal Emperor. Lord Hastings abolished both the formalities, so as to 'extinguish the fiction of the Mughal government'.[15]

Lord Hastings also turned down outright the suggestion, while touring the precincts of Delhi, to pay a formal visit to the Emperor Akbar II, who had succeeded his father Shah Alam in 1806. He (Hastings) was not prepared to wait upon the Emperor as a "liege lord of the British possessions".[16] To reduce the authority of the Emperor Lord Hastings encouraged the Nawab Wazir of Oudh and Nizam of Hyderabad to disown the authority of the Emperor by dropping their titles which denoted their being a minister to the Emperor. Nawab Wazir dropped his title 'wazir', and proclaimed himself an independent monarch. But the Nizam was more shrewd to defy the authority of the Emperor.[17]

The tough line adopted by Hastings bore two important results. First, the de jure sovereignty of the Emperor *vis-a-vis* the Governor-General was extinguished along with the court ceremonials in 1827. Second, in 1835 the old coins were replaced by new ones bearing the name and image of the British sovereign.[18]

Thus, Lord Hastings raised the Company to the position of the Paramount Power in India. The subsequent Governors-General followed the lead until 1848, when the new Governor General Lord Dalhousie gave a fresh orientation to the foreign policy of the Company. His principle was "not to put aside or neglect such rightful opportunities of acquiring territory or revenue as may from time to time present themselves".[19] He changed the map of India with the speed of a lightning.[20] Had he been allowed a freehand, there would not have been left a single Indian State and the Mughal Emperor would have been deprived of his title.[21]

Lord Dalhousie completed the work of Lord Wellesley and Lord Hastings. His annexations added to the British dominions in India, a territory equal in area to Russia, with a revenue totalling four million and a half sterling.[22]

But there were sane voices within the Company itself which were against the outright annexation of the "Native States". One such man was Sir John Malcolm, one of the most human Anglo-Indian statesman with a deep understanding of Indian affairs. He said, as early as 1825: "I am decidedly of opinion that the tranquility not to say security of our vast oriental possessions is involved in the preservation of native principalities......These are also so obviously at our mercy, so entirely within our grasp that besides other and great benefits we derive from their alliances their co-existence with our rule is of itself a source of political strength, the value of which will never be known till it is lost.[23]

The fears of the non-expansionist school proved true, when the dispossessed chiefs rebelled against the Company in 1857.[24]

SECTION 2: INDIAN STATES AFTER THE REVOLT OF 1857

The revolt of 1857 in some way proved a blessing for the survival of the remaining states in India. Malcolm's sane advice had its echo in the famous words of Lord Canning, the first Governor-General of the post-rebellion period of the British India, who described the princes as the "breakwaters of the storm which would otherwise have swept over us in one great wave".[25] Queen Victoria's proclamation of 1858, dispelled the misgivings of the Indian Princes, when she said, "We desire no extension of our present territorial possession".[26] The proclamation also assured the maintenance of the existing rights, prerogatives and dignity of the princes.[27] The Government of India rewarded liberally those princes, who stood by it through the hazards of 'mutiny' with honours,[28] distinctions,[29] and rewards.[30] To scatter away the "the clouds of mistrust",[31] the Government issued *Sanads,* some 140 in all to each of the principal states of India in 1860, assuring them that in case of failure of natural heirs, their adopted sons would be recognised as their successors. Similar assurance was given to the Muslim states that every form of legitimate succession allowed under Islamic law, would be honoured.[32] Thus the era of unrestrained and unbridled annexation was over.

However, little did the Princes at that time realise that they had bartered away their freedom in exchange for security. The Princes lost their independent entity.[33] From the *de facto* sovereigns and *de jure* dependents they found themselves metamorphosed into *de facto* dependents though possessing treaties many of which recognised them as *de jure* sovereigns.[34] The *Sanads* of adoption carried with them the obligation to be loyal to the Crown.[35] Lord Canning's eulogy of the Indian Princes was a stroke of diplomacy.[36] In fact, he enunciated the principle of intervention in the internal administration of the States, as henceforth it was the moral responsibility of the British Government to protect the lives and liberties of the people in the Indian States.[37] Similar sentiments were also repeated by Lord Elgin and Lord Lawrence.[38] Lord Mayo established three principles with regard to the Princely States. First, the paramount power had to interfere in those states which were misgoverned. Second, if a well-meaning ruler was opposed to the establishment of good government by his "petty baron, mutinous troops or seditious classes of subjects", it was the imperative duty of the British Government to crush the insurgent elements and support the

Ruler. Third, a civil war within the state was not to be permitted. Speaking to an assemblage of Rajput princes, Lord Mayo said, "If we support you in your power in return we expect a good government". Thus it effected "a remarkable if a silent revolution". The position of the princes was reduced akin to that of the government officers who are punished for the neglect of duty.[39] He also started the process of bureaucratisation of administration. He encouraged his Residents to streamline the administration of the States, whenever opportunity came in the wake of regencies and minority administrations. A tradition of residential domination was created. It was a proverbial saying that the whisper of the residency was the thunder of the State. King Edward VII, when he came to India as Prince of Wales, noticed the rude and rough manners with which the British Residents treated the rulers.[40] Lord Mayo's intervention at Alwar and Tonk set the precedence. The famous example of intervention was the Baroda case. Malhar Rao Gaekward, who stood by the English during the revolt of 1857, was deposed on the fabricated charge of misgovernment, when he incurred the displeasure of the Resident.[41] This "inconvenient precedent" of deposition as an adequate punishment on grounds of "misconduct, mismanagement, and incompetency" was used indiscriminately as a model by the masterful and reforming Residents.[42]

Wardship of minor princes and their education was also the charge of the British Government. Similarly no succession to the *gaddi* was valid until approved and ratified by it.[43] The British Government had also the authority to depose, dispossess, and degrade the Indian princes. The famous cases of arbitrary deposition had taken place in Mysore,[44] Kashmir[45], Bharatpur,[46] Alwar.[47] Besides these, there have been forced abdications of political and constitutional import in Sirohi,[49] Indore,[50] Nabha[51] and Udaipur.[52]

The Crown, as the successor to the Mughal Emperor, had assumed the right of awarding the Princes titles, honours, salutes and precedence. Thus, the Nizam was honoured with the title, 'His Exalted Highness', and was permitted to add along with his other titles the designation of the Faithful Ally of the British Government. Hereditary titles were conferred and advanced on the Princes as an exclusive right of the sovereign. The title of 'His Highness' was confined only to those Princes, who enjoyed more than eleven gun salutes. The salutes indicated the status or rank of the Ruler. The highest salute consisted of twenty-one guns. The Government also reserved the right for itself of decreasing or depriving the rulers of their salutes as a punishment.[53] In 1866, the Maharaja of Datia and in 1870 the Maharaja of Jodhpur were punished by reducing the number in their salutes. The title of His or Her Highness was confined to the ruler and his consort. Such titles could not be used by the relatives of the ruling family outside the State, without the specific permission of the Crown. Thus, the *yuva Rajah* of Mysore has been given the title of His Highness. The word "Prince" was scrupulously avoided by the Government to the sons of the Princes. The sons, if they happen to be the heirs apparent, were addressed as *Maharajah Kumar* and that of the ruling nawab as *Nawabzada*. The word royalty as a generic term was not recognised for the Indian Princes. Their families were officially addressed as ruling families and not as royal families. Their governments were called '*Darbars*'.[54] The paramount power decided the precedence among the Rulers at the Imperial *Darbars*. Their decision was final.[55]

SECTION 3: INDIAN STATES VERSUS PARAMOUNTCY

The renowned jurist Sir Lesli Scott defined paramountcy as arising "out of the agreed cession of attributes of sovereignty,[56] to the Crown. This control was defined as "single charge" or "one charge". Lord Canning explained these terms meaning that the Indian States and British India had become, under the new setup, members of a single polity, presided over by the Governor-General with a dual personality.[57] In other words, the Governor-General held two offices, one, that of governing British India as an appointee of the Crown and the other looking after Indian States as a representative of the Crown. 'Single charge' or 'One charge' operated in the field of economic development of India, as a whole, *e.g.*, building of railroads, canalisation, customs, currency, salt, opium, construction of telegraph lines, and the growth of the public press.[58] The railroads from British India passed through the Indian States, and the land for the building of railroads was surrendered to the Government of India by them. The Imperial Post Offices functioned in the Indian States like the rest of India, except Gwalior, Patiala, Nabha and Jhind. The Imperial Telegraph system was extended to every state, except Kashmir, which had its own system. The British coinage was the legal tender in the Indian States. In those states which had their own coinage, the British coinage had the pre-eminence.[59] The monetary policy of the States was under the control of the Government of India.

The Indian States did feel the encroachment over their authority not only in material development but in the moral progress also. The educational institutions in the Indian States were affiliated to the Universities of nearby British Indian provinces. The High Courts in British India and the British jurisprudence became the model and type of legislation and judicial system for the States. During the minority administration and regencies, the framework of British Indian revenue administration was introduced into the States.[60]

In the international matters, the Princes had no *locus standi*. Their subjects were treated as British-protected subjects and their maritime boundaries were accepted as the British boundaries. They were bound to accept all international obligations undertaken by the Paramount Power.[61]

The Paramount Power had even the right over life of the princes. The case of Manipur was the living example. The ruling Prince of Manipur along with his supporter, also a prince were executed after trial, which pronounced them guilty of murder, despite the objections of the Queen.[62] The Government of India in a notification of August 21, 1891, pointed out that, "the principles of international law have no bearing upon the relations between the Government of India as representing the Queen Empress on the one hand, and the Native States under the suzerainty of Her Majesty on the other".[63] The Manipur affair also evolved a new constitutional doctrine that "the allegiance of the subjects of a Native State is due first to

Paramount Power and only in second degree to the authorities of his own State."[64] For the first time the claim was put forward to the direct allegiance of the subjects of the Indian States to the British sovereign.[65]

To classify the bigger and smaller states in the same category was another subtle policy of the paramountcy to curtail the powers of the bigger states. The single classification emanated from the principle of "reading all Indian treaties together."[66] This was even opined by the legal expert of the Prince, Sir Lesli Scott, who said, "The rights and duties arising from paramountcy are uniform throughout India".[67]

Lord Curzon did not allow the Indian Princes frequent travels and long periods of stay in foreign countries. He categorised such absence of the Indian Princes from their States as "a dereliction of duty".[68]

The State of Gwalior was granted permission for recruiting police battalions for internal maintenance of law and order and also to look after the revenue administration in May 1858. The condition was that "they were to constitute a police and not a military force".[69] The Maharaja Jayaji Rao Sindhia had a passion for the army. He trained his police force to the efficiency of an army. "The army was his idol; its discipline his constant occupation; the only books with which he has any acquaintance are those connected with drill and military pursuits".[70] Major Meade, Governor-General's Agent to Central Indian states, grew alarmed in April 1866, while inspecting one of the police battalions. He found it so well drilled as to be fit to take its place in line with the regular army. The Government ordered in 1867 to break-up the *Nijeebs* (police) as a military force and to refrain in future from maintaining masses of men at his capital. The Maharaja was also directed not to maintain at Gwalior more than one-half to two-thirds of his regular army. The remaining portion of the army was to be cantoned in different parts of the country.[71]

The all comprehensive nature of the British paramountcy was emphasised by Lord Curzon, when he said at Bahawalpur in 1903 that the political system of India did "not always rest upon a treaty…the sovereignty of the Crown is everywhere unchallenged. It has laid down the limitation of its own prerogative."[72] That is why Sir Charles Tupper defined the relations between the States and the Crown as feudatory.[73] There is an ample truth in the observation of Sydney Owen: "The native Prince being guaranteed in the possession of his dominions, but deprived of so many of the essential attributes of sovereignty," sinks in his own esteem, and loses that stimulus, to good government, which is supplied by the fear of rebellion and deposition. He becomes a *roi faineant*, a sensualist, an extortionate miser, or a careless and lax ruler, which is, equivalent in the East to an anarchist."[74]

References

1. Shastry, K.R.R., *Indian States,* Kitabistan, Allahabad 1941, p. 35. From the point of view of population and income, the States ranged from Hyderabad with a population of 1.4 crores and an annual income of ₹8.50 crores, to the State of Bilbari, a tiny speck too small for map, having a population of 27 and an annual income ₹ 80.00.
2. Stratchey, Sir John, *India Its Administration and Progress,* 1888, Reprinted in India, 1977, p. 483. (*Contd. on Page 11*)
3. Keene, H.G., *The Fall of the Mughal Empire,* p. 28.
4. Chandra, Satish, *Parties and Politics at the Mughal Court*, p. 259.
5. Muir, Ramsay, *The Making of British India,* Manchester, 1923, pp. 36-39.
6. Lee Warner, W., *The Protected Princes of India,* London, Macmillan & Co., 1894, p. 86.
7. CH 1, Vol. V.
8. Spear, Percival, *The Oxford History of India,* pp. 515-16.
9. PP. 1831-32, Vol. XVI, P. 240.; Thompson, Edward, Garratt, G.T., *Rise and Fulfillment of British Rule in India,* pp. 230-238; Arnold, Sir Edwin, *The Marquis of Dalhousie's Administration of British India*, London, 1862-65, ii, pp. 7-8.
10. PP. 1831-32, Vol. XVI, p. 240.
11. *British Paramountcy and Indian Renaissance,* I, p. 15. The *modus operandi* of the annexation of the Indian States is thus described by the Marquess of Hastings: "In our treaties we recognise them as independent sovereigns. Then we send a Resident to their Courts. Instead of acting in the character of an ambassador, he assumes the functions of a dictator; interferes in all their private concerns; countenances refractory subjects against them; and makes the most ostentatious exhibition of this exercise of authority. To secure to himself the support of our

(Contd. from page 10)

The following list shows the area, population, and approximate revenue of the Principal Native States:—

	Square Miles	Population	Approximate Revenue	Religion of Ruler
Haiderabad (Nizam)	82,700	11,141,000	3,300,000	Mohammedan
Bhopal	6,990	666,000	270,000	-do-
Bahawalpur	17,300	720,000	137,000	-do-
Gwalior (Sindhia)	25,000	3,000,000	1,092,000	Hindu
Indore (Holkar)	8,400	851,000	570,000	-do-
Baroda (Gaekward)	8,100	1,950,000	1,130,000	-do-
Mysore	29,400	5,539,000	1,250,000	-do-
Travancore	7,100	2,950,000	663,000	-do-
Jaipur	15,500	2,700,000	455,000	-do-
Jodhpur	35,000	2,000,000	343,000	-do-
Udaipur	12,700	1,000,000	247,000	-do-
Bikaner	23,300	584,000	143,000	-do-
Rewah	12,600	1,320,000	107,000	-do-
Kutch	7,600	450,000	131,000	-do-
Patiala	5,400	1,597,000	411,000	Sikh
Kashmir	80,900	2,906,000	460,000	Hindu

Government, he urges some *interest* which, under the colour thrown upon it by him, is strenuously taken up by our Council and the Government identifies itself with the Resident not only on the single point but also on the whole tenor of his conduct. In nothing do we violate the feelings of the native princes so much as in the decisions which we claim the privilege of pronouncing with regard to the succession to the *musnud*".

12. *The Private Journal of the Marquess of Hastings,* pp. 30-a; Singh, Raghubir, *Indian States and the New Regime,* Bombay, Taraporewala, 1938, p. 22; *Thompson, Edward, The Making of the Indian Princes,* p. 285; Mehta, *M.S. Lord Hastings and the Indian States*, p. 242.
13. *The Private Journal of the Marquess of Hastings*, pp. 26-27.
14. Punaiah, K.V., *The Constitutional History of India*, p. 16.
15. Keith, A.B., *A Constitutional History of India,* p. 117; Spear, P., *Twilight of the Mughal Empire,* p. 45; Blandenburg, Major Ross, *The Marquess of Hastings,* p. 191; B.P.I.R., I, pp. 17-18.
16. *Ibid.*
17. MH, p. 190, Lord Hastings encouraged the Rulers of Oudh and Hyderabad with the motive "that it would benefit British interests, by dividing the Muhammadans among themselves, and by weakening the moral power of the house of Timur which nominally reigned at Delhi".
18. CHI, V, p. 606.
19. Dalhousie's Minute, dated August 30, 1848, quoted in Lee Warner's '*Life of Marquis of Dalhousie*', London 1904, ii, p. 116.
20. THG, p. 353.
21. Keith, A.B., *op. cit.*, p. 124.
22. Arnold, Sir Edwin, *The Marquis of Dalhousie's Administration of British India,* London, 1862-1865, II, p. 5. At another place he says; In 1853 "The Nizam came into our power by a process which has been often and successfully repeated in our Indian annals. There is a curious phenomenon in the insect world where an egg is deposited in the body of living creature which nourishes itself upon the substance of its unwilling nurse, gradually taking up all the fat, flesh and tissues of the victim, till it dies, or drags on a futile existence. Our Government in India has frequently laid such an egg in the shape of 'a Contingent' within the confines of friendly states. Oudh, Gwalior, and the territories of Scindia were thus treated, and by no other means were the dominions of the Nizam brought within the grasp of Lord Dalhousie."
23. Panikkar, K.M., *An Introduction to the Study of the Relation of Indian States with the Government of India*, 1927, p. XXIV.

24. Sen, Surendra Nath, *Eighteen Fifty Seven,* Delhi, Publications: Division, 1957, pp. 38-39.
25. White Paper on Indian States, *n* 2, 12.
26. C.H.I., VI, p. 493.
27. White Paper on Indian States, *n.* 2, 12.
28. For. Pol. Dept., Nos. 607-52, Part A, April 1860, *e.g.*, in case of Sirohi, half the yearly tribute with all arrears; of Jhalawar, one year's tribute; and of Karauli, a portion of the debt of the State, were remitted.
29. In 1861, the order of the Star of India was founded and bestowed on many of the leading princes. CHI, VI, p. 495.
30. Maharajas of Benaras and Rewa were rewarded, For. Pol. Dept., Political Despatch from the Secretary of State to the Government of India, No. 2, 12 January, 1860. Besides *Khillats* valued in tens of thousands of rupees were granted to the Rulers and, in the case of the Ruler of Tonk, his gun salute was increased from 15 to 17; *Ibid.,* Progs. Nos. 607-52, Part A, April 1860; No. 2, January 12, 1860, and No. 18, March 1860; Phadnis, Urmila, *Towards the Integration of the Indian States,* 1919-1947, 1968, p. 9.
31. *Ibid.,* No. 261, Part A, June 1860.
32. Pannikar, K.M., *op. cit.*, p. 57; Stratchey, *op. cit.*, pp. 462-63.
33. Pannikar, *op. cit.*, p. 34; B.P. I.R., I, p. 961, "The Crown of England", Canning declared, "was for the first time brought face to face with the *feudatories,* and there was a reality in the suzerainty of the sovereign of England, which never existed before, and which was eagerly acknowledged by the chiefs"; Lee Warner, *Native States of India,* p. 164.
34. CHI, V, p. 492; Selections, *Nasim-i-Agra,* June 23, 1888, the conduct of the British Government resembles that of the old man in the *Gulistan,* who saved a lamb from a wolf, but subsequently killed and ate it himself; *Ibid., The Tuti-i-Hind* (Meerut), July 8, 1888; *Ibid., The Azad,* July 13, 1888.
35. For. Pol. Dept., No. 376-82, Political A, March 18, 1862.
36. Walrond, T., ed., *Elgin's Letters and Journals,* London, John Murray, 1872, pp. 422-3.
37. For. Pol. Dept., Political Despatch of Lord Canning to Sir Charles Wood, No. 43 A, April 30, 1860.
38. *Philips, C.H., Evolution of India and Pakistan,* p. 417.
39. Pannikar, *op. cit.*, pp. 35-37.
40. Low, Sydney, *A Vision of India,* p. 136.
41. For. Pol. Dept., Progs., No. 9-86, July 1875.
42. Mallet, B., *Earl of Northbrook—A Memoir,* London, Longmans: Green & Co., 1875, p. 96.
43. Parliamentary Papers, Vo. 59, Paper 392, p. 413.

44. Stratchey, J., *op. cit.*, p. 459.
45. Lansdowne to Hutchins, No. 198, November 9, 1891, Lansdowne Letters to Persons in India; Resident to Maharaja Pratap Singh 11C, April 17, 1889, For. Sec. E. Pros., May 1889, No. 563.
46. F.P.D. Progs., No. 284-97, Internal, August, 1889.
47. Pannikar, *op. cit.*, p. 61.
48. CHI, p. 498; Aitchison, C.U., *Treaties, Engagements and Sanads,* III, p. 322. With Alwar there was a treaty of 1803, by which the Company became "guarantee........for the security of his country against external enemies", and at the same time engaged not to "interfere with the country" of the Raja.
49. For. Pol. Dept., No. 142-4, Part A, December 1861.
50. All India States Peoples Conference, *Memorandum of Indian States' Peoples,* Bombay, p. 35.
51. Pannikar, *op. cit.*, *n.* 77, pp. 60-67.
52. *Ibid.*
53. Pannikar, *op. cit.*, p. 73.
54. Pannikar, *op. cit.*, p. 74.
55. Keith, *op. cit.*, p. 221.
56. *Butler Committee Report*, p. 64.
57. B.P.I.R., I, p. 964.
58. Pannikar, *op. cit.*, pp. 53, 124.
59. B.P.I.R., I, p. 963.
60. *Ibid.,* p. 964.
61. Phadnis, Urmila, *op. cit.*, p. 15.
62. Appeal to the Governor-General in Council by the ladies of the royal family of Manipur (Proceedings of the Indian Historical Records Commission, Vol. XXXV), p. 35; Lansdowne Papers, Cross to Lansdowne No. 26, July 19, 1891; *The Amrit Bazar Patrika,* May 12, 1981.
63. Keith, A.B., *op. cit.*, p. 215.
64. Lansdowne Papers, to the S.O.S., No. 33, June 23, 1891.
65. Pannikar, K.M., *op. cit.*, p. 57; Misra, J.P., *The Administration of India Under Lord Lansdowne,* p. 96.
66. Lee Warner, *op. cit.*, p. 256; Raleigh, *Curzon in India,* p. 226.
67. *Butler Committee Report*, p. 70.
68. Ronaldshay, *Life on Curzon,* II, p. 91.
69. B.P.I.R., I, p. 995.
70. Daly, Major H., *Memoirs of General Sir Herbert D. Daly*, 1905, p. 267.
71. Thoronton, T.H., *General Sir Richard Meade and the Feudatory States of Central and Southern India*, 1898, p. 116.

72. Raleigh, Thomas, ed., *Lord Curzon in India,* Being a Selection from his speeches as Viceroy and Governor-General of India 1898-1905, Vol. I, p. 247.
73. Tupper, C., *Our Indian Protectorate,* quoted in Lee Warner, pp. 3, 376.
74. Owen, Sydney, *A Selection from the Despatches of Wellesley,* p. XXVII; Selections, *The Kannuj Punch,* October 15, 1888, prints a Cartoon: A strong and stout European is represented as conversing with a *Nawab* and a *Raja,* who are mere skeletons. The letter-press is as follows:

    European—"Why are you so lean"?

    Nawab & Raja—"We have become so lean owing to the mischievous proceedings of the Residents."

2

British Paramountcy and Kashmir

"Who has not heard of the vale of Cashmere, with its roses, the brightest earth ever gave,..........Its temples, and grottos, and fountains as clear as the love-lighted eyes that hang over the waves?"[1]

Kashmir-*be-nazir* (without an equal), Kashmir-*Junat-i-puzir* (equal to paradise) is an extensive alluvial vale bounded on the west by the Suleiman mountains, on the east, south-east by the river Sutlej, and on the north by the Himalayas, the most elevated and stupendous of the mountain systems in the world. This biggest Valley on the earth is noted for its flora and fauna, for its shimmering and sparkling springs, for its *chinars* and, *safedas* (poplars), for its snow capped mountains and emerald green jungles, and for the beauty and elegance of its maidens with doe eyes and black hair. This earthly paradise in reality is without a peer, and is created for the poets to sing its praises. Naturally, it made Bernier, the first European who entered Kashmir in 1665, to write: "In truth, the Kingdom surpasses in beauty all that my warmest imagination had anticipated."[2] In form it is irregularly oblong, lying northwest and south-east, with 84 miles in length and 20 miles in breadth at its broadcast part. It has an area of 4,800 square miles, and an average height of 5,200 feet above the seal level.[3]

Ironically, its beauty and charm is the cause of its misfortune. For centuries together it has suffered the tyrannies of an unwanted rule. In 1846, the land was sold to Gulab Singh, a vassal of the Sikh rulers, during the first Anglo-Sikh war by Lord Hardinge, the Governor-General of the East India Company for 75 lakhs of rupees or £750,000 as a price for his perfidy against his masters.[4] According to Article 1 of the treaty, the East India Company made over to Gulab Singh and the heirs male of his body forever, in independent possession, all the hilly and mountainous country, situated to the eastward of the river Indus and westward of the river Ravi including Chamba and excluding Lahoul, being part of the territories ceded to the British Government by the Lahore State, according to the provision of Article VI of the Treaty of Lahore dated March 9, 1846.[5] But much water had washed down the Jhelum since 1846 to 1884. The Russian expansion towards Central Asia[6] gave shudders to the Anglo-Indian bureaucracy, which resulted in a policy known as the 'Forward Policy.'[7] During the late seventies of the nineteenth century this policy was experimented by Lord Lytton in his second Anglo-Afghan war,[8] which by its utter failure crushed his political career in India.[9] Nevertheless, the policy was not abandoned, and it formed one of the items of the political manifesto of the Conservative party. Despite of Lord Lytton's *faux pas* in the Afghan imbroglio, he was a strategist... par...excellence. He formulated a new policy of checking the advance of Russia towards India by controlling the trans-frontier of Kashmir. He was guided in this Policy by P.D. Henderson of the Foreign Department, who favoured the appointment of a Resident in Kashmir.[10] The Government of India, evinced a keen interest in the region, since 1870, when it despatched Doughlas Forsyth on a commercial mission to Yarkand. He was instructed to explore the area on his way. He was sent for a second time also. This time he made startling discoveries. He explored that the Baroghil and the Karambar or Ishkaman were the principal passes of the great range separating Chitral and Yasin from the Valley of Oxus. The first pass led from Sarhad in Wakhan to Chitral and second to Yasin and the Gilgit valley. The second pass held a great strategic value, as it commanded the first pass.[11] Doughlas Forsyth's mission corrected a mistake held for a long time that Gilgit and not the Pamirs was really the roof of the world. His fresh and scientific knowledge of the trans-Kashmir frontier made him to suggest that an Agent at Gilgit to be stationed to elicit correct information of the region which until then were a closed book for them. The proposed Agent would be able to communicate with the Amir of Wakhan.[12]

SECTION 1: GILGIT— THE NORTHERN GATE OF INDIA

Gilgit, the Gibraltar on land was known as Sargin in ancient times.[12A] In ancient Sanskrit literature the place was probably known as Gohalta and the area was ruled by Hindu Rajas with the title *Ra*. Shri Badat was the last of the Hindu rulers.[13] The importance of Gilgit to any ruler of northern India lay in its strategic position. It's difficult terrain rugged and inhospitable physical features lend Kashmir an impregnable frontier. Located in the lap of the Himalayas its numerous deep valleys and mountains make it inaccessible and invincible. Within a radius of 56 miles around Gilgit, there are innumerable peaks. Eleven peaks varying from 18,000 feet to 20,000 feet, seven from 20,000 to 22,000 feet, six from 22,000 to 24,000 and eight from 24,000 to 26,000 feet.[14] It covers all the passes over the Hindu Kush, from the eastern most one, the Shimshal to those at the head of the Yasin River in the west. All these passes descend to the Valley of the Gilgit River and its tributaries. Further, "it affords us a direct communication through Kashmir territory to the protected State of Chitral, which would be otherwise removed from our influence by the interposition of countries at present close to us."[15]

SECTION 2: THE MADHOPUR SETTLEMENT

The recent knowledge of the Hindu Kush region made the Government of India keen to control over the Baroghil pass and especially Ishkaman pass[16] to contain the Russian offensive on the north-west frontier. The best course to get control over the passes was through the State of Jammu and Kashmir. Lord Lytton, the Governor-General of India, whose life ambition was to give a scientific frontier to the Indian Empire, gladly took over the project. To him both Afghanistan and Kashmir were "indivisible parts of a single imperial question."[17] It would indirectly secure for the British, "a vicarious but virtual" control over the tribal territories without costing anything.[18] The Maharaja of Kashmir was not to be given unbridled authority to bring the tribes under his control. But the consent was circumvented with the condition that

British officers were to be located in Gilgit or elsewhere in his territory throughout the year. Moreover, the British troops were also to be stationed at Gilgit, when deemed necessary, by the Indian Government. The Foreign Department sagaciously enough tried "to gild the pill still more" by bestowing a number of favours on the Maharaja.[19] The concessions were to grant the Maharaja and his successors the title of "Maharaja Adhiraj", presenting of a mountain battery and 1,000 Enfield rifles and stripping off the Officer on Special Duty in Kashmir of all political powers, except to maintain law and order among the visitors.[20] With these intentions Lord Lytton called upon the Maharaja Ranbir Singh on November 17 and 18, 1876 at Madhopur.[21]

Lord Lytton apprised the Maharaja of the alarming and volatile situation in the region in the wake of the galloping Russian imperialism. In order to check it the Maharaja ought to procure control over Chitral and Yasin. The Maharaja was overjoyed, but he requested that the agreement should be put in writing—to empower him to commence negotiations. Lord Lytton then broached the real issue of stationing of a Political Officer at Gilgit. The Maharaja had qualms over the appointment. He had the bitter taste of the Political Officer at Leh a decade earlier. Dr. Cayley, the Political Officer at Leh, had acted as an open sesame to the entire frontier of Kashmir to the British surveillance. At one stage the negotiations were about to breakdown, but the diplomat in the Maharaja triumphed and he accepted the British Agent at Gilgit, while Lord Lytton shelved his plan for a British Resident in that State.[23] Thus, the Madhopur settlement was made in a spirit of give and take. It resulted in the establishment of the Gilgit Agency and Captain Biddulph became the first Political Agent at Gilgit in 1877.

SECTION 3: STATIONING AND WITHDRAWAL OF THE BRITISH AGENT

Lord Lytton charged John Biddulph, in contravene of the written assurance made to the Maharaja, to involve, himself in active politicking in the neighbouring tribes and to obtain reliable information in regard to occurrences beyond the border.[24] Biddulph took over the charge with a dedicated mission. The attitude of the tribes was unfriendly towards the British. A systematic and continuous propaganda against the British was carried on at the behest of the acting Governor, Bhai Gurbuksh Singh of Gilgit, long before the arrival of Biddulph.[25] He was harassed, and all sorts of troubles were created for him.[26] Being distraught, he complained against the Governor of Gilgit to the Maharaja. Maharaja immediately replaced the Governor, but took no responsibility for the safety of the Resident.[27]

Biddulph got involved in the tribal politics, without any knowledge of their flexible nature, volatile temperament and changing loyalties or allegiances. He was not actively helped by the Maharaja. There were transit difficulties. The Maharaja made no efforts towards the construction and repairs of the roads towards Gilgit. Even the Chief of Yasin, Pahelwan Bahadur, who was friendly to him, unpredictably became hostile and mounted on offensive. The Chiefs, Jaffar Khan of Nagar and Aman-ul-Mulk of Chitral, formerly distrusted by Biddulph came to his rescue. By their timely help and prompt action, Pahelwan Bahadur's moves were foiled. He was forced to fly almost alone into Wakhan.[28] Though the danger was averted, the new Governor-General, Lord Ripon, allergic to the strategy of "Forward Policy", withdrew temporarily the Gilgit Agency.[29] He was of the opinion that the British Agency at Gilgit could only be kept at the expense of embarrassment and dangers quite disproportionate to the gain arising out of it. The conditions were such that its continuance was neither beneficial to the Imperial Government nor to the Maharaja.[30] Moreover, it was impolitic to leave altogether in the hands of the Kashmir Darbar the management of affairs on the northern frontiers of the state.[31]

The Gilgit Agency failed because of lack of co-ordination and trust between Biddulph, the Agent at Gilgit and Henvy, the Officer on Special Duty in Kashmir. Henvy was indiscreet in his dealings with the Maharaja. Similarly, Biddulph flirted with the most impracticable schemes of sowing dissensions among the tribes, disobeyed orders on a number of occasions, mishandled his dispute with the Governor of Gilgit, and failed to gain any influence over the tribal chiefs.[32] His arrogance earned him the title "The Emperor of the Age."[33] Second, the position of Agency in the most inhospitable and uncongenial region, with the people past master in double dealings, intrigues and squabbles hampered the smooth functioning of the Agency.[34] Third, the Gilgit Agency was involved into the petty intrigues of local politics, and lost credit and respect. Fourth, the means of communications between Srinagar and Gilgit were inadequate and inefficient. Timely supply of men and material to Gilgit in any emergency was impossible.[35] Fifth, the Gilgit Army, the mainstay of the Agency was utterly incompetent and weak. It was, "ill-paid, ill-fed and ill-disciplined" and majority of the men were sick and old, and thus "unfit for an active service in a mountainous country."[36] Lastly, Ripon terminated the Gilgit Agency as he took it as a part of the forward policy, which contained the danger of involvement in the petty intrigues of the small states beyond the Kashmir border, and at the same time it was likely to excite the suspicions of the Maharaja as well as of the Afghan Amir. Yasinee attack on Gilgit in October 1880 further reinforced his resolve.[37]

Even Lytton admitted towards the fag end of his Indian career that the Gilgit arrangement was a complete muddle.[38]

Biddulph reacted strongly against the Government's decision for withdrawing the Gilgit Agency, as it would give a lever to the Maharaja "to prosecute his intrigues to greater advantage." He would boast to the Indian princes that he had got rid of the presence of a British Political Agent, deriving lessons from the examples of the King of Burma and the Amir of Kabul.[39]

Under the Madhopur settlement the Government of India gave a written assurance to the Maharaja to deal with the tribes beyond his borders. Maharaja also profited by the grant of five thousand rifles and a well-equipped battery. Lack of rapport between the Agent at Gilgit and Maharaja was responsible for the breakdown of Madhopur Settlement, when the Gilgit Agency was withdrawn in 1881. However it was a temporary measure. The Madhopur Settlement was a precursor to the British Residency in Jammu and Kashmir State, and the posting of a permanent Agency at Gilgit.

SECTION 4: BRITISH RESIDENT IN KASHMIR

Biddulph's warning was catalytic. The Government of India for a long time was thinking of posting a Resident in Kashmir. But the treaty concluded, with Gulab Singh had no provision for installing a Resident in the State. Moreover, the Government of India was afraid of the powerful personality of Ranbir Singh, and it did not dare impose a Resident. The idea was in the air since 1848 from the time of Lord Hardinge. In 1851 the idea again dominated the official circles, when an Officer on Special duty for the summer months was appointed without any political duty. In the meantime the Officer on Special Duty was designated Political Agent and Justice of Peace in 1872.[40] Mixed courts were established under the authority of the Officer on Special Duty.[41] Prior to 1872, European visitors without the permission of the Maharaja were not allowed to stay beyond the middle of October. Lord Northbrook, the Governor General of India revoked it, in spite of the severe remonstrance's from the Maharaja.[42] Until 1877 the affairs of Kashmir were conducted through the Punjab Government, but the Government of India in the same year took over direct charge. In 1877, the Government of India divested the Punjab Government, of the charge of Kashmir affairs. This was the prelude to the appointment of a Resident in Kashmir. Lord Northbrook tried to station a Resident in Kashmir in 1873.[43] But the proposal was stoutly opposed by the Maharaja.[44] He submitted a Memorandum clarifying his stand against the appointment of a Resident.[45] He reminded the Government of India of the services of his father Gulab Singh to the British Empire. His father rendered valuable services to the Government of India during the revolt of Sardar 'Chuttur Singh' in alliance with Amir Dost Mohammad of Kabul. Further, during the revolt of 1857, his father remained not only faithful but rendered active help also. After the suppression of revolt the Government of India awarded territories and *jagirs* in grateful acknowledgement to the services of the loyal princes. The Maharaja of Kashmir declined to receive any gift either in the form of territory or *jagir*, instead he solicited that in future the Government of India in its dealings, with his state 'should keep its eyes upon my services.' Lord Canning then acquiesced in. The Maharaja further cited the cases of the States of Patiala, Jhind and Nabha, which were not only awarded *jagirs* and extension of powers in lieu of their services during the mutiny, but were still more favoured by the removal of the agencies in their respective States. But the reward for his loyalty was in depriving him of the privilege he had before and had all along been enjoying by posting a Resident in his state.[46] In his memorandum he made two important concessions to the Government of India. The first was that the Joint Commissioner of Ladakh could stay at Leh, while the second was to allow the Officer on Special Duty in Kashmir to stay at Srinagar for eight months instead of six months. Nevertheless, he opposed the stationing of the Resident. He also submitted that to prove his sincerity he was prepared to "allow one of his sons to be detained in the British territory as hostage".[47]

Lord Northbrook, meanwhile, was apprised of a startling disclosure that, before the Treaty of Amritsar was concluded in 1846, Lord Hardinge had decided "after full consideration" with Sir Henry Lawrence and Sir F. Currie, who later on negotiated the Treaty, to promise to Maharaja Gulab Singh that "as long as His Highness remained faithful to the conditions of the treaty and loyal to the British Government, no interference with his Government would be attempted by us and no Resident established at his capital".[48] This promise was conveyed to Maharaja Gulab Singh by Sir F. Currie in the presence of Sir Henry Lawrence and Jwala Sahai, the Diwan of the State. Currie was against the stationing of the Resident. The Secretary of State, Lord Argyll concurred with Currie that such a course would be virtually a penal measure.[49] Lord Northbrook bound down by the dictates of the Secretary of State,[50] ransacked the files of the Foreign Department in a bid to find out Hardinge's letters in question, but failed to trace it in them the supposed promise.[51] He conveyed his misgivings to Lord Salisbury, the Secretary of State, who appreciated his reasoning and stand.[53] Hence the matter was not closed and options were open.

P.D. Henderson of the Foreign Department in his note of November 8, 1879 again opened the matter.[53] The note contained that the chief interest in Kashmir was presumably to secure the services of the Maharaja in dealing with the trans-frontier politics. Therefore, the important question was, "how will this object be effected by the appointment of a Resident". Maharaja Ranbir Singh had a prognostication of such a possibility.[54]

The note further said that the absence of a Resident had given a free hand to the Maharaja in his dealings with the trans-frontier states. The 'Foreign States' would not have intrigued with him against the Government of India, if his subordinate position would have known to them.[55] A.C. Lyall, the Foreign Secretary, on November 19, 1879, wrote his own Memorandum on receiving the above-mentioned note. In his Memorandum, A.C. Lyall fully agreed with Henderson that the Maharaja was most solicitous for pressing his position as an independent *Sirdar*. He aimed at extending his influence and establishing relations with neighbouring powers. He also, probably, considered it prudent to maintain good relations with Russia. Still, the Foreign Secretary did not think worth his while to post a Resident with large powers, as it would amount to direct interference in the internal administration of Kashmir. Thus, the deputation of a permanent Resident to superintend such interference would put in the reverse gear the whole policy up to date with regard to Kashmir. It would be strongly protested by the Maharaja, and would damage the reputation of the Government of India in the eyes of the Indian States.

For two years the matter was hanging fire. The issue was opened up by H.M. Durand, who clarified that Northbrook never shut the door for the appointment of a Resident. He consented not to call the Officer on Special Duty a Resident. But there was no doubt that he regarded the Officer on Special Duty as a political officer, and intended him to be treated as such in all respects. Durand opined that the designation of the Officer on Special Duty ought to be changed to Resident and sooner the better.[57] A.C. Lyall, who was still the Foreign Secretary agreed with his Deputy's suggestion, but both of them did not insist upon it.[58]

In June 1882 the Foreign Department received a report from its Officer on Special Duty on the serious condition of Ranbir Singh and of his imminent death.[59] H.M. Durand again raked up the matter.[60] C. Grant, who was the new Foreign Secretary, differed with his Deputy saying that the exigencies of the situation did not warrant forcing a Resident Political Officer on the new Maharaja. The Viceroy Lord Ripon agreed with his Foreign Secretary.[61]

Meanwhile the ailing Maharaja, who in 1882 had already made a request to the Government of India to nominate his youngest son Amar Singh as his successor—as the latter was "wiser" than his other two brothers, Pratap Singh and Ram Singh—repeated it in 1884 as well.[62] Lord Ripon, had, with the approval of the Secretary of State, decided to proclaim Pratap Singh, the eldest son of Maharaja Ranbir Singh, as the Maharaja of Kashmir, and to post a Resident in the State, who should replace the Officer on Special Duty on the new Maharaja.[63] The new Maharaja was also to be instructed to carry out a set of reforms.[64] Thus, before his departure Lord Ripon had laid down the blue print of the policy for the appointment of the Resident in Kashmir, after the death of Ranbir Singh.

Maharaja Ranbir Singh breathed his last at 4.30 p.m. on September 12, 1885.[65] On September 13, 1885 St. John, the Officer on Special Duty informed Pratap Singh in the presence of Diwan Anant Ram, Babu Nilambar Mukherjee and Govind Sahai, the councillors of the late Maharaja, that he was recognised as the Maharaja by the Government of India. Maharaja was directed to introduce certain reforms forthwith and he (St. John) was promoted to the rank of the Resident.[66] The last message was received as an unexpected blow. In the evening Babu Nilambar called on St. John and asked for the clarification for the Maharaja's information, the meaning of the "assistance of a Resident." St. John replied that he would leave all the active work of administration to the Darbar, but he should be informed of any matter in detail, which he thought proper to know. He would give advice, if asked for, and if he thought proper he would also give advice on his own, which was to be obeyed.[67] On September 16, Babu Nilambar called on St. John, and delivered a message from the Maharaja. The Maharaja desired that the appointment of the Resident should be deferred for some time, so that he should streamline the administration according to his plan, which he had thought of long ago. Babu Nilambar finally came to the point that main objection was to the name of 'Resident'. The Resident replied that he regretted that under the present circumstances he could not recommend to the Governor General any delay in the formal appointment of a Resident.[68]

Maharaja Pratap Singh knocked at the door of the Governor-General to get the appointment of the Resident cancelled. On September 18, 1885 he wrote that he was very much pained to learn that he was given no time to show his merits as an administrator. He had certain plans to improve the administrative setup. The change in the designation from the Officer on Special Duty to the Resident would lower his position in the State.[69]

The Government of India rejected the appeal, as it was not an innovation to appoint a Resident in a Princely State. The great Princes and Chiefs of India had Residents in their courts.[70]

Lord Dufferin assured the Maharaja that the appointment of the Resident was not made with any ulterior motive to interfere in his administration unnecessarily and improperly. Sir Oliver St. John would assist him with friendly advice only and implementation of the reforms would be left, as far as possible, to his government.[71]

Maharaja Pratap Singh was formally proclaimed the ruler on the afternoon of September 25, 1885. The same day St. John became the first Resident in Jammu and Kashmir State.[72] Babu Nilambar Mukherjee read out a manifesto in English, an

48. Currie to Argyll, November 27, 1873, also Northbrook to Davies, December 27, 1873, For. Sec., Nos. 19-29, Progs., March 1875; Argyll to Northbrook, November 28, 1873, Northbrook Papers, 9, pp. 103-5.
49. Northbrook Papers, 9, pp. 103-4, Argyll to Northbrook, November 28, 1873.
50. For. Sec., Nos. 19-29, Progs., March 1875, Northbrook to Davies, December 27, 1873, and March 25, 1874. Northbrook wrote, "... I should be exceedingly sorry to urge upon the Maharaja any course which should be distasteful to His Highness's feelings".
51. Northbrook Papers, 11, pp. 12-18, Northbrook to Salisbury, March 27, 1874.
52. *Ibid.,* pp. 12-15, Salisbury to Northbrook, April 24, 1874.
53. Henderson to A.C. Lyall, November 8, 1879, For. Sec., No. 86, Progs., March 1883.
54. Digby, William, *Condemned Unheard,* 1890, pp. 7-8. An instance of Maharaja's foresight is provided by the account of Mr. Edward E. Meakin's informal meeting with Maharaja, when he asked, "Sahib, what do you call that little thing between the railway carriages? It is like a button stuck on a sort of gigantic needle that runs through the train, and when the carriages are pushed at one end on the other you hear a "houff, houff", and bang they go against the poor button. I felt very sorry for the poor little button, but it is doubtless useful in its way. What do you call it?" I replied that I believed it was called a "buffer". "Buffer Buffer", repeated the Maharaja in earnest tones. 'Yes, buffer, that is just what I am, and that shall henceforth be one of my titles". "......On one side of me there is the big train of the British possessions and whenever they push northward they will tilt up against me, then on the other side is the shaky concern Afghanistan, and on the other side of it is the ponderous train and engine called Roos. Every now and then there is a tilting of Roos towards Afghanistan, and simultaneously there is a tilting upwards of the great engine in Calcutta, and I am the poor little button between them. Someday, perhaps not far distant, there will be a tilting from the North, and Afghanistan will smash up. Then there will be a tremendous tilt from the South, and I shall be buried in the wreck and lost! It may not come in my time, but it is sure to come when that poor little button is on the pin'... Pointing to his son, the present Maharaja......".
55. For. Sec., No. 86, Progs., March 1883.
56. R.P./I.S. 290/7, Vol. IV, pp. 180 (a)—(b), Ripon to Halifax November 17, 1883.
57. For. Sec., Nos. 518-25, K.W., Progs., August 1881.
58. *Ibid.*
59. Officer on Special Duty to Foreign Secretary, June 28, 1882, For. Sec. E. No. 427, Progs., January 1883.

60. For, Sec, E. Nos. 427-30 (K.W.), Progs. January 1883.
61. *Ibid.*
62. Henvy to C. Grant, December 14, 1882. For. Sec., No. 353, K.W., Progs., May 1884.
63. Despatch of the Govt, of India, April 7, 1884, and Despatch of the Sec. of State, May 23, 1884, Par. Papers, 1890, Vol. IV, pp. 231 ff., Government of India to Secretary of State, April 7, 1884, For. Sec., E., No. 354, Progs., May 1894.
64. *Ibid.*
65. For. Dept., Sec. E., March 1889, No., 107-200; D.P., Reel 518, No., 243, to the S.O.S., September 17, 1885.; K.G.R., Jammu, Private Department, Records of Maharaja Pratap Singh.
66. D.P., Reel 519, p. 85, Letter to the S.O.S.. September 17, 1885.
67. From Resident in Kashmir to Secretary to the Government of India, Foreign Department, Jammu, September 16, 1885, vide Gadru, S.N., *Kashmir Papers,* pp. 198-201.
68. Gadru, S.N., *op. cit.*, pp. 198-201.
69. *Ibid.,* Enclosure 3, in No. 3, From Mian Partap Singh to His Excellency the Viceroy and Governor General of India, Jammu, September 18, 1885.
70. Secretary of State of Govt. of India, November 27, 1885, *Ibid.*
71. File No. R-2, Part II, 1885 (J & K State-Archives).
72. For. Sec. E, Nos. (235-300) (K.W.), Progs., October 1886.
73. D.P., Reel 528, Resident of India, September 26, 1885: Selections, *The Shafiq-i-Hind,* Lahore. February 13, 1886.; K.G.R., Jammu, Chief Secretariat, Pol. Dept., File No. 22 of 1900.
74. D.P., Reel 529, encl. in No. 354, pp. 231-32, Maharaja to Aitchinson, April 11, 1886.
75. *Ibid.*, p. 231, Aitchinson to Wallace, April 14, 1856.
76. *Ibid.*, No. 362, p. 237.
77. Ghose, D.K., *Kashmir in Transition*, p. 39.
78. Selections, *The Shafiq-i-Hind*, May 15, 1886.
79. PSLE 1/45, pp. 1-19, Durand to St. John, October 5, 1885, encl. 21 in GOI to S.O.S., October 19, 1885.

3

Pratap Singh and the Residents

SECTION 1: PRATAP SINGH AND THE RESIDENTS

Pratap Singh ascended the throne at the time when the British had already made up their mind to bring the state firmly under their control. They were only waiting for the time *i.e.,* the death of Ranbir Singh. Misrule in the state was a good excuse for planting a Resident in the state. Pratap Singh's humility and affability were taken as his weaknesses to be exploited. Unluckily, nature had not gifted him with a regal charm and virile physique which had been lavishly gifted to his younger brothers.

During the viceroyalty of Lord Ripon the Foreign Department had already decided that the following "principal measures" were to be implemented.[1]

(*a*) "the introduction of a reasonably light assessment".

(*b*) "the construction of good roads".

(*c*) "the cessation of state monopolies".

(*d*) "the revision of existing taxes and dues".

(*e*) "the abolition of the system of farming the revenues".

(*f*) "the appointment of respectable officials".

(*g*) "the establishment of a careful system of financial control".

(*h*) "the removal of all restriction upon emigration".

(*i*) "the reorganisation and regular payment of the army".

(*j*) "the improvement of the judicial administration."

The Anglo Indian press was also voicing its concern for reforms in the administration of Kashmir. The accession of Pratap

Singh was taken as the opportune time.[2] It also recommended the "stationing of a Political Resident of the first class" for guiding Pratap Singh, who appeared to be a weak ruler.[3] St. John, the first Resident handed over to Pratap Singh the above-mentioned list of reforms to be carried out.

Pratap Singh, who was familiar with the misgovernment in Kashmir, had already made up his mind to overhaul the administration. He wanted the freedom and time to make his country "a model of a well-governed state" in alliance with the Government of India.[4] The Maharaja made two representations for getting the appointment of the Resident cancelled, but to no avail.[5]

Lord Churchill, the Secretary of State for India desired that the proposals made during Ripon's Government to be implemented without delay. Moreover, his thinking was that there were "many reasons" for bringing the Kashmir State "in our hands". Though his views were not shared by the Government of India.[7]

Colonel Sir O. St. John— First Resident of Kashmir

With the appointment of St. John as the Resident in Kashmir, a form of dual government started in the State. The death of Wazir Punnu, the most powerful figure in the late Maharaja's council, six days before his master's death was a tragic blow to the stable functioning of the government. Had he been alive he would not have allowed the faction fight in the Court. His death was rejoiced by the pro-Pratap Singh party of Diwan Anant Ram and Nilambar Mukherjee.[8]

St. John reported that the death of Wazir Punnu was *tabula rasa* for Pratap Singh to carry out the reforms according to his plan.[9] "The general prosperity of the country" as far as it could be after the recent famines also favoured Pratap Singh. The agricultural output was satisfactory in 1884, and prospects for the coming harvest were expected to be good. The Punjab Trade Reports showed that the commerce was gearing up.[10]

A day after Pratap Singh formally took his seat in the *darbar,* on September 26, 1885, St. John enquired of the Maharaja about the reforms proposed to initiate.[11] About the reforms the Maharaja handed over to St. John the

Urdu translation of which was read subsequently. The Darbar announced certain concessions, which were "a valuable boon to the people",[73] especially to the cultivating classes of Jammu. Some relief was also given to the peasants of Kashmir, but the artisans of the towns, whose needs were greater,-got relief in the reduction of levy on fruit and vegetables.

The Maharaja Pratap Singh, in accordance with the calculations of his astrologers, had fixed the date for the installation ceremony as May 10, 1886. By this time St. John, the first Resident had been transferred, and was replaced by T.J.C. Plowden. Maharaja expected that Lord Dufferin would personally bless and congratulate him as the new Maharaja.

The absence of Lord Dufferin at the installation was conspicuous. The Maharaja had invited both Dufferin and Aitchison to grace the occasion. Aitchison had accepted the invitation anticipating that Viceroy would also go. On coming to know that the Viceroy would not go,[74] he requested the Government of India to inform him whether he was permitted to go or not.[75] The Government of India did not permit him to attend the installation ceremony.[76] Pratap Singh was very disappointed. He had special attachment with Aitchinson, as prior to the appointment of the Resident, the Punjab Government carried out the communications between the Government of India and Kashmir, therefore in spite of his absence he thanked Aitchinson profusely.[77] Plowden did not like it. The vernacular press predicted that the absence of Lord Dufferin and Aitchinson was ominous.[78]

The Maharaja was also instructed to withdraw his agent from the headquarters of the Government of India, as all political relations with the Kashmir State in future would be carried out through the British-Resident, the accredited representative of the Government of India.[79]

References

1. Moore, *Lala Rookh, q*uoted in Wakefield, W., M.D., *The Happy Valley*, 1879, on the opening page.
2. Younghusband, Francis, Sir, K.C.I.E., *Kashmir*, p. 1.
3. Wakefield, W., *op. cit.*, p. 9., *Encyclopaedia Britannica*, Vol. XII, p. 867. The territory [86,023 sq. mi. (222,798 sq. km.)] is bounded

on the north-west by Afghanistan; on the north by Sinkiang-Uigur Autonomous Region of China; on the east by Tibet; on the south by India and on the west by Pakistan.

4. Aitchison, *Treaties Engagements and Sanads,* See Appendix II.; CHI, V, p. 552.
5. Gadru, S.N., Ed., *Kashmir Papers*, p. 124.
6. *The Cambridge Modern History*, 1934, Vol. XII, p. 464.
7. Tytler, K.K. Fraser, *Afghanistan,* Oxford 1859, p. 130 ff.; Wyllie, J.W.S., *Essays on the External Policy of India, 1875*, Chapters, I-III.
8. *Political History of England*, Vol. XII, p. 306.
9. BPIR, I, p. 697.
10. Henderson to A.C. Lyall, November 8, 1879, Foreign Secret, No. 86, Progs, March, 1883. On November 8, 1879, P.D. Henderson wrote, "The Chief object of our relation with Kashmir, is presumably to secure the Maharaja's services as a political ally with reference to trans-frontier politics. The important question is, therefore, how will this object be effected by the appointment of a Resident."
11. For, Sec., Nos. 34-60B, (K.W.), Progs., July, 1877.
12. For. Sec., Nos. 68-81, Progs., August, 1875.

12A. *Gazetteer of Kashmir and Ladak*, p. 328. "The ancient name of the place was Sargin. Later the name of Gilit was given to it, and this has been changed to Gilgit by the Sikh and Dogra' conquerors; but among the inhabitants it is still known as Gilit or Sargin-Gilit. Its identity with Gahalata of ancient Sanskrit literature has been suggested. A few remains still exist of ancient stone buildings, apparently of the same description as the *Martund* and *Pandrathan* temples in Kashmir. Their presence indicates that a considerable amount of wealth and scientific skill must have once existed in this remote valley of which not even the tradition has survived.

13. Bajpai, *The Northern Frontier of India*, p. 9. The remains of ancient stone building and Buddhist carvings suggest that Gilgit was once the seat of a Hindu, or a Buddhist dynasty, while traces of abandoned cultivation point to the fact that the population in early times was far larger than it is at present. For many centuries the inhabitants of Gilgit have been Muhammadans, and nothing definite is now known of their Hindu predecessors. Tradition relates that the last of the Hindu Ras, Shri Badat, known as *Adam Khor, t*he 'man-eater, was killed by a Muhammadan adventurer, who founded a new dynasty known as Frakhane. Shri Badat's rule is said to have extended to Chitral, and the introduction of Islam seems to have split up the kingdom into a number of small states carrying on a fratricidal warfare and incessant slave raiding. The Frakhane dynasty is now extinct, though it is claimed that the present titular *Ra* of Gilgit has a slight stain of Trakhane blood. In the early part of the

nineteenth century we find Yasin giving a *Ra* to Gilgit. He was killed by the ruler of Punial, who in turn was killed by Fair Shah, Chief of Nagar. Fair Shah was succeeded by his son, who was killed by Gauhar Aman, ruler of Yasin vide *Imperial Gazetteer of India.* Vol. XXI Oxford, 1908. The Dards (Daradae) were located by Ptolemy with surprising accuracy on the west of the upper Indus, beyond the headwaters of the Swat river (Gr. Soastus), and north of Gandarae, *i.e.*, the Gandharans, who occupied Peshawar and the Country North of it. The region was traversed by two Chinese pilgrims, Fa-Hsien, coming from the North about A.D. 400, Hsuan Tsang, ascending from Swat, in A.D. 629, and both left records of their journeys. Gilgit, as far back as tradition goes, was ruled by rajas of a dynasty called Trakhane. When this family became extinct the valley was desolated by successive invasions of neighbouring rulers, and in 20 or 30 years ending with 1842 there had been five dynastic revolutions. The Sikhs entered Gilgit about 1842 and kept a garrison there. When Kashmir was made over to Maharaja Gulab Singh of Jammu in 1846 by Lord Hardinge, and a boundary commission was sent that included the first: Englishmen to visit Gilgit Vide *Encyclopaedia Britannica* Vol. X, p. 487 *Chamber's Encyclopaedia* Vol. VI, p. 351, *Great Soviet Encyclopaedia.* Vol. VI, p. 408. In the *Gazetteer of Kashmir and Ladakh* the name of the last Hindu Ruler is given as Shri Badutt.

14. *Biddulph, Maj. I., Tribes of Hindu Koosh.*
15. Knight, E.P., *Where Three Empires Meet*, 1905, pp. 290-291.
16. For. Sec., 34-60B. K.W., Progs., July 1877.
17. Political and Secret Letters and Enclosures from India, Government of India to Secretary of State, 23rd March 1877, pp. 235-47; Lytton Papers, 518/1, Lytton to Salisbury, September 18, pp. 460-67.
18. Balfour, Lady Betty, *The History of Lord Lytton's Indian Administration*, 1899, p. 187.
19. For. Sec., Nos. 34-60B, K.W., Progs., July 1877; Kapoor, M.L., *Kashmir Sold and Snatched, 1968*, pp. 77-78.
20. For. Sec., Nos. 34-60B, K.W., Progs., July 1877. As regards this concession, the Foreign Secretary observed: "With an officer at Leh and Gilgit, we should get all the information we require.......while the abolition of the Political Officer at Srinagar would not, in my opinion, diminish our political influence".
21. For. Sec., No. 38, Progs., July 1877.
22. Biddulph's Memo on the present condition of affairs in Gilgit, March 31, 1881, For. Sec., July 1881, Nos. 314-99.
23. Balfour, Lady Betty, *op. cit.*, pp. 144-8.
24. Ripon to Kimberley, July 15, 1881, For. Sec., July, 1881, No. 396; Bajpai, *op. cit.*, p. 79.

25. Bajpai, *op. cit.*, p. 80.
26. Biddulph's memo on the present condition of affairs in Gilgit, March 31, 1881, *n. 10*.
27. Bajpai, *op. cit.*, p. 80.
28. For. Sec., December 1880, Nos. 83-153; Alder, G.J., British India's Northern Frontiers, 1865-95, London, 1963, *n. 9*, pp. 140-44.
29. Ripon to Kimberley, July 15, 1881, For. Sec., July 1881, No. 396.
30. Henvy to Foreign Secretary, March 30, 1881, For. Sec., No. 380, Progs, July 1881.
31. For. Sec., December 1880, Nos. 83-153.
32. Alder, G.J., *op. cit.*, p. 132; For Sec. F.,-January 1888, Nos. 115-118.
33. Memorandum, November 22, 1880, by Henvy, For. Sec., No. 137, Frogs., December 1880.
34. Government of India to Secretary of State, July 15, 881, For. Sec., No. 393, Progs., July 1881.
35. Kapoor, M.L., *op., cit.*, p. 93.
36. Biddulph's Report on Kashmir Army, For. Sec., E, No. 346, July 1883.
37. R.P., I.S. 290/5, Vol. I, p. 43, Ripon to Hartington, 27th July, 1880; For. Sec., July 1881, No. 396, Ripon to Kimberley, 15th July 1881; PSLEI/29, G.O.I. to S.O.S., July 27, 1880.
38. Robert Papers, Box file L7, Lytton to Roberts, March 20, 21, 1880.
39. Biddulph's memo, *op. cit.*, No. 10.
40. Bajpai, S.C., *op. cit.*, p. 84.
41. Aitchison, *op. cit.*, *n.* 1, Vol. XII, pp. 29-30; Foreign Political A, October 1872, Nos. 374-77; *Ibid.*, April 1873, Nos. 187-96.
42. For. Pol. A, January 1873, Nos. 88-89, "Maharaja' Remonstrances;" For. Sec., August 1877, Nos. 73-75, from Secretary, Punjab to Secretary Government of India, November 25, 1872, From Secretary, Government of India to Secretary, Punjab December 27, 1872.
43. Northbrook Papers, 11, pp. 12-18, Northbrook to Salisbury, March 27, 1874; *Ibid., 21/2*, pp. 168-69, Northbrook to Rawlinson, December 25, 1873; For. Sec., Nos. 19-29, Progs., March 1875.
44. For. Sec., No. 19-29, Progs., March 1875, when H. Lep Wynne, the then Officer on Special Duty in Kashmir, tried to assure him of the Government's genuine intentions of non-interference in his internal affairs by the appointment of a Resident, the Maharaja said, "Nay Sahib, when a man has a tree which he cherishes, of course he looks after it, and people do not call that interference."
45. *Ibid.*
46. *Ibid.*
47. *Ibid.*

48. Currie to Argyll, November 27, 1873, also Northbrook to Davies, December 27, 1873, For. Sec., Nos. 19-29, Progs., March 1875; Argyll to Northbrook, November 28, 1873, Northbrook Papers, 9, pp. 103-5.
49. Northbrook Papers, 9, pp. 103-4, Argyll to Northbrook, November 28, 1873.
50. For. Sec., Nos. 19-29, Progs., March 1875, Northbrook to Davies, December 27, 1873, and March 25, 1874. Northbrook wrote, "... I should be exceedingly sorry to urge upon the Maharaja any course which should be distasteful to His Highness's feelings".
51. Northbrook Papers, 11, pp. 12-18, Northbrook to Salisbury, March 27, 1874.
52. *Ibid.,* pp. 12-15, Salisbury to Northbrook, April 24, 1874.
53. Henderson to A.C. Lyall, November 8, 1879, For. Sec., No. 86, Progs., March 1883.
54. Digby, William, *Condemned Unheard,* 1890, pp. 7-8. An instance of Maharaja's foresight is provided by the account of Mr. Edward E. Meakin's informal meeting with Maharaja, when he asked, "Sahib, what do you call that little thing between the railway carriages? It is like a button stuck on a sort of gigantic needle that runs through the train, and when the carriages are pushed at one end on the other you hear a "houff, houff", and bang they go against the poor button. I felt very sorry for the poor little button, but it is doubtless useful in its way. What do you call it?" I replied that I believed it was called a "buffer". "Buffer Buffer", repeated the Maharaja in earnest tones. 'Yes, buffer, that is just what I am, and that shall henceforth be one of my titles". "......On one side of me there is the big train of the British possessions and whenever they push northward they will tilt up against me, then on the other side is the shaky concern Afghanistan, and on the other side of it is the ponderous train and engine called Roos. Every now and then there is a tilting of Roos towards Afghanistan, and simultaneously there is a tilting upwards of the great engine in Calcutta, and I am the poor little button between them. Someday, perhaps not far distant, there will be a tilting from the North, and Afghanistan will smash up. Then there will be a tremendous tilt from the South, and I shall be buried in the wreck and lost! It may not come in my time, but it is sure to come when that poor little button is on the pin'... Pointing to his son, the present Maharaja......".
55. For. Sec., No. 86, Progs., March 1883.
56. R.P./I.S. 290/7, Vol. IV, pp. 180 (a)—(b), Ripon to Halifax November 17, 1883.
57. For. Sec., Nos. 518-25, K.W., Progs., August 1881.
58. *Ibid.*
59. Officer on Special Duty to Foreign Secretary, June 28, 1882, For. Sec. E. No. 427, Progs., January 1883.

60. For, Sec, E. Nos. 427-30 (K.W.), Progs. January 1883.
61. *Ibid.*
62. Henvy to C. Grant, December 14, 1882. For. Sec., No. 353, K.W., Progs., May 1884.
63. Despatch of the Govt, of India, April 7, 1884, and Despatch of the Sec. of State, May 23, 1884, Par. Papers, 1890, Vol. IV, pp. 231 ff., Government of India to Secretary of State, April 7, 1884, For. Sec., E., No. 354, Progs., May 1894.
64. *Ibid.*
65. For. Dept., Sec. E., March 1889, No., 107-200; D.P., Reel 518, No., 243, to the S.O.S., September 17, 1885.; K.G.R., Jammu, Private Department, Records of Maharaja Pratap Singh.
66. D.P., Reel 519, p. 85, Letter to the S.O.S.. September 17, 1885.
67. From Resident in Kashmir to Secretary to the Government of India, Foreign Department, Jammu, September 16, 1885, vide Gadru, S.N., *Kashmir Papers,* pp. 198-201.
68. Gadru, S.N., *op. cit.*, pp. 198-201.
69. *Ibid.,* Enclosure 3, in No. 3, From Mian Partap Singh to His Excellency the Viceroy and Governor General of India, Jammu, September 18, 1885.
70. Secretary of State of Govt. of India, November 27, 1885, *Ibid.*
71. File No. R-2, Part II, 1885 (J & K State-Archives).
72. For. Sec. E, Nos. (235-300) (K.W.), Progs., October 1886.
73. D.P., Reel 528, Resident of India, September 26, 1885: Selections, *The Shafiq-i-Hind,* Lahore. February 13, 1886.; K.G.R., Jammu, Chief Secretariat, Pol. Dept., File No. 22 of 1900.
74. D.P., Reel 529, encl. in No. 354, pp. 231-32, Maharaja to Aitchinson, April 11, 1886.
75. *Ibid.*, p. 231, Aitchinson to Wallace, April 14, 1856.
76. *Ibid.*, No. 362, p. 237.
77. Ghose, D.K., *Kashmir in Transition*, p. 39.
78. Selections, *The Shafiq-i-Hind*, May 15, 1886.
79. PSLE 1/45, pp. 1-19, Durand to St. John, October 5, 1885, encl. 21 in GOI to S.O.S., October 19, 1885.

manifesto, but at the same time he stressed that for the reforms and the constitution of the ministry he needed time. When pressed hard he disclosed that he had entrusted Babu Nilambar Mukherjee with all business connected with finance, while Diwan Anant Ram would be in-charge of Foreign Affairs, which he defined as Ladakh and Leh, and correspondence with the Resident. Before his departure he impressed upon the Maharaja that relieving the manufacturing classes of Kashmir from the heavy taxation on trade should be the prime consideration of his government.[12]

H.M. Durand, the Foreign Secretary to the Government of India instructed St. John that the Governor-General had desired that the Resident should inform the Maharaja personally that owing to the inflammable situation beyond the north-west frontier and strategic considerations—the location of a British force at some point or points within his state had become imperative, as the Government of India was bound by treaty to protect Kashmir from foreign aggression and in the general interests of the Empire also.[13]

Durand also drew the attention of the Resident to a point which he thought of immediate political importance. The Viceroy had come to know that the subjects of Maharaja were strongly discouraged from taking military service under the British Government, and that men who did take service were imprisoned or otherwise ill-treated when they visited their homes in the State. Though the Viceroy did not believe it, still the Resident was instructed that he should without delay inform the Kashmir Darbar that such complaints should cease altogether.[14] St. John conveyed the message. About the second point the Resident[15] informed Durand that during his recent visit to Jammu he apprised the Maharaja that to put obstacles in the way of his subjects joining the British army was contrary to the traditional loyalty of his house to the British Crown, and in marked contrast to the policy of Nepal and other states. The Maharaja assured him that the late Maharaja's only object had been to provide the efficiency of his own army as an instrument always at the service of Her Majesty, and that immediate orders would be issued to give every assistance to recruiting parties from regiments of Her Majesty's service. At the Maharaja's request he (St. John) wrote privately to this effect to the Commander-in-Chief of the Government of India referring to an announcement in the newspapers that several of the new troops of cavalry would be formed of Dogras. At the same time the Maharaja asked the Resident that the deserters from his army should not be allowed to take service under the British army. On this the Resident assured the Maharaja that the enlistment rolls of recruits would be sent to the Darbar for verification as before, which would help him ascertain whether the recruit was a deserter or not.[16]

With the proposal for the establishment of a British cantonment in Kashmir, Pratap Singh was very annoyed. He immediately left for Calcutta accompanied by Babu Nilambar to discuss the matter personally with Dufferin. On his way, the Maharaja met Aitchinson, the Governor of Punjab, at Lahore. Pratap Singh requested him to get his old connection with the Punjab Government restored for the smooth working of the Government. Aitchinson was sympathetic, but he did not want to interfere in any way with appointment of Resident in Kashmir. Nevertheless he wrote to Dufferin urging him to reconsider the request of the Maharaja, if it was possible.[17] Dufferin referred the matter to his Foreign Secretary, Mortimer Durand, who was vehemently opposed to it and, presumably under his advice, declined to revert to old order of a link between Kashmir and the Punjab Government.[18]

The meeting between Dufferin and Pratap Singh took place in Calcutta in the middle of January 1886. Mainly three points were discussed.[19] (A) Establishment of a British Cantonment in Kashmir territory. (B) Plea for the restoration of a Kashmir Vakil at the headquarters of the Government of India. (C) Right of British traders to purchase land in Jammu and Kashmir.

With regard to B and C Maharaja's request was not considered. The Viceroy ruled out any other channel except that of the Resident.[20] He further said that the British traders had a right to purchase land in Kashmir.[21] He said no Indian

State could prevent European British subjects from buying or hiring suitable buildings for carrying out their business. "The colony would be equally resident in Kashmir and equally free from the jurisdiction of your courts".

With regard to point A, Pratap Singh registered more formidable resistance. He also argued that the establishment of the army was contrary to the treaty of Amritsar. He offered to raise his own army to help the British Government to repel any foreign aggression, provided it was subsidised by the Government of India, like Afghanistan. For subsidy the Viceroy did not agree, saying that under the treaty stipulations Kashmir was a feudatory state created by the British Government and owing allegiance to it. Hence, it was the obligation of the State of Kashmir to place before the Government of India the whole of its military resources against an enemy operating from the North-West Frontier. Nevertheless, the Viceroy assured the Maharaja that a British cantonment would not be established in Kashmir without due regard to his wishes. It was also possible that the development of communication and other circumstances might obviate that necessity. But in case the Government of India decided to quarter its army the Maharaja should come forward to accept the decision with readiness and goodwill.[22]

St. John before his departure presented a damaging report on January 1886 about the functioning of the new government.[23] He passed strictures against the Maharaja in every way. He wrote that in his private life the Maharaja was under the sway of backstairs influence of three persons Miran Baksh, A Muslim of ill-repute, Seth Ramanand, an astrologer (*Jotishi*), and a Hindu named Sawal Singh, considered as *dewana* or mad man. This man pretended to have spiritual communion with the ghost of the departed Raja, which was influencing the destiny of the present Maharaja. Maharaja acted according to the dictates of the spirit, whose orders were communicated to him through Sawal Singh. The overpowering influence of Sawal Singh was an anathema to many people, including the Maharani Bishen Devi, Pratap Singh's wife, who had complained of it to Lord Dufferin and to the Lieutenant Governor of Punjab.[24]

During the last four months Pratap Singh had headed the government the condition of Kashmir had steadily deteriorated.[25] He dissolved the council of his father and thus had dispensed with the services of Raja Moti Singh, his cousin, Rajas Ram Singh and Amar Singh, his brothers, and Sheikh Wahab-ud-Din, the only Muslim member. He worked through Dewan Anant Ram as Prime Minister, Babu Nilambar Mukherjee as Finance Minister, and Diwan Gobind Sahai as Vakil at the Headquarters of the Government of India. Diwan Anant Ram[26] was Prime Minister only in name. All power was usurped by Gobind Sahai and his party consisting of his son Lakhpat Rai, his cousin Amar Nath, and a Kashmiri Pandit, Muhanand Jee, who had incurred the displeasure of the late ruler for his corruption and depravity.[27] Diwan Lachman Dass, the most capable man in the whole of state and a personal favourite of Ranbir Singh, was forced to resign, as Gobind Sahai, Amar Nath and Nilambar were against him.[28]

St. John's opinion was that the Maharaja was "unfit to rule" and, instead of reform and improvement, the administration of the country would continue to grow worse and worse. No material progress was possible under him. He would fight for the curtailment of his authority and the reforms would be retarded. Such measures as might be "forced upon the Darbar would be grudgingly carried out and evaded in every possible way", while the resources of the State would be "squandered on unworthy favourites".[29]

Diwan Gobind Sahai as Prime Minister

The hard work told upon the health of Diwan Anant Ram.[30] He suffered from 'disorder of the brain', and was obliged to quit his post. Diwan Gobind Sahai became the next Prime Minister, and Babu Nilambar was again made the Finance Minister. The whole administration was entrusted to these two persons.[31] St. John was unhappy over it, as he wanted a ministry of his choice. He predicted its failure. About finances St. John has reported on September 27, 1885, that although the late Maharaja was "said to have left considerable wealth", the public treasuries were empty at the time of his death.[32]

St. John's forebodings about the ministry were on account of loyalty of Gobind Sahai and Babu Nilambar towards the Maharaja and not to the Government of India.[33] His impression was that both were incompetent administrators. Curiously enough St. John was also not above board. It was alleged that the Maharaja's Government had bribed him.[34]

Besides Lord Ripon's suggestions for reforms, St. John was also asked to convey to the Darbar to take up following reforms:[35]

1. "The position of European traders in Kashmir".
2. "The postal arrangement of the State".
3. "The Coinage".
4. "The question of jurisdiction over-Europeans in Kashmir who are not British subjects".
5. "The extradition of criminals".
6. "The Kashmir railway question".
7. "A British cantonment in Kashmir".

About the first the Viceroy had already intimated to the Maharaja that the European. British subjects were entitled to all sorts of facilities as enjoyed in other feudatory states.[36]

About the second the Resident reported in November 1885, that the Darbar had desired to enter into a postal convention with the British Government. In February 1886, he was informed that the Government of India was prepared to consider a convention similar to those with other 'Native States'.[37]

About the third and fourth the Government of India itself was not keen, as it thought that they 'are not burning questions'.[38].

The fifth was taken up with the Government of Punjab and was to be decided soon by it.[39]

For the sixth Colonel De. Bourbel was surveying the area for laying down the railway line in Kashmir.[40]

The seventh was open and had been reserved for the present.[41]

About the reforms suggested by Lord Ripon and handed over to the Maharaja by St. John, the latter had reported in March, 1886, that the reform under the head[42] (*d*) For the revision of existing taxes and dues, the Darbar had abolished all taxes and cesses on land except the revenue demand. St. John had remarked that the relief thus afforded to cultivators would be great if the burdens were not reimposed under different names.[43]

Besides these, Pratap Singh had undertaken many other reforms.[44] The Darbar was spending a large amount of money in the construction of the Muree-Kohala cart road for the defence of the British empire.[45] But St. John was not happy. His recommendation was that the ministry should be composed of Diwan Lachman Dass as the Prime Minister, and brothers of Maharaja, who formed a caucus against the Maharaja and his men.

T.J.C. Plowden the Second Resident

Dufferin was not happy with the functioning of St. John.[46] Plowden was appointed as his successor and was ordered to take over personally from the out-going Resident as these were "matters requiring personal explanation."[47]

Fall of the Ministry

The Prime Minister Gobind Sahai and the Finance Minister Babu Nilambar, the two pillars of the ministry had fallen out against each other. Gobind Sahai was very jealous of the influence of Nilambar over the Maharaja.[48] Diwan did not know English, therefore all the correspondence was scribed by Nilambar to the Resident. Gobind Sahai confided it to the Resident. He broached upon the question of the private servants of the Maharaja, on which the Resident expressed his inability to get rid of them. Plowden also shared St. John's opinion about Gobind Sahai that he had no administrative experience, was detested by all the parties alike, and was shamelessly corrupt.[49]

Babu Nilambar also laid before the Resident his grievances. He said that when Gobind Sahai had gone to Calcutta to meet Dufferin, he had taken four lakhs with them to bribe the

Foreign Department. As a Finance Minister he had asked Gobind Sahai for a statement on ₹65,000 found unaccounted. The Babu confided to the Resident that the Viceroy also enquired about St. John's debt. At first both he and the Maharaja were taken aback, but later on they admitted that the money had been offered.[49A] . The next thing was that the Maharaja had contracted debts during his father's lifetime, which had been forged to the value of ten lakhs of rupees. The Maharaja had recently instructed him to settle the debts to which he agreed if due consideration was shown in each instance. But his endeavours were defeated by Sawal Singh, who got the Maharaja's consent to settle them for eight lacs, which amount had been paid out of the treasury. He felt let down and tendered his resignation. Maharaja did not accept it, and he issued a *parwana* conferring on him (Babu) full powers in all administrative matters with leave to dismiss and appoint as he pleased. Babu had refused to accept this, but he wanted to ascertain his (Resident's) opinion whether he would be supported by him as he was very unpopular with the officials, who held him responsible for the misgovernment in Kashmir.[50] The Resident wrote to Durand sooner or later the Babu, Gobind Sahai, and the private servants must be got rid of, especially the Babu. He must never come back.[51]

The atmosphere was rife with the rumours that sooner or later there would be a change in the ministry as the news of growing *fissure* between Gobind Sahai and Babu had gained currency. *The Pioneer* was in the forefront in this regard. Babu also felt uncomfortable on account of Sawal Singh's influence on the Maharaja,[52] and an open rupture between the two was reported by *The Pioneer.*[53] Babu had come to the tether's end and he again tendered his resignation, but Maharaja instead of accepting it, issued a second *parwana,* giving him full powers. After a few days the Babu submitted various proposals, including the reduction of his own salary to ₹1,500, which were not approved. On August 13, there was a scene between him and Gobind Sahai, whereupon the Babu again tendered his resignation and this time the Maharaja accepted it.[54] The Resident was very happy as the Babu was the man, who acted as the stumbling block to the imperialist designs of the British.

It was officially announced in the month of September 1886, that the Babu had resigned and was going back. After a few days Babu Nilambar left Kashmir along with a few other Bengali officials, who also resigned with him.[55]

The ministry broke down.

SECTION 2: MANIPULATIONS TO BRING ANTI-MAHARAJA GROUP INTO POWER

The Kashmir Darbar had requested the Punjab Government to select for them some officers specialised in Law and Revenue Settlement. Plowden resented being overpassed. He complained to Durand that the Maharaja had directly approached the Punjab Government for the loan of the British officers in contravenes to the wishes of the Viceroy, conveyed to him in the *Kharita* enclosed in the Foreign Department Confidential letter, dated August 1, 1884. He also expressed his resentment against the Punjab Government which had taken into consideration the request of the Kashmir Darbar wrongly addressed to it. The Punjab Government ought to have referred the Darbar to the Government of India through the Resident. This was the proper procedure laid down in the orders of the Government of India to the Government of Punjab in 1881, which had been confirmed and expanded by the confidential instructions on August 1, 1884 and subsequent letters. These defined the position and powers of the Resident in Kashmir as the local representative of the Viceroy and channel of communication with the British Government. The Foreign Secretary should be intimated that it is the 'Governor-General in Council' not the Government of Punjab which was empowered to place at the disposal of the Darbar the services of any British Officer, who might seem best suited for the work in view.[56]

Plowden wrote to Aitchinson, the Punjab Governor, to wait until he had ascertained whether the Maharaja had any definite scheme for the reorganisation of the judicial administration. Meanwhile, Plowden took the Maharaja to task for ignoring the Resident. The Maharaja explained that he had done so because he had a quarrel with St. John. The Maharaja evidently was puzzled why Aitchinson had not sent the official he had promised to send. Plowden wrote to Durand that the conduct of the Maharaja shows clearly that he understood fully the use to which he could put the Government orders leaving him a means of access to the Punjab Government. "It was evidently to score off the Resident."[57]

Babu Nilambar was a thorn in Plowden's flesh, as he was always outwitted by him. He was crestfallen when he came to know that a Bengali, Rishibar Mukherjee, a brother of Nilambar had already been appointed Chief Justice of the *Sadar Adalat* at Jammu. If Plowden was checkmated in the judicial appointment he used his influence to get the man of his choice, Mr. Wingate, to conduct revenue survey and settlement operations in Kashmir.[58] The Maharaja accepted the appointment with the condition that with regard to the proportion of the Government's demand on land and other matters connected with settlement, "he shall act entirely under such instructions as may, from time to time, be issued by my Government".[59]

On the whole Plowden's thinking was that the Darbar was not serious about the reforms. It was more interested in impressing the Government of India with its reform projects by creating a few nominal posts and filling them with the British officers on loan.[60]

Ironically enough a false propaganda was carried on by the Resident's Reports and the Anglo Indian press that Kashmir was seething with corruption and misgovernment.[61] Durand apprised Mackenzie Wallace that he could not "help what *Pioneer* says,.......but what is said is probably true." The Maharaja was evading the wishes of the Government of India. He had let himself to be guided by Nilambar Mukherjee and Gobind Sahai, to preserve his 'independence from control'. He would be a happier man and "Cashmere will greatly benefit" if the Maharaja did not bother with the "working of the Native Press" and left his reliance on the Punjab Government.[62]

Meantime *The Pioneer* circulated that there were straws in the wind towards a change in the ministry, after the proposed meeting between Dufferin and Pratap Singh had taken place.[63]

Lord Dufferin, who was touring the Indian States, invited Pratap Singh for talks to Lahore. The meeting took place on November 4, 1886. The Viceroy outright directed Pratap Singh to dismiss Diwan Gobind Sahai and constitute another Council composed of Rajas Ram Singh and Amar Singh, and Diwan Lachman Dass. Maharaja struggled hard to retain Gobind Sahai at least in the capacity of a general adviser, but Dufferin did not agree.[64] Evidently, the composition of the new council was suggested by Plowden, as all its members were anti-Pratap Singh. All the pleas of Pratap Singh to bring his own men fell flat and he complied with the directives of the Viceroy.[65]

Pratap Singh tried to evade the constitution of the new Council. Plowden administered the Maharaja a stern warning that his reluctance to constitute a new council would necessitate the handing over of the administration to Raja Moti Singh of Punch believed to be hostile to the ruling family. Plowden observed that the warning worked like a magic.[66] Maharaja issued a *parwana* for the constitution of the new council and a *Khillat* was sent to Lachman Das's house. The new council was to be composed of Lachman Das, as the Resident and Rajas Amar Singh and Ram Singh as members.[67] The Viceroy in March 1887 sent his congratulations to the Maharaja.[68]

The vernacular press presented a mixed reaction. Some defended Lord Dufferin,[69] while *The Punjab Punch* published a cartoon in which the new council in the shape of a vile hag was beheading with a sword the Maharaja's Government.[70]

The new Council started its work by taking stock of the state treasuries to check useless expenditure. It separated the legitimate public expenditure of the state from the private and personal disbursements of the Maharaja. The private servants of the Maharaja were excluded from interfering in the administration. The Council placed a check on the Maharaja's extravagance by depriving him of his right to sign public bonds independently. Accordingly, he was made to issue an order that no bills would be cashed at the public treasury which were not countersigned by the Council and that his own unsupported signature would be valid only against his private exchequer.[71]

Wingate, the Settlement Officer, with the assistance of Lala Nursing Das and four others, lent by the Punjab Government, began his work at Jammu in April 1887 and completed within a year the preliminaries of the settlement work in Jammu and Kashmir provinces of the State at a cost of ₹35,048.[72]

The Darbar, undoubtedly at the behest of the Resident completed a preliminary survey for a railway into Kashmir on its own expense.[73] Colonel (afterwards Major General) R. de Bourbel was appointed for this purpose,[74] and later on was made the Chief Engineer in-charge of the Public Works Department.[75] In August 1887, Lachman Dass made a proposal for the construction of a railway line from Sialkot to Jammu.[76] The agreement over it between the Government of India and Kashmir Darbar was finalised on July 4, 1888.[77]

Besides, the Cart road which had been constructed during the period of previous ministries was thrown open to traffic.[78]

The Council from the beginning had paid its whole attention to punishing the Maharaja's friends and ex-councillors for corruption and peculation. Miran Baksh was charged for pilfering *pushmina* to the tune of ₹84,000/- from the State Store. The Maharaja wanted to save him, but he could not.[79] The case was given to a Commission headed by Rishibar Mukherjee. Miran Baksh was found guilty and was sentenced to seven years' imprisonment.

The Medical Department in Kashmir for a long time was in a disarray. On Maharaja's request the Resident lent the services of Surgeon-Major Deane of the British Residency for supervising the Medical Department in his spare time on an honorarium of ₹250/- per mensem.[80] He systematised the medical expenditure of the State, and increased the efficiency without any extra expenditure.[81] He also made arrangement for educating the boys of the State at the Lahore Medical School, to enable them to take charge of the dispensaries of this State.[82]

The Maharaja and his Council came to a break, when the latter decided to act against Sawal Singh. The Maharaja wrote to the Viceroy and the Resident,[83] about the highhanded and arbitrary functioning of the Council, alleging that the

Council had been acting like a Council of Regency and treated him like a minor. He favoured a Council to advise him but was thoroughly dissatisfied with the dictatorial attitude of the present Council.[84] The Resident tried a *rapprochement*[85] between the Maharaja and the Council, but it was short lived.

The Council also took up the case against Diwan Gobind Sahai for peculation in not submitting the account for ₹65,000/-. Gobind Sahai, who had gone to the Punjab, was ordered to appear before the Council to stand trial. But he declined to appear as the President of the Council, Diwan Lachman Dass was hostile to him.[86] The case was tried in absentia, and Gobind Sahai was held guilty. He was fined ₹40,000/-, which together with embezzled money was to be realised from his property in the state. He was debarred from holding any office in the State. The Council put the decision for the Maharaja's signature and he signed it.[87]

The '*Bakidar* question'[88] heralded the doom for the Council.[89] The people belonging to every walk of life *i.e.,* officials, merchants, shawl bearers, shop-keepers, and cultivators had taken loan from the State amounting to three crores of rupees.[90] When the Council wanted to recover them from those who could pay it, it found itself pitted against a powerful opposition mounted by Mia Lal Din at Srinagar. This led them to drop '*Bakidar* question'.[91] The reputation of the Council suffered a decline.

Financial reform was the crying need of the time. Plowden drew the attention of the Council towards it. The Council prepared two draft budgets for Kashmir and Jammu. But the prepared draft was a labour in vain as according to Plowden the task was far beyond the administrative capability of the Council.[92]

Meanwhile, Raja Amar Singh had fallen out with Lachman Dass, as he aspired to become Prime Minister of the Council. The Maharaja sided with Amar Singh because, on one hand, he wanted to settle his scores with Lachman Dass and on the other, his (Lachman Dass) morals had become a bazaar gossip. Measures of reform proposed and adopted were rarely carried out in their true spirit.[93] The reforming zeal of the Resident and the Council had made the state completely bankrupt so much so that, in the beginning of March 1888, Amar Singh confided to Plowden that at the moment the total cash in the public treasuries was ₹800/- only.[94] Plowden also admitted that Lachman Dass Ministry was a spent force.[95] On March 19, 1888, Maharaja summarily dismissed Lachman Dass Ministry, and handed over the charge to Amar Singh as Prime Minister.[96] He simultaneously communicated the decision to the Resident and the Viceroy[97] stating the charges that the Prime Minister had failed to discharge his duties satisfactorily and to control the expenditure of the State which had exceeded the income, leaving the civil and military establishments in arrears of pay. Lachman Dass appealed to the Resident to save him from this discomfiture.[98] The Resident rebutted the charges of the Maharaja by attributing the bankruptcy of the state to its military expenditure, and to the personal expenditure of the Maharaja and his two brothers.[99]

Plowden tried his best to malign Pratap Singh for dismissing Lachman Dass, without consulting the Paramount Power.[100] He convinced Durand, the Foreign Secretary with his reasoning, who accepted his contention.[101]

An Assessment

The dismissal of the Lachman Dass ministry was challenged by Plowden. He said that the military expenditure and personal extravagance of the Maharaja and his brothers were responsible for the rifling of the treasury. But Plowden conveniently forgot that he himself was responsible for the expenditure on military affairs, as he had directed Lachman Dass that the strategically position of Kashmir did not warrant any economy on this score.[102] He also forgot the loan of ₹25 lakhs taken by the Government of India from the Darbar, which was a shattering blow to the already crashing state treasury.[103] Plowden was grieved to see that his game to set aside the Maharaja had not only misfired but backfired.

The Press in India took keen interest in the dismissal of Lachman Dass, and came out with various interpretations. The Anglo-Indian Press squarely put the blame on the shoulders of the Resident for his failure.[104] The Resident having secured his man as the Prime Minister of Kashmir, made him his stooge and interfered too much in the affairs of the state, "both small and great". It was said that, once the protege was removed for his failure, the man (Plowden) who was actually responsible for all this should also be recalled.[105] Still, the Resident hoped that the Viceroy would intervene and would order the Maharaja to retire from active politics.[106] But Dufferin totally ruled this out.[107] He cancelled his trip to Kashmir,[108] as he was not happy with the working of the Residents. He dismissed them as "a very poor lot".[109]

A section of the Vernacular newspapers blamed Plowden for "the present unsatisfactory state of things in Kashmir".[110] It recommended the recall of Plowden. He was charged with the pillage of a number of pieces from the Museum at Jammu.[111] Some newspapers were critical of Diwan Lachman Dass for instituting a case against Gobind Sahai.[112] Diwan was also very impertinent towards the Maharaja.[113] The mutual enmity between Diwan Lachman Dass and Diwan Gobind Sahai was the root of the evil. The former dismissed capable officers, such as Pandit Moti Lal and Pandit Pyare Lal, and had shabbily treated Gobind Sahay, Sheikh Miran Baksh and his brother Sheikh Inayat-ullah.[114] *The Ravi* printed its issue in golden letters publishing Maharaja's proclamation dismissing Lachman Dass.[115] *The Civil and Military Gazette* blamed Diwan Lachman Dass for rifling the State treasury. Some papers favouring Lachman Dass bitterly refuted it.[116] They praised the administration of Lachman Dass and said that law and order was restored during his regime and that the canard against the Diwan by *The Civil and Military Gazette* was spread with the purpose of installing an European as the Prime Minister.[117]

On the whole the vernacular press held the opinion that the establishment of the Council was a great mistake.[118] Before the dismissal of Lachman Dass the press was happy that Lord Dufferin was going to Kashmir, and recommended that Aitchinson should also go there and see the highhanded administration of the Council.[119] Raja Amar Singh sided with Lachman Dass and the Resident, as he wanted to become the Maharaja.[120]

Referring to the hallucination of the Russophobia with which the Government of India was obsessed, the press said that it was following a wrong policy in alienating the Maharaja instead of strengthening its friendship with him. *The Charpaz* published a cartoon in which the British lion was represented as casting a wistful glance at a lamb called Kashmir. In the letter-press the editor "warns the lion if he devours the lamb, he will find it difficult to digest the animal, and that other lambs will be put on their guard".[121] The annexation of Kashmir would also be against the proclamation of 1858, and would greatly dampen the zeal of the Indian Princes, who were vying with one or other in their loyal offers for the defence of the North-West Frontier.[122]

The Council failed as it had bitten much more than it could chew. Its haste also heralded its ruin. The Resident's rashness in bringing Kashmir at par with the other feudatory states complicated and muddled the situation, and compromised the British position. The Council consisted of anti-Maharaja faction, and thus the Council and the Maharaja were moving in opposite directions. Lachman Dass arrogated himself to such an extent with the support of the Resident that he dismissed the Kashmiri officials known to be pro-Maharaja from the State service, and they due to the fear had fled to the Punjab. Colonel P.D. Henderson reported that most scandalous reports probably exaggerated were rife in the Punjab for months together regarding the unrestrained and profligate conduct of the three members of the Council.[123]

Though the Council was the creation of Plowden and acted as his handmaid, his report about the working of the Council was startling. He wrote: "that the administration of every department is effete and corrupt".[124] It is an enigma that he was still fighting for its life.

The most glaring defect of the Council was that neither its powers were defined nor the position of the Maharaja with regard to it. Thus, in the absence of clear cut division of the power, responsibilities of each could not be determined. Mere establishment of a Council was not a panacea for all evils.[125] Even the members also need not to be brilliant administrators.

But the crux of the point was to establish a system in which definite responsibilities and powers were assigned and which could be worked by men of average calibre. The need of Kashmir was a system. The administrative machinery was old fashioned, cumbrous, out of order, and too large and too complicated to be worked by any one man however energetic and able.

Plowden's Report

After the dismissal of the Lachman Dass ministry, Plowden despatched to the Government of India's Foreign Department a translation of paper signed by the Maharaja's two brothers, Diwan Lachman Dass, Wazir Sahib Saran, and the notorious Mian Lal Din. Plowden in the forwarding note wrote that the paper was handed over to him in March 1887, when the Lachman Dass ministry was functioning, but he kept the paper with himself, as the Maharaja promised to work in collaboration with Lachman Dass and his colleagues.[126] Like his predecessor Plowden also submitted to the Government of India an adverse report about the functioning of the administration under the Maharaja. About the Maharaja he wrote, "is not merely profligate, but of a degraded and miserable character, whose weakness borders on imbecility, and in whom decent motives or conduct cannot reasonably be expected.[127]

He put forth three alternatives, as:

(A) Making over the administration with Raja Amar Singh as the Prime Minister.

(B) To import a Prime Minister.

(C) To continue the old Council, along with Lachman Dass, making the Resident its temporary head, and strengthening it by the addition of two selected Indians.

He himself rejected A and B alternatives. For the A, his objections were:[128]

1. Raja Amar Singh was too young, about 24 years old, hence was inexperienced to carry out the important reforms without the aid of a British Officer, whether European or Indian as Secretary.
2. Raja aimed to become what his father at one time intended him to be Maharaja of Kashmir, and would use power unscrupulously to that end.

3. The Raja would be sure to quarrel soon with His Highness and with the second brother Ram Singh.

For the B, his objections were:

1. That the imported man would have to be exceptionally strong and honest.
2. That he could not stand without "full support" from the Government of India.
3. That the Maharaja's brothers would oppose him tooth and nail and would be excluding him from the administration altogether.

He favoured the C alternative. He thought that within three years the essential reforms would be introduced after which the Resident might withdraw. Apart from the form of the new administration, Plowden insisted upon two measures, to exclude the Maharaja from the administration, and to employ honest and capable officials in place of the present staff. He justified his recommendations on the grounds of misrule, failure of the Maharaja in introducing reforms, and that a misgoverned Kashmir was a disturbing element on the frontier of the Indian Empire.

The Foreign Secretary gave his mind to the various alternatives and thought that the C alternative would have, "the particular advantage of ensuring the proper direction of matters affecting political arrangements for the North-West Frontier of Kashmir. An imported Minister would not understand this question".[129]

The Maharaja Sought Sanction for his Proposed Council

The Maharaja sent to the Viceroy a *Kharita*, on April 13, 1888, through the Resident,[130] in which the Maharaja observed that the "circumstances obliged" him to dismiss Lachman Dass and hence he was putting forth a proposal for constituting another council, with the following office-bearers.[131]

1. President—the Maharaja.
2. Vice-President and "Prime Minister with executive powers"—Raja Amar Singh.
3. Military Member—Raja Ram Singh.

4. Revenue Minister—Babu Nilambar Mukherjee.
5. Miscellaneous Member and Secretary—Diwan Janaki Prasad.

The Council was to be "consultative", and the executive powers were to be vested in Raja Amar Singh.

Plowden had serious objections to the scheme.[132] His version was that the Maharaja was "wholly unfit to be entrusted with any power whatever", and suggested his deposition in favour of the infant son of his brother Ram Singh. Raja Amar Singh was not only too young but also "shifty and untrustworthy". Both the younger brothers of the Maharaja should be sent away to their respective *jagirs,* and should not be allowed to interfere with the administration of the State. Ram Singh was perhaps harmless but "certainly useless". Janki Prasad was a "non-entity". Nilambar Mukherjee "thoroughly disloyal to us" and wholly ignorant of revenue work. Thus Plowden totally ruled out the establishment of the proposed council. He suggested that the Government of India should interfere "decidedly and effectually". In a nutshell, his recommendation was that the Maharaja should reign, but not rule, instead the country should be administered through a Council by the Resident.[133]

The Maharaja was bent upon the recall of the Babu notwithstanding Plowden's aversion for him. To checkmate the Maharaja, Plowden raised constitutional implications against the appointment of the Babu[134] to which the Maharaja submitted grudgingly and helplessly.

Though rejecting the appointment of Babu Nilambar, Dufferin approved of the Maharaja's proposal for the new constitution. There was a feeling in the Foreign Department that the Maharaja should be given a fair trial, despite the skepticism in all quarters about the success of the new venture.[135]

The Maharaja was to be told that this was his last chance in active administration. He should immediately reorganise judicial and executive services. At the same time Plowden was also warned to sink his own views and do his utmost to help the Maharaja. His right attitude perhaps would smooth out the situation.[136] Plowden informed the Maharaja about the Government's decision, but he suspected that the Maharaja had no idea of the budget and thought that, as the land revenue formed the principal source of income, nothing much could be done until the new settlement was concluded.[137]

Accordingly the Maharaja constituted his Council, dropped the Babu, and requested the Government of India to lend him the services of two able and experienced officials, preferably from the Punjab, for the Judicial and Revenue Departments.[138] The new order of the Council would be as following:

1. The Maharaja — President
2. Raja Amar Singh — Vice-President and in-charge of Judicial and Foreign Departments
3. Raja Ram Singh — Military Department
4. Diwan Janki Parshad — Secretary and Miscellaneous Department.

New Additions

5. Diwan Amar Nath — Nizamat Department.[139]
6. Vacant — Revenue Department
7. Vacant — Judicial Department.

On the appointment of a new member from outside, Raja Amar Singh would be relieved of the charge of Judicial Department.

Plowden had misgivings about the appointment of Diwan Amar Nath, although he was also included in the Lachman Dass ministry. He was informed on the authority of the confidential report of St. John, that he was a young boy of 17 years, in 1886, and wielded a great influence upon the Maharaja, and was also devoid of administrative experience.[140]

About the Maharaja's request to lend him two Punjab officers, Plowden pointed out that to encourage a connection between the Darbar and Punjab officialdom was inexpedient. The Foreign Department agreed with his point, as it was also trying to sever connection between the Darbar and Punjab officialdom for some time past. The newly-appointed Judicial Member, Pandit Bhagat Ram was a Panjabi, but had long been separated from the Punjab. He was a capable and seasoned: Officer.[141]

This was the last contact between Plowden and Kashmir. Dufferin was not happy with Plowden's dabbling in the Kashmir politics. He apprised his views to the Queen.[142] He did not discount Plowden's abilities, but he disliked his "*Zubberdust*" demeanour. A week after this he informed the Secretary of State, Lord Cross of his decision to replace Plowden by Colonel Trevor, the Commissioner at Ajmere.[143] But the circumstances shaped in such a way that he had to change his choice.

Colonel Nisbet, the Commissioner of Rawalpindi at this time was manipulating to be appointed the Resident of Kashmir.[144] He expressed this to Wallace that he was very much interested in the promotion of the welfare of Kashmir, and even frankly acknowledged that the Maharaja and his brothers had often applied to him for coming to their assistance.[145] The Foreign Secretary, Durand was very much opposed to this appointment. He complained to Wallace that the Kashmir Darbar had always tried to play off the Punjab Government against the Resident, and Nisbet's appointment would merely encourage them to believe that they were in future to be entrusted to the charge of the Punjab officials, if not of the Punjab Government.[146] But the Viceroy thought that Nisbet was the right man to be appointed as the Resident, to guide the Maharaja, and whom the Maharaja 'likes and trusts'![147] He thought that Nisbet would put the administration back on the rails.[148]

Plowden laid down the office in November 1888,[149] on the 13th of the same month Colonel Parny Nisbet assumed the office of the Resident.[150] The Maharaja presented him a thundering ovation. At the outset Nisbet formed a favourable impression of the Maharaja.[151]

In spite of all this the future was bleak for Pratap Singh, and very soon he was forced to resign.

References

1. For. Dept., Sec. E., Cons., October 1886, Nos. 235-300.
2. *Civil and Military Gazette*, September 16, 1885, p. 1; *Englishman*, September 23, 1885, p. 5.
3. *Englishman*, September 25,1885, p. 5.
4. D.P., Reel 519, Pratap Singh to Dufferin, September 18, 1885, encl. 17, To the S.O.S., October 19, 1885.
5. For. Dept., Sec. E., December 1886, Nos. 192-245, No. 238, From Dufferin to Pratap Singh, dated October 5, 1885; PSLE1/45, p. 1019, Memorandum of September 28, 1885, on the meeting between Dufferin and Gobind Sahai, encl. 20 in GOI to S.O.S., October 19, 1885.
6. D.P., Reel 517, p. 183, From the S.O.S., September 16, 1885.
7. Ghose, D.P., *op. cit.*, p. 25.
8. PSLE1/45, p. 1019, *Civil and Military Gazette,* September 16, 1885, p. 1; G.M.D. Sufi, *Kashmir*, ii, p. 805.
9. *Ibid.,* St. John to Durand, September 16, 1885, encl. 14 in GOI to SOS, October 19, 1885.
10. Punjab Administrative Reports, 1884-85, Nos. 168, p. 104.
11. For. Dept., Sec. E, December 1885, Nos. 133-245, No. 233.
12. *Ibid.*
13. For. Dept., Sec. E, December 1885, Nos. 192-245, No. 243. Durand wrote: "You should, if necessary, explain that the British Government has placed cantonments in all the principal states of India, and that therefore His Highness need not entertain any apprehension on account of the proposed measure. It will be carried out in Kashmir as it has been elsewhere, with the utmost consideration for the privileges and feelings of the chief......You will understand that no immediate movement is contemplated, and that the troops need not necessarily be stationed at or near Srinagar; but it will be desirable to avoid committing yourself to any promise in this respect.
14. *Ibid.*
15. For. Dept., Sec. E, December 1885, Nos. 192-245, No. 245, No. 617-C, Dated Srinagar, October 27, 1885 (Confidential).
16. *Ibid.*
17. D.P., Reel 529, pp. 460(a)-62, Aitchinson to Dufferin, December 30, 1885.
18. *Ibid.,* pp. 22(c)-(d), Durand to Wallace, January 6, 1886.
19. For. Dept., Progs, Sec. E, July 1886, Cons. 426, Memorandum of a Conversation between Lord Dufferin and Pratap Singh, dated January 15, 1886; *Ibid.,* Sec. I, December 86, Nos. 16-143.
20. File No. R-2, Year 1885, STATE ARCHIVES, Kashmir, Lord Dufferin wrote on March 16, 1886, "I could not consent to retain a

Kashmir representatives at the Headquarters of Government, and to this decision I must adhere."

21. *Ibid.*
22. *Ibid.,* For. Dept., Progs, Sec. E, July 1886, Cons. 427, Dufferin to Maharaja, March 16, 1886.
23. For. Dept., Progs, Sec. E, March 1889, Cons. 108, Memo of January 8, 1886.
24. Bishen Devi to Dufferin, No. 20, 1886, and Bishen Devi to Lt. Governor Punjab, November 25, 1886, PSDOC/3, First Series, p. 816; PFP/2923, Native States, Part B, February 1887, Cons. 3-9, and Cons. 29-30.
25. For. Dept., Prog, Sec. E, March 1889, Cons. 108, Memo January 8, 1886; For. Dept., Sec. I, March 1889, Nos. 107-200.
26. *Ibid.*
27. For. Dept., Progs, Sec. E, March 1889, Cons. 108, Memo of 8th January 1886.
28. *Ibid.,* Report of the Kashmir Correspondent, September 13, 1885, *Englishman*, September 23, 1885, p. 5.
29. For. Dept., Progs, Sec. E, March 1889, Cons. 108, Memo of 8th January 1886; PSDOC/3, First Series, p. 823.
30. For. Dept., Progs, Ext. A, June 1886, Nos. 90-93, No. 91.
31. India For. Prog., 2783, June 1886, Cons. 91, Maharaja to Viceroy, March 3, 1886; For. Dept., Sec. E, March 1889, Nos. 109-200, External A, June 1886, No. 90.
32. For. Dept., Sec. E, Cons., October 1886, Nos. 235-300, Sec. E, December 1885, No. 233.
33. *Ibid.,* External A, June 1886, Nos. 42-48.
34. *Ibid.,* No. 275, From Plowden to Dufferin. Then he (Nilambar) spoke about St. John's bribe, and said that when the Viceroy spoke about this to the Maharaja, he and the Maharaja were taken aback, but had been obliged to admit that the money had been offered.
35. *Ibid.,* No. 243, Sec. E, December 1885, Foreign Dept., Letter No. 1629 C.
36. For. Dept., Progs, Sec. E, July 1886, Cons. 426.
37. For. Dept., Sec. E, October 1886, Nos. 235-300, External A, February 1886, Nos. 88-91.
38. *Ibid.*
39. *Ibid.*
40. *Ibid.*
41. *Ibid.*
42. *Ibid.,* External A, June 1886, Nos. 42-48.
43. *Ibid.*

44. Indian For. Progs, 2783, June 1886, Cons. 90, St. John to Durand, March 20, 1886.
45. For. Dept., Progs, Sec, E, July 1886, Cons. 423, Maharaja to Dufferin, January 14, 1886.
46. Cross Papers, 24, No. 96, Dufferin to Cross, June 1, 1888.
47. Indian For. Progs, 2791, July 1886, Cons. 148.
48. D.P., Reel 530, pp. 130-33, Plowden to Durand, August 8, 1886; *Civil and Military Gazette,* October 13, 1886, p. 6.
49. For. Dept., Sec. E, October 1886, Nos. 235-300, No. 275, Kashmir Residency, August 8, 1886; For. Dept., Progs, Ext. A, June 1886, Nos. 90-93, No. 90.

49A. See F.N. 34.

50. For. Dept. Progs, Sec. E., October 1886, Cons. 287, Nos. 235-300.
51. D.P., Reel 530, pp. 130-33. Plowden to Durand, August 8, 1886. "If I can get the Babu depart, even on leave on his own accord, it will be a great gain."
52. D.P., Reel 530, pp. 130-33, Plowden to Durand, August 8, 1886.
53. *The Pioneer,* July 31, 1886, p. 1.
54. For. Dept., Sec. E, October 1886, Nos. 235-300, No. 287, August 15, 1886, From Plowden to Durand; For. Dept., Sec, E, October 1886, Nos. 435-441, No. 437, From Plowden to H.M. Durand, "I telegraphed to you about Nilambar's resignation; next day it was confirmed and appears to be true—for his *ruksatwana khillat* has been ordered".
55. *The Pioneer,* September 22, 1886, p. 1, *The Englishman,* September 27, 1886, p. 5, and October 2, 1886, p. 4; Bose, J.C., *op. cit.*, p. 32.
56. For. Dept., Sec. E, Progs, October 1886, Nos. 235-300, No. 239.
57. *Ibid.,* From Plowden to H.M. Durand, No. 268, August 1, 1886. "I have already written my views about the impasse to which existing orders on the subject might inevitably lead, and you knew that I am not singular in holding that opinion; Henvey and St. John held them as strongly as I do. Therefore, I hope very much that the orders you told me are coming and will put the matter right."
58. For. Dept., Sec. E, October 1886, Nos. 235-300, No. 289, Dated August 19, 1886.
59. *Ibid.*
60. For. Dept., Sec. E, March 1889, Nos. 109-200, External A, June 1886, Letter No. 261, Cons. 239, June 17, 1886.
61. D.P., Reel 529, No. 633, From Aitchinson to Dufferin, December 30, 1885, "Maharaja complained bitterly of the attacks made on him in the *Pioneer* and the persistent way the paper abuses him".
62. D.P., Reel 529, No. 319, From Durand to Mackenzie Wallace, January 6, 1886.

63. *The Pioneer,* October 21, 1886.
64. For. Dept., Progs, Sec. E, December 1886, Cons. 73, Memorandum of interview on November 4, 1886.
65. Cross Papers, 22, No. 47A, Dufferin to Cross, June 24, 1887.
66. PSLEI/54, pp. 855-918, Plowden's Report, March 5, 1888, encl. 1 in GOI to SOS, August 18, 1888.
67. For. Dept., Sec. E, March 1889, Nos. 107-200.
68. For. Dept., Sec. E, March 1887, Nos. 46-48; *Ibid.,* April 1887, Nos. 510-12.
69. Selections, *The Aftab-i-Punjab,* March 23, 1887.
70. *Ibid., The Punjab Punch*, March 19, 1887.
71. For. Dept., Progs, Sec. E, March 1887, Cons. 46-48, D/o No. 2, Plowden to Cunningham, February 14, 1887.
72. Lansdowne Papers, IB(1), pp. 923-72, Preliminary Report by Wingate, August 1, 1888, encl. in GOI to SOS, July 26, 1889; PFP, 2923, Native States B, April 1887, Cons. 16 and 126-27.
73. IFF, 3738, February 1890, Cons. 307-308, DE Bourbel's General Report.
74. PSLEI, 48, p. 765, encl. in GOI to SOS, October 25, 1886, IFP, 2791, Nov. 1886, p. 19; For. Dept., Sec. E, October 1886, Nos. 235-300.
75. IFP, 3036, August 1887, Cons. 156, Plowden to Government of India, March 26, 1887.
76. IFP, 3278, March 1888, Cons. 586A, Lachman Dass to Plowden, August 4, 1887.
77. IFP, 3280, August 1888, Cons. 94.
78. IFP, 3278, Lachman Dass to Plowden, August 4, 1887, Cons. 586A.
79. For. Dept., Progs, Sec. E, March 1887, Cons. 46-48, D.O. No. 2, Plowden to Cunningham, February 14, 1887.
80. IFP, 3275, January 1888, Cons. 42-44.
81. *Ibid.,* 3501, January 1889, Cons. 116, Plowden to GOI, November 12, 1888.
82. *Ibid.,* October 14, 1888, Cons. 117, Report of Surgeon Major Deane.
83. For. Dept., Progs, Sec. E, April 1887, Cons. 510-12, K.W. 2, Plowden to Cunningham, March 18, 1887.
84. *Ibid.,* Maharaja to Plowden, March 11, 1887.
85. For. Dept., Progs, Sec. E, March 1887, Cons. 48, February 28, 1887; *Ibid.,* Sec. E, April 1887, Cons. 510-12, and K.W. 2.
86. PSDOC, 2, First Series, pp. 254(a)—(d), Gobind Sahai to Wallace, June 8, 1887; For. Dept., Progs, Sec. E, June 1887, Cons. 171, Plowden to Durand, April 29, 1887.

87. For. Dept., Progs, Sec. E, June 1887, Cons. 171; *Ibid.,* Sec. E, June 1887, Cons. 179-92.
88. Bakidar means debtor.
89. For. Dept., Progs, Sec. E, K.N., June 1887, Nos. 171-194.
90. PSLEI, 40, p. 27, Henvey's Report, May 15, 1880, encl. 2, in GOI to SOS, April 7, 1884; *Ibid.*; 54, p. 855, Plowden's Report, March 5, 1888.
91. PSLEI, 54, pp. 855-918, Plowden's Report, March 5, 1888, encl. 1 in GOI to SOS, August 18, 1888.
92. *Ibid.*
93. PSLEI, 54, p. 855, Plowden's Report, March 5, 1888, encl. 1 in GOI to SOS, August 18, 1888; *Ibid.,* sub-encl. in encl. 2 to GOI to SOS, Lachman Dass to Plowden, August 18, 1888; *The Pioneer,* January 26, 1888, p. 6.
94. PSLEI, 54, p. 855, Plowden to Durand, March 23, 1888, encl. 2 in GOI to SOS, August 18, 1888.
95. For. Dept., Sec. E, March 1889, Nos. 107-200.
96. *Ibid.*
97. PSLEI, 54, p. 855, Pratap Singh to Dufferin, March 19, 1888.
98. Ghose, D.K., *op. cit.*, p. 67.
99. PSLEI, 54, p. 855.
100. For. Dept., Sec. E, March 1889, Nos. 107-200, Nos. 15C, and 19C. Plowden's letters dated March 23, April 4, 1888 to Durand.
101. *Ibid.,* PSLEI, 54, pp. 825-918, Durand to Plowden, March 22, 1888, sub-encl. in encl. 3, to GOI to SOS August 18, 1888.
102. *Ibid.,* pp. 855-918, Sub-encl. I to encl. 1 in GOI to SOS, August 18, 1888.
103. *Ibid.,* p. 855, Plowden's Report, March 5, 1888;. Bose, J.C., *Cashmere Prince,* p. 69.
104. *The Pioneer,* March 21, 1888, p. 1.
105. *Ibid.,* March 21, 1888, p. 1, and March 1888, p. 1.
106. *Ibid.,* March 23, 1888, p. 1.
107. *Ibid.,* March 26, 1888, p. 1, Lord Dufferin's Speech at the Town Hall, Calcutta, March 23.
108. Roberts Papers, Box File D3 No. R27/159, Dufferin to Roberts, April 9, 1888.
109. Cross Papers, 24, No. 89, Dufferin to Cross, April 16, 1888. Dufferin wrote about the cancellation of his trip. "For some reasons, I was glad, for others sorry. I was sorry not so much on account of missing a sight of that wondrous valley, as because I am not satisfied with the condition of public affairs in the State. We have tried Agent after Agent there, and none of them had done well. The fact is our political are a very

poor lot. They are either lazy or stupid, or vulgar-minded bullies, or disreputable or amicable gentlemen, devoid of any real grasp or energy".

110. Selections, *Hindustan,* May 13, 1888.
111. *Ibid., Khair Khwah-i-Kashmir,* October 16, 1888. "He was kind to low and mean persons, and opposed to friends and well-wishers of the State".
112. *Ibid., The Aftab-i-Punjab,* (Lahore) February 16, 1888.
113. *Ibid., The Punjab Punch,* March 10, 1888. 'When Maharaja expressed a desire (when powerless he might retire to Utar-bahni), Diwan impertinently replied that His Highness might go on a pilgrimage to Gaya and Prayag, if he pleased'.
114. *Ibid., The Aftab-i-Punjab,* (Lahore), February 16, 1887.
115. *Ibid., Rafiq-i-Hind, (Lahore), March 5, 1887, The Vazir-i-Hind,* February 13, 1887. *Ibid., The Ravi,* March 21, 1888.
116. *Ibid., Akhbar-i-Am,* June 24, 1887, *The Najmul Hind*, September 15, 1887; *Koh-i-Nur*, March 22, 1887.
117. *Ibid., The Punjab Akhbar*, March, 7, 1888; *The Aftab-i-Punjab,* May 27, 1887, March 5, 19, 1888.
118. *Ibid., The Rafiq-i-Hind*, October 15, 1887.
119. *Ibid., The Punjab Punch*, March 17, 1887.
120. *Ibid.*
121. *Ibid., The Charpuz,* August 21, 1888.
122. *Ibid., The Punjabi Akhbar,* March 24, 1888.
123. For. Dept., Sec. E, March 1889, Nos. 107-200, Henderson wrote about the Council, "rumours, not without foundation, have been rife of neglect of state business and of scenes of debauchery... the two Rajas are young and inexperienced and not given to hard work; that Raja Amar Singh is not friendly to the Maharaja; that Raja Ram Singh and Lachman Dass detest him and are detested by him, that all of them said to be dissolute; and that Lachman Dass is a notorious free-liver".
124. *Ibid.*
125. *Ibid.*
126. PSLEI, 54, p. 855, Plowden to Durand, March 28, 1888, encl. 3 and sub-enclosures in GOI to SOS, August 18, 1888; For. Dept., Sec. E, March 1889, Nos. 107-200.
127. For. Dept., Sec. E, March 1889, Nos. 107-200.
128. *Ibid.*
129. *Ibid.*
130. *Ibid.*, Letter No. 26C, dated April 21, 1888; PSLEI, 54, p. 855, Sub-encl. 4, GOI to SOS August 18, 1888.
131. *Ibid.*

132. For. Dept., Sec. E, March 1889, Nos. 107-200.
133. *Ibid.*
134. D.P., Reel 533, No. 398, p. 304, Resident to India, March 30, 1888; *Ibid.,* Durand to Wallace, March 31,1888.
135. For. Dept., Sec. E, March 1889, Nos. 107-200, Durand wrote: "I am well aware that the course I propose is not unlikely to prove a failure. The Maharaja will not improbably fall back into the hands of unworthy favourites and personal servants. Indeed it would appear from Mr. Plowden's Report that brothers felt too weak to stand against such influences". Dufferin wrote: "I see no objection to allowing the Maharaja to remain President of the Council, at all events as an experiment; but the criticism which I am inclined to make on the suggested arrangement is that we are delivering over the State to a half-witted Prince and to his two young brothers, who are obviously unfitted for any serious administrative responsibility."; PSDI/14, pp. 55(*a*)-60, SOS to GOI, October 12, 1888, Lord Cross, was also of the opinion that "to try Pratap Singh to the last", so that if it should "become necessary hereafter to remove the Maharaja as incapable of ruling his State, it will not be possible to charge the Indian Government with acting in an arbitrary manner................ ."
136. For, Dept., Sec. E, March 1889, Nos. 107-200. Durand wrote: "If he (Plowden) interferes authoritatively at every turn and practically rules the State, we incur and justly incur, misrepresentation, and the odium of all existing evils .... It is unfortunate that he has hitherto taken so strong a line in the opposite direction, and made the Maharaja afraid of him".
137. For, Dept., Sec. E, March 1889, Cons. 177, September 21, 1888.
138. For. Dept., Progs., Sec. E, March 1889, Cons, 178.
139. For. Dept, Sec. E, March 1889, Nos. 107-200. In Mr. Crawford's Kashmir precis on page 119, the Nizamat is described as follows: "This is a local force of infantry which was formed about 1871, and is distributed among the seven zillas of Jammu. Each zillah contains one regiment under a Commander, of the same strength, officered and equipped in the same way as a battalion of the Jungi Fauj. The men are the sons of Zamindars and are employed within the limits of their own zillahs on revenue and tehsil work. They are a drilled force, and are armed like the lunge Fauj. The whole force is commanded by a Colonel, and is administered directly by the Wazir of Kashmir and the Chief Diwan. The men spend four or five months in every year at their homes. The Nizamat is largely drawn on from time to time to fill up gaps in the Jungi Fauj, to which it acts as the principal source of supply for recruits".
140. *Ibid.*
141. *Ibid.*
142. D.P., Reel 510, No. 98, Dufferin to the Queen, May 21, 1888.
143. Cross Papers, 24, No. 96, Dufferin to Cross, June 1, 1888.

144. D.P., Reel 533, No. 5, Nisbet to Wallace, July 3, 1888.
145. *Ibid.*
146. *Ibid.,* B.P., Reel 533, pp. 174-75, Durand to Wallace, September 5, 1888.
147. PSDOC, 2, First Series, pp. 1731-32, GOI to SOS, October 15, 1888.
148. Cross Papers, 25, No. 121, Dufferin to Cross, December 3, 1888. Dufferin hoped, "that our new man in Cashmere will put everything to rights in that most important corner of the world".
149. IFP, 3508, February 1889, Memo., November 13, 1888, Cons. 3, 5.
150. *Ibid.,* Cons. 5, Memo. No. 13, 1888.
151. D.P., Reel 534, No. 656, Nisbet to Dufferin, December 8, 1888. "The Maharaja is not the least wanting in intelligence, far from it, being very shrewd in all his remarks, and he can reason and argue with much force and good sense".

4

Nilambar Mukherjee and Bengalis in the Jammu and Kashmir

In the mid-eighties of the nineteenth century there arose a controversy over the appointments of the Bengalis on lucrative posts in Kashmir and they were also charged for stalling the progressive reforms. The most eminent among them was Nilambar Mukherjee, who cut a prominent figure in Kashmir politics for a period of nearly two decades. He was popularly known in Kashmir as Babu. One of the most distinguished graduates of the University of Calcutta, he went to Lahore in 1867 to join the bar of the Punjab Chief Court. In the following year, Diwan Kripa Ram, having heard the fame of Mukherjee recommended him to Maharaja Ranbir Singh, who appointed him as the Chief Justice of Kashmir. While working in that capacity, he was deputed to make arrangements for His Highness's property in Lahore. He did both of his works so creditably that the Maharaja as a token of appreciation almost doubled his salary. When the Silk industry was started in Kashmir, Babu, was placed in-charge of it. The industry rapidly developed and expanded, and Babu was favoured with the commendatory notices of the Government of India and the Secretary of State. He rose very high in the estimation of his master to the envy of his colleagues, who started a whispering campaign against his management of the silk concern. This disgusted him, and he prayed his master to be allowed to retire from his charge. Maharaja Ranbir Singh, while granting his prayer, showed a due appreciation of his valuable past services by promoting him to the rank of a Minister, which he held until the death of the Maharaja. Pratap Singh in his younger days was not favourably inclined towards Babu. But, as he grew up, he came to understand him. The late Maharaja also, on his death-bed, enjoined upon Pratap Singh to regard Babu as his most faithful servant and trusted councillor.[2]

After the death of Ranbir Singh, Babu pleaded to the Resident the case of Pratap Singh for stay put the order of the imposition of the Resident in Kashmir.[3] Being a distinguished lawyer he had the capability to draft any legal case in a systematic way embellished with jurisprudistic dialectics. Perhaps this was the reason that the first two Residents had given adverse reports about him. In St. John's opinion he was "clever and well-intentioned, but without practical experience of administration and deficient in force of character." When Babu was made the Finance Minister, after Prime Minister Anant Ram lost his mental balance, St. John was not happy over this choice. He wrote to Durand, the Foreign Secretary that Babu was believed to be a mere theorist, anxious perhaps for reforms, but ignorant of the way to carry them out. His influence over the Maharaja was solely due to his instant pretexts for resisting the supremacy of the British Government and "for evading compliance with its advice".[4]

At this time there arose a sharp controversy over the appointment of the Bengalis in the State. According to Durand, "the greatest obstacle to progress of any kind was the presence of so many useless and mischievous Bengalis."[5] The Second Resident, Plowden felt defeated when his plan to implant his own man as Chief Justice was foiled, as Rishibar Mukherjee, a brother of Nilambar was appointed the Chief Justice of the Sadar Adalat at Jammu. Plowden was revengeful. He bore pressure upon Durand to issue orders to eliminate objectionable persons or to place a limit to their employment. Aitchison was also of the opinion that Kashmir was "rapidly becoming the happy hunting ground of Bengali Babus."[6] Babu Raj in Jammu, was a subject of common talk in the Punjab. He himself suspected that the Maharaja—a man with no force of character—-was completely under the thumb of the Bengalis. The Maharaja and St. John had requested him to supply a good 'native' settlement officer for

Kashmir, but he wrote to Wallace, "I cannot agree to lend Kashmir my officers if they are liable to be ousted in favour of Bengali Babus and returned on my hands without notice."[7] Plowden got bolstered up. He emphasised, "the employment of Bengalis, unless they were government servants, in the Native States was highly objectionable". He agreed with Aitchison that the introduction of the Bengali element into Kashmir—especially the high position that Nilambar occupied— was the cause of great dissatisfaction.[8] The Foreign Secretary supported his political agents. *The Pioneer* also mounted opposition against the Bengali element in the Kashmir Government Service.[9]

The Maharaja had appointed a number of Bengalis at the suggestion of the Babu, which excited the jealousy of Punjab officials. A section of the Punjabi Press took up the side of the Punjabi officials. A Lahore-based paper[10] drew up a cartoon with the caption 'Present State of Affairs in Kashmir', which purported to show that the Bengalis are eating up the grapes and the Diwan-family helplessly looking at them. In another of its issue it wrote that the Bengali officials dismissed 'Natives' in order to accommodate their 'countrymen'.[11] The same paper in another issue advised the Maharaja against trusting the strangers and published a cartoon in which a Bengali is carrying a camel represented as Kashmir, his own way, while an English-man endeavours to pull the animal back by the tail.[12] *The Liberal* published a list of the Bengalis employed in the State.[13] However, another paper rebutted the allegations of *The Delhi Punch* and *The Victoria Punch* that Maharaja had largely employed Bengalis in his service. The Maharaja had dismissed Six Bengalis, who were employed in his father's time, and had appointed five new Bengalis. There were in all only eleven Bengalis in the State including the Babu.[14] But if the Bengalis were not the state subjects, the Diwan's family which occupied even the lucrative posts of the Prime Minister (Gobind Sahai and Lachman Sahai were relatives and both were Prime Ministers) were also not the state subjects. Besides, one point goes in favour of the Babu, that the personnel which he got appointed were men of calibre and integrity, *e.g.*, Rishibar Mukherjee disobeyed an order from Amar Singh when he tried to invade the independence of the Judiciary. Though the Resident who desired a show-down of the Bengalis and the Maharaja, kept quiet,[15] but he later reported that one of the worst judicial abuses in Kashmir was the Executive pressure brought to bear upon it, "to decide cases at the sacrifice of conscience and fairplay.[16] Another Bengali, Jogendra Bose, who served the state only for four months, wrote an able defence of the Maharaja in his pamphlet 'Cashmere and its Prince,[17] which helped Pratap Singh in his restoration to the power, as it attracted the attention of the British Parliamentarians. Babu, himself was a man of integrity. During Pratap Singh's rule he was working as the Finance Minister under Diwan Gobind Sahai's Prime Ministership, but he had the courage to ask the Diwan to account for ₹65,000/-, which had been embezzled by him. This coupled with the capability of the Babu incurred the wrath of the Diwan, who conspired against him.[18] Babu was so fed up with intrigues that he resigned thrice, the Maharaja turned those down each time and accepted his resignation on the fourth time with great reluctance. The Babu met Plowden and apprised him that he had resigned, as his suggestions for reforms were ignored, and that his conscience would not allow him to continue to draw pay for doing nothing while holding such a responsible position. Gobind Sahai, though a non-entity in the administration of the state, contrived to get the Babu ousted in combination with Suraj Bal, Sawal Singh, and others. Sawal Singh told the Maharaja that the '*Mandleek*' would not be satisfied until Nilambar was cleared out of Jammu. Babu did not get the pension, and showed the *sanad* on which he relied to Plowden. He agreed with Plowden that the *sanad* had a loophole, and admitted that it entirely depended upon the Maharaja to give him or withhold the pension. He pleaded for a *Jagir* from the Government of India in recognition of his services, as he had always furthered the views and policies of the paramount power. Plowden replied that he knew of no precedent for a grant to a man in his position.[19]

Controversy over the Appointment of the Foreigners in Kashmir

To improve the administration of Kashmir State, the Government of India in 1884 prescribed "the appointment of the respectable officials" amongst the principal measures of administrative reform.[20] In June 1886, Plowden urged that for the speedy implementation of reforms, it was "essential that the Government of India should control the appointment of British subjects to offices in Kashmir".[21] The Resident was directed to obtain from the Darbar a statement showing the appointments held by "foreigners" in the Kashmir State.[22] Plowden reported that a large number of officials, and especially the senior officials, were British subjects whose employment was not sanctioned by the Government of India. The Darbar was requisitioning the services of the 'foreigners', as it did not possess a trained and efficient bureaucracy. He suggested that the term of the British officials loaned to the Darbar, should be fixed for two years, as it had become customary for the Darbar to regard a sanction once given as unlimited in time.

The Residents' proposals were based upon Article 7 of the Treaty of Amritsar, whose English version was as follows: "The Maharaja Gulab Singh engages never to *take or retain* in his service any British subject, nor the subject of any European or American State, without the consent of the British Government". The English version of the treaty was authoritative, but the Persian version forbade the employment to "the people of the foreign country of England and other European people or residents of America".[23] There occurred also a similar discrepancy in the Nepalese treaty as well.[24] In practice the Persian version had been acted rather than the English.[25]

Article 7 was a matter or discussion since 1881.[26] Sir Alfred Lyall's observation was that although the treaty had given them power to interfere in the employment of British Indian subjects in Kashmir, it was practically not possible *to limit* the 'influx of natives' from the British India. They in any particular case could interfere, but it would be more proper to request the Darbar to inform the Government of India when it employed the British subjects.

Lord Ripon thought that the matter should be dealt with carefully. He agreed with Sir Charles Aitchison's opinion that, though the treaty had authorised them to veto the employment of the British subjects in the Kashmir State, the right had not been exercised so far. It would certainly lead to controversy to assert it without specific cause or until they had a strong case.[27]

The moot question was whether the latest position in Kashmir warranted 'a really strong case' for 'the assertion of hitherto dormant treaty right'. The decision arrived at was that the statement[28] showing the list of the Foreigners in the employment did not make a strong case. As Nilambar and his assistants had left the State there were only seven Bengali servants in the employment of the Darbar, the list does not give good grounds for an immediate and strongly marked communication, to the Darbar.[29] The Foreign Office was of the opinion that it was rather a straining of the language to call Punjabies "foreigners" in the Jammu region at least.[30]

This decision of the Foreign Office was not convincing that the Bengalis were Foreigners' and the Punjabis were not, while both of them hailed from the British India.

After the fall of Lachman Dass Ministry the Maharaja telegraphed Babu to resume his duty in Kashmir. Plowden, on getting information sent him a counter-telegram, intimating him not to come without the sanction of the Government of India.[31]

The Maharaja was so much impressed by Babu that he tried his utmost to get him back. He submitted the list of the members of the reconstituted council, in which the Babu was given the charge of Revenue Department, but Plowden opposed it tooth and nail.[32] Maharaja in the last resort requested Plowden for permission to appoint Babu under a provisional arrangement. But Plowden remarked that this meant that the Maharaja wanted to make Babu a permanent employee.[33] Pratap Singh asserted that the Article VII of the

Persian version of the Treaty of Amritsar, which bore only the signature of his grandfather Gulab Singh, authorised the State to appoint any British subject without the consent of the Indian Government. On his part Plowden held the English version of the treaty, as authoritative and any denial of it by Pratap Singh would mean from the British point of view, forfeiture of his right to continue as the Ruler of Kashmir.[34] The Maharaja left the matter to the Government of India,[35] which enjoined upon the Maharaja that it should be informed beforehand, if he wanted to employ any person, "formerly in their service, or to give an important post to any native subject of Her Majesty".[36]

Thus, Babu was not allowed to take up service in Kashmir, although even Durand held a good opinion of Babu.[37] Colonel Henderson, also upheld the same opinion. He even supported the request of the Maharaja to get the Babu back. He wrote, "For myself I have not such a bad opinion of the Babu as Plowden apparently has; he is perhaps too theoretical, but he is certainly to think the most honest".[38] Digby says that Babu worked with "the zeal, honesty, devotion, and single-mindedness that characterises him".[39]

Thus, the bogey that Nilambar Mukherjee and the Bengali officials were eating up the vitals of the state was a false propaganda. The boot was on the other leg.

References

1. Gadru, S.N., *Kashmir Papers*, p. 135.
2. *Ibid.*
3. From Resident in Kashmir to Secretary to the G.O.I., For. Dept., Jammu, September 16, 1885.
4. For. Ext., A., 90, Progs., June 1886, St. John to H.M. Durand, March 20, 1886; IFP, 2783, June 1886, Cons. 90.
5. For. Sec. Progs., October 1886, Nos. 235-300 (K.W.).
6. D.P., Reel 529, pp. 464-65, Aitchison to Wallace, June 16, 1886, No. 688 and enclosure.
7. *Ibid.*
8. For. Dept., Progs, Sec. E, October 1886, Cons. 238, Plowden to Durand, D.O., June 14, 1886.

9. For. Dept., Sec. E, Progs, October 1886, Nos. 235-300, No. 237, Telegram, No. 1185-E, Dated Simla, June 10, 1886, *The Pioneer* of June 9, 1886.
10. Selections, *Delhi Punch,* (Lahore), May 26, 1886.
11. *Ibid.,* April 14, 1886.
12. *Ibid.,* February 24, 1886.
13. Ghose, D.K., *Kashmir in Transition,* p. 40.
14. Selections, *The Rafiq-i-Hind,* (Lahore), May 29, 1886.
15. *Pioneer,* June 9, 1886.
16. PSDOC, 3, First Series, pp. 633-60.
17. PSDOC, 3, First Series, pp. 811-51, Cunningham's Review.
18. For. Dept., Sec. E, October 1886, Nos. 235-300.
19. For. Dept., Progs, Sec. E, October 1886, Nos. 435-441, No. 439, Plowden to Durand, Dated October 9, 1886.
20. For. Dept., Progs, Sec. E, October 1886, Nos. 235-300, K.W. *Kashmir,* p. 2.
21. *Ibid.,* No. 238, From Plowden to H.M. Durand, June 14, 1886 ".....In order to carry out the instructions in the Foreign Department Confidential No. 1, dated 1st August 1884, and subsequent letters, it appears to me essential that the Government of India should control the appointment of British subjects to offices in Kashmir. The sooner this is done the better. Action might be taken on the VII article of the treaty of Amritsar, and I might be instructed to intimate to the Darbar that no British subjects can be taken or retained in the Maharaja's service except with the consent of the British Government, and to call upon the Darbar for a list of all such persons now in the service of the Darbar."
22. *Ibid.,* No. 247.
23. For. Dept., Pol. A., February 1872, Nos. 39-49.
24. For. Dept., Int. A., September 1886, Nos. 321, p. 24.
25. For. Dept., Sec., December 1881, Nos. 526-532.
26. *Ibid.,* K.W., p. 1.
27. For. Dept., Sec. E, Pros, February 1887, Nos. 10-13, "It does not of course follow that the justice of the particular decision on which we chose to take our stand would reconcile the Darbar to the assertion of a hitherto dormant treaty right; but at any rate they would not be able to object that we were raising difficult and distasteful questions without sufficient reason".
28. *Ibid.,* See the Appendix II.
29. *Ibid.,* For. Dept., Sec. E, October 1886, Nos. 235-300, K.W., No. 247.
30. Moreover, many of these so-called 'foreigners' have been domiciled for years in the Maharaja's country—notably the "Diwan" family from

Eminabad in the Gujranwala district of which Gobind Sahai is an illustrious member.

31. D.P., Reel 533, No. 398, p. 304, Resident to G.O.I. March 30, 1888.
32. For. Dept., Sec. E, March 1889, Nos. 107-200.
33. PSLEI, 54, pp. 855-918, Maharaja to Resident, June 22, 1888, Sub. encl. in enl. 8 to GOI to SOS.
34. For. Dept., Progs, Sec. E. March 1889, Cons. 157-160.
35. *Ibid.*
35. For. Dept., Progs, Sec. E, February 1887, Nos. 10-13.
37. For, Dept., Prog, Sec. E, July 1886, Cons. 426.
38. For. Dept., Sec. F, March 1889, Nos. 107-200.
39. Gadru, *op. cit.*, p. 135.

5

Deposition of Pratap Singh

Colonel Parry Nisbet, the new Resident, was a friend of the late Maharaja Ranbir Singh, and the present Maharaja. Ironically, enough the Maharaja Pratap Singh suffered more humiliation and degradation under an apparently friendly Resident than under unfriendly ones. In the beginning Nisbet reported that the Maharaja and his brothers were eager to co-operate with him in carrying out the reforms.[1] The Maharaja apprised the Resident of his desire to meet the Viceroy, Lord Lansdowne, which was very much appreciated by Nisbet, as he thought that such a meeting would help the settlement of frontier problems and other matters.[2] Accordingly, he informed Durand about it and suggested that in case the desired meeting could not take place, he himself could go to Calcutta along with Raja Amar Singh. The Viceroy was so busy that the meeting could not take place.

SECTION 1: THE DEPOSITION

While Nisbet was busy in negotiating a close rapport between the Viceroy and Darbar on February 25, 1889, a batch of 34 letters in Dogri script, alleged to be in the Maharaja's own handwriting, to the Tzar of Russia, Maharaja Dalip Singh, and to his favourites fell in the hands of Nisbet.[3] Nisbet, without any proper verification, jumped at the conclusion, on the authority of Amar Singh, that the letters were in the handwriting of the Maharaja, and this tantamount to be a treason on the part of the latter. Nisbet gloated over his discovery. He wrote to Durand that the Maharaja 'with lucid intervals of good sense and propriety' was utterly incapable of being trusted to run the administration. He advised the Resident that, since 'the Maharaja is a timid and very superstitious man' and being in the hands of unscrupulous scoundrels, he should be dissociated from the administration.[4]

The enthusiasm of Nisbet was not shared either by the Viceroy or by the Foreign Secretary, Durand. Though the latter appreciated the gravity of the matter, he could not swallow the whole affair, being aware of the intrigues of Amar Singh against the Maharaja. He rightly thought that in the removal of the Maharaja, 'we should have to wash a great deal of dirty linen in public.'[5] The Viceroy ordered that Nisbet should make a full enquiry into the matter and afterwards present his case.[6] Nisbet, the man on the spot, was so much excited that he thought no investigations were needed in the case, as the Maharaja's signatures have been verified by his two younger brothers, therefore the powers of the Maharaja should be entrusted to a Council composed of the Maharaja's brothers and other members approved by the Government of India.[7]

Afterwards, Nisbet proceeded for Jammu and had two interviews with the Maharaja on March 7 and 8. According to his version, in both of these meetings the Maharaja had expressed his desire to retire from public life, delegating his powers to a Council which should include the Resident himself. Resident Nisbet knew that this proposal was not feasible, instead he suggested inclusion of an English member in the Council, which would ensure freedom from intrigue and continuity of the Kashmir administration. Nisbet's impression was that the Maharaja by this time was thoroughly tired of the worry and troubles his officials had given him. A few hours after his second meeting on March 8, Amar Singh brought to the Resident an edict or *Irshad* of the Maharaja in which the latter had declared his intention to retire voluntarily for a period of five years, and authorised the work to a Council consisting of five members.[8] Of these five members two were his brothers, Ram Singh and Amar Singh, a third was to be an English member selected by the Government of India, and the two others were Pandit Suraj Kaul and Bhag Ram.

The Government of India was not inclined to give undue importance to the letters, but the news leaked out and the press gave it a wide circulation.[9] Lansdowne was exasperated.[10] Durand also doubted the sagacity of the Resident, who had seen so much of the Princely States. He advised the Viceroy to restrain Nisbet.[11] Durand approved the Resident's plan of the proposed Council, but disapproved of the appointment of an English member for it would seem the appearance of annexation. Durand advised the Viceroy that in issuing orders he should specifically lay down that the proposed change was not based either on the letters or voluntary resignation but, keeping in view both of them and maladministration, it was desired that the Maharaja for a time delegate his powers to the State Council.[12] Lansdowne agreed with his Foreign Secretary that the whole change should be made as quietly and unostentatiously as possible, so that it might not appear that the Maharaja was being publicly degraded.[13] He also attached little importance to the letters.[14]

Accordingly, the Viceroy issued instructions to the Resident on April 1, 1889,[15] that Maharaja was to retain his rank and dignity as the Chief of the State, but full powers of Government were to be vested in a Council consisting of the Maharaja's brothers and three or four officials selected by the Government of India. The appointment of an Englishman on the Council was not thought desirable. Amar Singh was made the President of the Council. Besides his rank and dignity the Maharaja would receive from the revenues of the State an annual grant sufficient to maintain his household in due comfort: and to defray any expenditure which might be rightly charged upon him. Nevertheless he would have no power of alienating the State Revenues, and the grant placed at his disposal, though adequate, must not be extravagantly large. The Council was granted full powers of administration, but they had to exercise their powers under the supervision of the Resident. They would take no steps of importance without consulting him, and they would follow his advice whenever it might be offered.[16]

The Resident also was directed that in communicating this order to the Maharaja and others, he should take care to avoid basing the decision exclusively either on the letters or on the Maharaja's resignation. The letters were repudiated by the Maharaja and were not of a very novel character, while on the other hand the Government of India are by no means prepared to make the present settlement a matter of compact with the Maharaja and to accept all the conditions laid down by his edict of the 8th March, for example the five years limit. Nisbet was to apprise the Maharaja that the decision of the Government was based on a full consideration of all the circumstances, the letters and the Maharaja's desire to resign being considered among other things, but only as portions of a difficult and complicated case, which it has been necessary to settle on broader grounds of general policy.[17]

The Resident was further ordered that, "you should remember that the Government of India has no desire to turn Kashmir into the semblance of a British district, or to place all administrative posts in the hands of the Punjabi foreigners." He should ascertain requirements of the State with regard to the subordinate services and should submit for the approval of the Government his views as to the steps to be taken for reorganising the administrative services.[18]

The appointment of Amar Singh as the Resident was not to the liking of the Resident, first, as he was young and inexperienced, second, passing over of Ram Singh in favour of his younger brother would create problems in the way of the smooth running of administration.[19] Though uncertain of Ram Singh's attitude, Nisbet was eager to keep the two brothers together. He thought he would be able to manage the New Council with his knowledge of the Indian character, which responded to a strong and vigorous policy, rather than the soft policy which 'they easily mistake for timidity.' Thus in reality the power of the administration of the State and of making important decisions was transferred to the Resident.[20] The decision of the Government of India was communicated to the Maharaja in a private Darbar on April 17 by Colonel Nisbet accompanied by Captain Ramsay.[21] Those present, besides the Maharaja, were his brothers, Rajas Ram Singh and Amar Singh, the two members of the Council, Pandit Suraj Kaul and Bhag Ram, Diwan Janaki Prasad, an old official of the State, and Sardar Rup Singh, the Governor of Kashmir... The Resident handed over to the Maharaja and the Prime

Minister, Raja Amar Singh, the written orders of the Government of India. The Maharaja said that he would consider the letter and would return an answer. The Resident told the Maharaja that a reply was not needed, as the message amounted to an order of the Government of India.[22]

SECTION 2: REPRESENTATION

The first meeting of the new Council took place on April 18, 1889.[23] The Maharaja was charged with serious offences and placed in abject misery. Dejected and disheartened the Maharaja represented his case to the Viceroy, explaining his pathetic and pitiable condition.[24]

The first letter was despatched on May 24, 1889, through Pandit Gopinath, the editor of the *Akbar-i-Am*.[25] The Maharaja wrote that he was writing the letter after suffering great humiliations, contempts, and even taunts at the hands of his inferiors. He should not at all take seriously the charges brought against him, about his secret correspondence with Russia, conspiracy with Dalip Singh, and an attempt to poison the British Resident and lots of other stupid stories. That the Governor-General himself also did not take them seriously had reinforced his faith in his justice. On receiving the orders of the Government of India to refrain from the administration of the State, he had complied with it, because he expected that some officer would be deputed by the Government to inquire into the false charges and would save him from humiliation. Raja Amar Singh was the cause of his misfortunes and mental suffering. He was the chief instrument in spreading rumours about his insanity and incompetence. To gain his end, he bribed the press and, taking advantage of his friendship with the Resident and the British Officers, he poisoned their hearts against him. His eventual plan was to calumniate the minds of the Government of India against him and thus to become the ruler of Jammu and Kashmir. He was disgusted with his brother's intrigues and designs. He twice snubbed him and resolved to remove him to his *jagir*. On both the occasions Amar Singh came to him and implored forgiveness.

He was moved. As a gesture of good will he bestowed upon him the rich *jagir* of Bhadderwa in exchange of the poor Bisoli, which he had got during his father's regime, and also made him the Prime Minister. Even then, he failed to change him. He created a strong party against him on regaining power. He promoted his adherents and degraded his well-wishers and faithful servants.

Colonel Nisbet, the Resident of Kashmir, was at first faithful and sincere to him, afterwards his mind was changed.

The Maharaja further submitted that his resignation was not a voluntary one, but was extorted out of him forcibly. His communication with Russia was nothing but a false story. The letters were written in Dogri script and it was never possible to communicate with Russia in that language. Still he was no fool or insane that, after getting high honours and all regards from the Government of India, he would give himself to the Russians, who were a by-name for tyranny and despotism. The Maharaja appealed to the Viceroy to make him a *de facto* ruler of the State, acting with the help of a just Resident. He should be given full powers to choose his Councillors and Ministers.[26]

Along with this letter the Maharaja wrote another to Sir Mortimer Durand, the Foreign Secretary, to save him from this discomfiture.[27]

At this time the *Akbar-i-Am* published a libelous attack upon Plowden, accusing him of gross treachery against the Maharaja, and the scraps of the letter of the Maharaja to the Viceroy were also published. The Viceroy, replying to the Maharaja on June 28, 1889, warned him that the letters should be delivered by ordinary post instead of through messengers.[28] The Viceroy placed no credence on the Maharaja's assertions. As a matter of fact the decision of the Government of India in alienating the Maharaja from the active participation in the administration of the State was not the result of recent events. The Government of India was eager to take a decisive step much before. The Viceroy also advised the Maharaja to bear with dignity his loss of power and to dissociate himself from the local intrigues and conspiracies, to prove that he had not entirely lost the qualities of a wise and prudent ruler.[29]

Earlier, Durand had replied, giving a friendly advice to Maharaja, that he should keep himself away from the undesirable elements, *e.g.*, Gopinath, who were not his well-wishers. He advised him to accept the decision of the Government of India with good grace, which was the only alternative to regaining his power and position lost through his mistaken policy.[30]

At Srinagar, the Maharaja expressed his desire to go to Jammu, as he had no say in the present administration. Nisbet did not like this. He was informed that the Maharaja wanted to go to Jammu to consult and employ lawyers to present his case either to the Government of India or to the Secretary of State.[32] The Resident tried his best to stop Pratap Singh, but to his dismay he learnt that not only Pratap Singh but Ram Singh, a member of the New Council, had also left for Jammu on June 1, 1889.[33] Plowden complained to Lansdowne, who in a letter, dated June 28, 1889 already referred to, as a reply to the Maharaja's representation, sent a warning to Ram Singh to resume his duties, otherwise some other arrangements would be made.[34]

The Maharaja replied on July 14, 1889.[35] He thanked the Viceroy for his letter and expressed his hope for the restoration of his powers. He referred to the *Kharita* of Lord Dufferin for the reforms in executive, judicial, and financial departments. Enough time was at his disposal also, but for several reasons he could not avail himself of the opportunity given to him. First, the two officials, whom he had asked for on loan reached late. Second, Raja Amar Singh, his minister and brother, opposed and checked his sincere measures, as he had an evil desire to enjoy the sole authority of the State. Third, he ordered that all the reforms in the respective departments to be implemented, but in the end he came to know that the heads of departments were the followers of Raja Amar Singh. They were the chief instruments in robbing his treasury and spreading disorders in the country. For his vulgar associates, he wrote that it was a false charge made by his enemies, especially by Raja Amar Singh, as his own officials were uneducated. Thus, in no way they could influence his mind. It was absolutely incorrect that he ever-acted on their initiative and even if he did, how could he have effected reforms in the State? He was not responsible also for the dismissal of Diwan Lachman Dass, which was due to the initiative of Raja Amar Singh.[36]

SECTION 3: REACTION OF THE INDIAN PRESS AND BRITISH PARLIAMENT

While the correspondence between the Viceroy and the Maharaja of Kashmir was thus going on some parts of the letters leaked out, and were published by the press.[37]

The Amrit Bazar Patrika in its issue of October 3, 1889, titling 'Cashmere and Gilgit—an extraordinary document', published Sir Mortimer Durand, the Foreign Secretary's note on Plowden's suggestion that Gilgit should be annexed. So Gilgit was the real motive behind the deposition of the Maharaja. At this time, Sir Lepel Griffin[38] made a controversial suggestion that the Government of India should colonise Kashmir with British settlers.[39] The Indian Press at once connected it with the deposition of the Maharaja, and forecast that Kashmir would be annexed before long.[40] It candidly said that Kashmir's strategically position, "is fatal to its being retained as an independent or even a tributary state".[41] *The Indian Mirror* published a long list of reform projects undertaken by the Government of India at the expense of the Darbar, thus depleting the state's exchequer.[42] *The Amrit Bazar Patrika* also reiterated the same charges. The appointment of British Officers on high salaries and their staff, the Jammu water works, a new Residency House at Jammu, and the building of the Gilgit Residency were some of the items which were draining the State treasury.[43] On the resignation of the Maharaja it said, that, "no one surrenders his kingdom for nothing" and pleaded for a full inquiry into the alleged resignation, which it feared was extorted from him.[44] *The Bengalee* pointed out that the plea of mal-administration was an excuse to remove the Maharaja and to take over the administration.[45] The paper suggested that if the Maharaja was guilty of misgovernment an open inquiry, like that against the Gaekwar, should be instituted.[46] Even the pro-government press also suspected that there was a skeleton in the cupboard. *The Pioneer* reported that the Kashmiris were pressed into forced labour in laying the telegraph line to Gilgit.[47] *The Statesman* said that if Gilgit was to be brought under British control, "it is difficult to see why the wishes of the Government were not communicated to the Cashmere Darbar and the permission of the Maharaja obtained. To have done so would have been a more manly and straightforward course than the roundabout and dubious method of getting in by the backdoor by first deposing the prince in order to put him out of the way".[48] When *The Indian Daily News* criticised *The Amrit Bazar Patrika* for publishing the document, *The Statesman* defended the latter,[49] J.C. Bose wrote an able defence of Pratap Singh.[50] In the Chapter VII of his pamphlet he demolished the charges against the Maharaja for depleting the state's treasury on account of prodigality and dissipation, and held that, instead, the Government of India was guilty of that charge. The latter had burdened the state treasury with an annual recurring expenditure of six lakhs rupees on the Jhelum Valley Cart Road. Thirteen lakhs and three lakhs of rupees were spent, respectively, on the Jammu-Sialkot Railway, and the Jammu water works. He further alleged that the Government of India took 25 lakhs of rupees as a loan from the State Government. Besides, a donation of ₹50,000/- was taken for Lady Dufferin's fund, and another of ₹25,000/- for Aitchison College at Lahore.[51] A lakh of rupees were spent during Lord Fredrick Robert's[51A] visit to Kashmir, and a further amount of ₹50,000/- spent on the Maharaja of Kapurthala's visit to the Valley.

Resident Nisbet contradicted Bose's charges one by one.[52] He wrote that the Jammu Valley Cart Road and the Jammu-Sialkot Railway were begun and estimated for under the late and the present Maharaja, long before he came to Kashmir and, therefore, he was in no way responsible for the expenditure. The estimates in neither case had been exceeded, and both were beneficial to the State. Second, the Jammu water works, were undertaken at the earnest request of the Maharaja and its beneficial character had been admitted by Bose himself.

Nisbet flatly denied that the Government of India had ever taken a loan of ₹2,50,000/- or any other from the Kashmir Darbar. Donations to Dufferin's funds and Aitchison college were given by the Maharaja voluntarily without any demand or pressure. About the alleged sum spent on the hospitality of Lord Roberts and Raja of Kapurthala the actual amount was much less. Kashmir had a reputation for hospitality, and it was Maharaja's wish to live up to that.

Lansdowne was happy at the counter reply of Nisbet to Bose's pamphlet,[53] but he did not consider it an indisputable document as a whole.[54] Nisbet's total denial of loan by the Government of India, according to Ardagh, was not correct, as at Plowden's suggestion a sum of twenty-five lakhs of rupees had been invested by the Darbar in India Government Paper.[55]

William Digby[56] censured the Indian Foreign Office, for its gross injustice to the Maharaja of Kashmir. It was guilty of such crimes as it, 'is in no way subject to that embodied conscience of present day civilization—an enlightened public opinion possessing furnitive power'.[57]

Abroad the Russians criticised the Government of India for its policy towards Kashmir, contending that the British seizure of Kashmir posed a serious threat to their interests in Central Asia.[58]

The Indian Press true to its moral obligation to stand as sentinel to protect the rights and liberties of individuals took up the cause of Pratap Singh in India and abroad. For getting the British Parliament acquainted with the disgraceful and unwarranted deposition of Pratap Singh, the Indian editors requested Charles Bradlaugh, when he came to India to attend the session of the Indian National Congress in 1889, to focus the attention of the Parliament to this grim episode. The editors between them raised a contribution which was supplemented by the Maharaja, and was sent to William Digby, to plead the case of the Maharaja in the British parliament.[61]

The Government of India alerted the India Office about it. The Under Secretary of State, Sir John Eldon Gorst got himself prepared.[62] Lord Lansdowne suggested, the line of defence to the India Office,[63] but in his heart of hearts he wished that papers on Kashmir should not be presented to the Parliament.[64] The Foreign Secretary, Durand, at that time was in London and was certain that nothing would come out of this 'paid agitation in England'.[65]

Bradlaugh on May 14, 1890, asked for the Kashmir Papers to be discussed in the Parliament. But the India Office, on the advice of the Viceroy of India, kept the matter hanging fire. Lansdowne requested the Secretary of State, Lord Cross, to show the papers to Bradlaugh, with an advice that by bringing the matter before the Parliament he would damage his client's case.[66] Bradlaugh was ready to withdraw the case from the Parliament if the Government of India agreed to give an opportunity to the Maharaja to defend himself.[67]

On July 3, 1890, Bradlaugh moved the adjournment in the House of Commons on the question of Pratap Singh's supersession.[68] Several members of the Parliament spoke in favour of Pratap Singh. The Kashmir Papers were not circulated amongst the members of the Parliament, but were simply laid on the table. He also attacked the posting of the Resident in Kashmir, which was a clear violation of the treaty stipulations. He made an impassioned oration: "I am not asking the House to say that this unfortunate man is guiltless, but I am asking them to say that he is entitled to be tried, and to have an inquiry before he is deprived of his rights. In 1889 the Government deprived this gentleman of his chieftainship. By what right? By no right save the right of force. By what law? By no law save the law of force. Upon what charges? Upon charges of vaguest description".[69]

About the charge of misgovernment in Kashmir, he said that five year's time was too short to reform a chronic mal-administration. He pointed to the Government's failure in not reporting it 'day by day, week by week, month by month and year by year'. But the fact was that the Maharaja had carried out the reforms.[70]

The Under Secretary of State ridiculed Bradlaugh for defending the cause of an oriental Hindu despot, while he a Tory was defending the right of the poor Muslim cultivators.

Mr. Macneill pointed out that the Under Secretary was raising a religious issue. The Maharaja was deposed as a result of an annexation policy, which in Ireland was known as "land-grabbing".[72]

Dr. Hunter also supported Mr. Macneill, on the religious issue.[73]

Sir R. Temple spoke against the motion. He defended the Government of India by saying that there was no annexation: "All that happens is the transfer of the sovereignty from one brother to another. England remains exactly in the same position as she was before and is in no wise benefited".[73] After the debate the motion was put to vote and was lost by an overwhelming majority.[74]

Lord Lansdowne was happy over the defeat, as he thought that the defeat on the floor of the British Parliament had taken the wind out of the sails of the Indian press.[75] But in India there was still a feeling that it was not the final verdict of the British nation.[76]

A final but unsuccessful attempt was made by William Digby to secure a re-hearing of the Maharaja's case by addressing a long letter to Sir U. Kay—Shuttleworth, M.P., in July 1890. The letter had become memorable with the matchless and befitting title 'Condemned Unheard'. He defended the case very ably, and tried his best to vindicate the Maharaja. He remarked that the Government of India's policy towards the Princes, 'is an advance on Jedburgh justice which hanged a man and then proceeded to inquire whether he was guilty'. About the diminishing population in Kashmir he compared the population returns of the census of 1881 with 1872 for the whole of India and proved that it was not a good record. Had a census record for Kashmir was available, the verdict would have gone in favour of Kashmir.[77]

These representations although did not help Pratap Singh directly, but they did create an atmosphere in favour of Pratap Singh.

References

1. For. Dept., Progs, Extl. B, April 1889, Cons. 27-33, K.W. 2, Nisbet to Durand.
2. *Ibid.,* Nisbet wrote to Durand on June 12, 1889, "I am satisfied that he only wants drawing out of his shell and being brought out of the background into which he had fallen of late to be both useful and complaint".
3. Lansdowne Papers, 7B(i), pp. 535-37. To the S.O.S., sub-encl. in encl. 8, pp. 535-37; For. Sec. E, Progs, April 1889, Nos. 80-98, No. 80. Nisbet wrote to Durand on February 27, 1889, "The gist of these other letters is that the Maharaja offers large sums of money to certain individuals on condition that they will murder or cause to be removed, Plowden, the late Resident, his own to brothers, Ram Singh and Amar Singh, and one of the Maharanis, who, for some reason, is personally objectionable to him".
4. Lansdowne Papers, 1B, (*i*), pp. 519-20, Nisbet to Durand, February 27, 1889; For. Dept., Sec. E, April 1889, Nos. 80-98, No. 89. "It surely is politically dangerous to leave the actual administration of this great State in the hands of an individual who may play us false at any moment, without, perhaps appreciating the disaster that would follow, and I believe, any steps Government may take short of the annexation will be right and necessary, and generally approved by the Princes and Chiefs India".
5. Lansdowne Papers, VII (*a*), p. 190, Durand to Wallace, March 3, 1889.
6. *Ibid.*, IB (*i*), p. 520, Viceroy to the Resident, March 4, 1889. encl. 2 in GO I to SOS, April 3, 1889.
7. *Ibid.*, p. 520, Nisbet's Report on Kashmir, March 16, 1889, to the S.O.S., April 3, 1889.
8. *Ibid.*, pp. 521-23, To the S.O.S., April 3, 1889, Maharaja's Irshad (edict), March 8, 1889, Sub-encl, in encl. 7, For. Dept., Sec. E, Progs, September 1890, Nos. 179-180; For. Dept., Sec. E, Progs, April 1889, No. 88; For. Dept., Sec. E, Progs, No. 555, May 1889.
9. *Amrit Bazar Patrika*, August 29, October 6, 1889; *Statesman*, March 11, 1889, Lansdowne Papers, VII (*a*), p. 125; *Pioneer,* March 11, 1889.
10. Lansdowne Papers VII (*a*), pp. 153-54. Lansdowne wrote to Roberts that Nisbet had made "a needless commotion about the letters".
11. For. Dept., Pol., Sec. E, April 1889, Progs, Cons. 80-98, Durand's note Dated March 16, 1889, on Nisbet's Report on Kashmir, March 16, 1889.
12. *Ibid.*
13. Robert Papers, Box File LI, R 34/18, Lansdowne to Roberts, March 30, 1889.
14. Cross Papers, 26, No. 16, Lansdowne to Cross, March 20, 1889.

15. Lansdowne Papers, IB(1), pp. 539-40, Instructions from the Government of India to the Resident in Kashmir, April 1, 1889; Teng, Kaul Bhatt, Kaul, *Kashmir Constitutional History and Documents*, pp. 261-63.
16. *Ibid.*
17. *Ibid.*
18. *Ibid.,* The want of good native officials makes it necessary to import some trained men from the outside, but the number of men so imported should be kept as low as possible, and your object should be to form with their help a class of Kashmiri officials, who will be capable hereafter of administering the State themselves. It is altogether against the wishes of the Government to interfere unnecessarily with the customs and traditions of a Native State, or to force upon it the precise methods of administration obtaining in British territory Administrative efficiency is not the only object to be attained in such case, nor, indeed the principal object.
19. For. Dept., Pol. Sec. E, May 1889, Cons. 556, Nisbet to Durand, March 29, 1889.
20. For. Dept., Sec. E., Progs, April 1889, Nos. 80-98, H.M. Durand's Note, March 16, 1889, See Appendix III.
21. Yasin, Madhvi, *Indian Administration,* pp. 91-98.
22. For. Dept., Sec. E, April 1889, Nos. 80-98, No. 89; For. Sec. E, Nos. 221-230, Progs, July 1890, Nisbet to Durand, April 19, 1889. The Resident repeated the orders of the Government of India to the Maharaja's brothers that, "they should let him thoroughly understand that the communication made to him were the definite orders of the Government of India which it was not necessary for him to answer."
23. Lansdowne Papers, IB (*i*), p. 915, Nisbet to Durand, April 19, 1889, to the S.O.S., July 26, 1889.
24. Ghose, D.K., *op. cit.*, p. 90.
25. For. Dept., Progs, Sec. E, April 1889, No. 80-98.
26. *Ibid.*
27. For. Dept., Progs., Sec. E, August 1889, Cons. 168.
28. PSLEI, 57, p. 1021, Lansdowne to Maharaja, June 28, 1889, encl. 1 in to the S.O.S.; Gadru, S.N., *op. cit.*, pp. 230-256.
29. *Ibid.*
30. For. Dept., Progs, Sec. E, August 1889, Cons. 173, Durand to Maharaja, June 11, 1889.
31. For. Dept., Progs, Sec. E, August 1889, Cons. 167, Maharaja to Nisbet, May 26, 1889; *Civil and Military Gazette,* June 15, 1889; Bose, J.C., *Kashmir and its Prince,* p. 42.
32. For. Dept., Progs, Sec. E, 1889, Cons. 62, Nisbet to Durand, May 17, 1889.

33. For. Dept., Sec. E, Progs, August 1889, No. 170, Nisbet to Durand, Demi Official, June 2, 1889.
34. See F.N. 28.
35. Cross Papers, 27, Pratap Singh to Lansdowne, July 14, 1889, sub-encl. in encl. 2A in No. 41.
36. For. Dept., Sec. E, August 1889, No. 190.
37. Lansdowne Papers, VIII (a), No. 76, p. 90, Ardagh to Godley, August 21, 1889; *Amrit Bazar Patrika,* August 15, 1889.
38. The Indian Civil Servant from England who for some years served as Secretary to the Punjab Government. He was a spirited officer who served long years as political agent in Central India, Kashmir, and Rajputana, and he showed scant regard for the privileges of Indian Princes and the sentiments of the Indian People.
39. Lansdowne Papers, (A) Lansdowne to Cross, July 19, 1889, pp. 121-25; Cross Papers, 27, No. 34; *Indian Mirror,* July 11, 1889; Bose, J.C., *Cashmere and its Prince,* p. 81.
40. *The Hindoo Patriot,* August 26, 1889, p. 399.
41. *Ibid.,* August 5, 1889.
42. *The Indian Mirror,* October 3, 1889.
43. *The Amrit Bazar Patrika,* Kashmir under the British Administration January 30, 1890.
44. *Ibid.,* July 11, 1889.
45. *The Bengalee,* March 30, 1889.
46. *Ibid.,* June 15, 1889.
47. *The Pioneer,* September 8, 1889.
48. *The Statesman,* October 6, 1889.
49. *Ibid.,* October 29, 1889. "As for part played by the *Patrika*, our own view, as we have already stated, is that he acted in perfect good faith in publishing the note, as he received it, and in the comments based there on. Whatever may have been 'policy and motives' of the Government, the Viceroy's admission in respect to the document clearly shows that the Political Agent in Kashmir did recommend a course with regard to Gilgit which was in open violation of our treaty engagements, and that instead of severely reprimanding Mr. Plowden and disapproving his unscrupulous suggestions in the strongest terms, the Foreign Officer merely recorded a mild dissent from his methods, and suggested instead a more straightforward way of attaining the same object".
50. *Bose, J.C., Cashmere and its Prince.*
51. For. Dept., Progs, Ext. B, February 1889, Nos. 168-171. The Maharaja also paid second contribution of ₹5,000/- to the building fund of Aitchison Chief's College at Lahore, vide, KGR, Jammu, Chief Secretariat, Pol. Dept., Old English Records, file No. 10, of 1888.

51A. Commander-in-Chief of India.

52. Lansdowne Papers, 1B(*iii*), pp. 417-78. To the S.O.S., encl. 4, January 29, 1890. Nisbet in compliance with the Viceroy's instructions, drew up his report on Kashmir, and added an appendix to it, which countered the charges of extravagance against the Government of India and himself in the capacity of the Resident.
53. Cross Papers, 28, Lansdowne to Nisbet, February 5, 1890, encl. in No. 62.
54. Lansdowne Papers, IX (*b*), pp. 13-15, Lansdowne to Cross, February 4, 1890.
55. PSDOC, 3, First Series, pp. 623-25, 721-807, Ardagh to Maitland, February 25, 1890.
56. The celebrated journalist, author, and politician, was the founder of the Indian Political Agency in London in 1887. He was its Director until 1892. Through this Agency he conducted extensive propaganda among the English people for the necessity of introducing reform in Indian administration and for inviting the attention of the British public to the sad economic plight of India. His book, 'Prosperous British India', though ill-arranged, was the chief source material from which Indian and American authors have dug their material for attacks upon the British administration.
57. *The London Times,* September 7, 1889, Letter to the Editor, entitled, Lord Lansdowne to Maharaja of Kashmir.
58. Novoe Vremya, Translation of an article 'Russian apprehensions about Kashmir', vide *The Pioneer,* October 2, 1889.
59. One of the most remarkable men in British history, who devoted his entire life to fighting for the cause of freedom of expression and conscience. He was a great orator. He took special interest in question relating to India and interested him so deeply in the social and political condition of the Indians that he was nick-named as 'member of India'. He attended the Bombay session of Indian National Congress in 1889 as the chief guest. He said in the course of a memorable oration, "For whom should I work if not for the whole people? Born of the people, trusted by the people, I will die for the people, and I know no geographical or race limitations".
60. Ghose, D.K., *op. cit.*, p. 109. Notable among them were Motilal Ghose of the *Amrit Bazar Patrika,* Calcutta, and Pandit Gopinath, and Jogendra Chandra Bose, respectively of the *Akbar-i-Am* and the *Tribune* of Lahore.
61. PSDOC, 3, First Series, p. 773, Motilal to Gopinath, January 10, 1890.
62. *Ibid.,* Gorst to Cross, February 12, 1890.
63. Cross Papers, 28, No. 65, Lansdowne to Cross, March 4, 1890.
64. *Ibid.,* No. 77, May 26, 1890.
65. Lansdowne Papers, VII (*b*), No. 36, Durand to Lansdowne, May 14, 1890.
66. Ghose, D.K., *op. cit.*, p. 111.

67. From the London Correspondent of *Bengalee*, July 19,1890.
68. Gadru, S.R, *op. cit.*, 270-299.
69. *Ibid.*
70. *Ibid.*
71. *Ibid.*
72. *Ibid.*, He said "But the right hon. gentleman laid stress on the word Moslem in order to excite those unhappy religious prejudices which unfortunately prevail in India. We know that in India, unhappily, both Moslems and Hindus are animated by strong fanatical opinions on the subject of religion, leading to collisions and breaches of the peace. And here is the Under Secretary for India in this House pointing his moral by the contrast between the Moslem and Hindu peasants, and trying thus to fan the embers of religious antipathy".
73. *Ibid.*
74. Parliamentary Debates, Hansard, Third Series, Vol. 346, July 3, 1890, Cal. 631.

    The House divided:

Ayes...	88
Noes...	226
Majority	138

75. Cross Papers, 28, No. 83, Lansdowne to Cross, July 7, 1890.
76. *The Friend of India*, August 9, 1890; *The Bengalee,* August 2, 1890.
77. Gadru, S.N., *op. cit.*, pp. 146-47.

6

Re-establishment of Gilgit Agency

Although established by Lord Lytton the Gilgit Agency was withdrawn by Lord Ripon in 1881, but the withdrawal by no means was final. The Government of India reserved full discretion to send back an officer to Gilgit if it was thought necessary. The India Office also had reservations over the withdrawal. Burne, the Secretary to the Political and Secret Department, commented that the withdrawal of the Agency was the removal of "a Sentry from a vulnerable point of the Indian Frontier".[1] Ripon's policy was to control the tribes on the north-west frontier of Kashmir through the Kashmir Darbar.[2] But his policy was short-lived.

The Afghan intrigues with the tribes[3], Russian expansion[4] and the capture of Chaprot and Chalt and the siege of Naomal by the Thums of the Hunza and Nagar[5] led to rethinking about the change in policy. In August 1886, it was reported that the Amir of Afghanistan was taking measures to annex to Kunar some of the passes held by independent chiefs as a prelude to onslaughts upon Kafiristan, Chitral and Bajaur. The Mehtar (ruler) of Chitral pressed hard for a treaty with the British Government.[6] The rulers of Dir and Jandol followed suit[7]. The new Viceroy, Lord Dufferin, who was at first unwilling to get involved in their affairs, revised his stand afterwards.

Simultaneously, reports about the Russian intrigues on the Kashmir frontier were rife. Russian surveyors were found in Shignan accompanied by armed escorts. It was reported that the Czar was making preparation for the navigation of the Oxus.[8] The trans-Caspian Railway was making rapid progress, and there was an apprehension that after its completion the Russian forces would be massed in Central Asia to pose a threat to India.[9] Waterfield, the Peshawar Commissioner suspected that a Russian emissary was working, in Bajaur and Chitral. There were recent reports that three Russian Officers disguised as merchants had visited Kashmir and had taken notes of the different routes to that state. The Peshawar report disclosed that Russia had sent two spies to India, one to Bombay and another to Calcutta, to collect reports and foment disaffection against the British Government.[10]

In 1885, there was also a startling information that the Russians were persuading Aman-ul-Mulk, the Mehtar of Chitral, to lease or to sell the Ludhkho Valley. Having failed in this they were "offering to lease the Darkot Valley for two lakhs a year with better prospect of success."[11] In 1887, some Russian travellers were reported to have visited Hunza, followed by Captain Gromchevsky's visit to explore the possibilities of Russian penetration across the Hindukush. In fact, the Russians had the notion that the area between the Afghan Wakhan and the Chinese Aktash was a sort of no man's land, and accordingly Gromchevsky had visited Hunza in the summer of 1888.[12]

All these developments were a prelude to the re-establishment of Gilgit Agency. The Foreign Secretary, H.M. Durand gave no credence to the report of the Russian offer to Aman-ul-Mulk of Chitral to get on lease Darkot Valley, nevertheless he thought it expedient to post an English Officer at Gilgit to gain information.[12A] Accordingly, Colonel Lockhart was despatched to visit Gilgit, Chitral, and Kafiristan.[13] Lockhart visited Chitral, but could not explore Kafiristan, owing to the opposition of the Amir.[14] He sent a memorandum, on February 27, 1886, to the Foreign Office, in which he laid down several proposals. The Mehtar of Chitral and Lockhart himself wished for a complete change in the old policy. The Mehtar asked for a treaty with, and subsidies from, the British Government. Lockhart supported these requests, and linked them with a scheme for "acquiring" Gilgit from the Kashmir Darbar, "erecting there a British Cantonment," establishing a garrison (the Gilgit Guide Corps) of locally raised troops, and carrying on "the district work" under the Commandant's orders. Lockhart describes the main objects to be attained by his proposals as: The acquisition of Gilgit would secure the continued loyalty of Chitral, carrying with it "Our right" of way through the Mehtar's dominions, and his active co-operation in time of need. In my opinion it would ensure the safety of Hindukush. It would have a very wholesome effect on the Indus Kohistan also, and would give them a *pied a terre* in a fresh quarter, from which tribes could be kept in check, "or on their complete subjugation ever becoming necessary." Independent Pathan tribes could be pressurised to render feasible an arrangement, similar to that of Khaibar, by which a military road would be run from Peshawar to Chitral and the Dora Pass by way of Swat and Dir.[15]

In a nutshell, Lockhart[16] stressed the importance of Gilgit as the defensive nucleus of Dardistan.[17]

At this time Panjdeh was attacked by the Russian troops, and was occupied by them from the Afghans. The Indian Princes reacted favourably to this danger and offered their military services to the Government of India. Plowden informed them that the Kashmir Darbar had also offered a sum of one million rupees in addition to all the troops and war materials of the state towards the defence of the Indian Empire.[18] At the same time he also wrote that the Thums of Hunza and Nagar have captured Chaprot and Chalt and laid the siege to Naomal.[19] The Government of China also laid claim upon Hunza, and this increased the insurgency of the Thum of Hunza.[20] Plowden, who had harboured serious resentment against the Maharaja on the dismissal of Lachman Dass, his protege, poured forth his venom in—these words: "Therefore I am justified in saying that the Gilgit disturbances indicate a serious collapse of the Darbar policy and testify to the inefficiency and weakness of its frontier administration, a point already noticed in my confidential report on the affairs of Jammu & Kashmir."[21]

Since the dismissal of Lachman Dass, the Darbar was sending Plowden further Gilgit Papers and requested him to advise Hakim-i-Ala directly without referring to it (Darbar) to avoid delay as to the action to be taken upon them. Plowden interpreted it as a lack of confidence and timidity on the part of the Darbar, which was a bad portent. He suggested that in Kashmir the same policy should be followed as was followed in the case of the Khan of Kalat in Baluchistan, in depriving him of the charge of frontier defence. In the name of the Darbar, the actual working of the scheme with regard to Gilgit, in all essentials, should be the British. He doubted the wisdom of retaining a Kashmir Governor at Gilgit as suggested by Durand. His proposal was to advise the Darbar, "to join the Government of India in the appointment of a Political Agent at Gilgit with supreme authority on the spot, civil, political, and military."[22] The Darbar and the Government of India should share half and half the salary of the Agent, but the salaries of all other officers should be borne by the Darbar as part of Kashmir's contribution to the Frontier Defence, as expressed by the Maharaja. He would select a Kashmiri official to be the Agent's Civil and Political Assistant. In all matters of a purely civil character the Political Agent might correspond with the Darbar directly through his Assistant, but in all other matters he should be subordinate to and correspond with the Resident alone, who would dispose of his references in communication with the Darbar and the Government of India as occasion required. He also suggested that the British troops to be stationed in Kashmir.[23]

The Foreign Secretary, Durand, did not approve of the memorandum of Plowden. His views were, "He (Plowden) is too much inclined to set Kashmir aside in all ways, and to assume that if we want a thing done we must do it ourselves." He opined that in liquidating the claim of the Darbar over the petty principalities in the neighbourhood of Kashmir, and stationing British troops in Kashmir, there was a risk "of turning the Darbar against us, and of thereby increasing the difficulty of the position. I do not think this is necessary. No doubt we must have practically the control of Kashmir—relations with these principalities, but this we already have.......We shall, I hope, in a short time have the whole thing in our hands without hurting anyone's feelings."[24]

According to Digby, "this proposal of Plowden was the main cause of his downfall."[25]

After the deposition of Pratap Singh the *Amrit Bazar Patrika,*[26] published the above document, vindicating the Maharaja and reinforcing his thesis that "it was Gilgit the Government wanted for which the Maharaja was pressurised to resign".

In the meantime, Dalip Singh, a son of Ranjit Singh had gone over to Russia in 1887, which made Dufferin and the Foreign Office jittery. It was alleged that the Kashmir State was intriguing with both Dalip Singh and Russia against the Government of India[27] and rumours were rife that Dalip Singh would settle in Kashmir.[28] Though the Officers of Dufferin, Durand, Aitchinson, and Henderson[29] did not believe in the canard that the Maharaja of Kashmir was in secret alliance with Russia, Dufferin had his reservations. To him it was, "one of those circumstances which must always remain a matter of conjecture."[30] Nevertheless the Government became more vigilant.

Both Dufferin and Durand were at first skeptical about the re-establishment of Gilgit Agency, but as the question was thrashed out it became clear that something ought to be done without much delay. Eventually, at the end of 1887, after the question of 'the Native States Armies' was raised. Dufferin sanctioned a modified scheme under which an English Officer was to be stationed at Gilgit with some picked Kashmiri troops.[31] At the same time he sanctioned a connected project...... the opening up if possible of the direct road from Peshawar to Chitral via Dir. Durand's brother, Captain Algernon Durand, an officer of the Quarter-Master-General's Department, was sent up to go to Gilgit to work out the arrangement in detail. At this time the situation had become complicated, as Hunza and Nagar had raised a banner of revolt against the Darbar. For the 'connected project', Merk, the Deputy Commissioner of Peshawar was appointed to supervise the construction of road.[32]

On December 5, 1888, A. Durand submitted his-report.[33] The military position at Gilgit was in a very bad shape. He laid emphasis on plugging the gap between the Afghan and Chinese frontiers, often called "Gromchevsky's wedge", through which Gromchevsky had visited Hunza in 1888.[34] It was a vulnerable point to the safety of Kashmir, as via this gap Russia could push down to Hunza at any time. He also recommended, like Lockhart, the re-establishment of a British Agency at Gilgit for the defence of Kashmir and the construction of a direct road to Chitral from the Peshawar frontier through Dir.[35]

Thus Plowden's proposal to re-establish Gilgit agency, which was discredited in the beginning, was accepted in the last resort. The spade work was done in the time of Dufferin, but it was established in 1889 during the Viceroyalty of his successor, Lord Lansdowne, when Pratap Singh was deposed and the Resident had become all-powerful. The Agency covered all the passes over Hindukush, from the eastern-most one, the Shimshal, to those at the head of the Yasin river, in the west.[36] A.G. Durand was appointed as the British Agent, with a couple of assistants, including Manners Smith and the Surgeon, Major G.S. Robertson.[37] He was asked to work in close cooperation with the Resident of Kashmir and to establish friendly relations with the States of Chitral, Dir, Dar, Hunza, and Nagar.[38] Durand visited Hunza, Nagar and Chitral. The subsidies of the ruling chiefs were increased.[39]

He invited the neighbouring chiefs to Gilgit to a Darbar to celebrate the re-establishment of the Gilgit Agency. The Chiefs were informed that in future their subsidies would be regularly paid every year, provided they faithfully adhered to the agreements they had undertaken to fulfil.[40]

Durand set himself to the task of strengthening the forts at Gilgit and to improve the transport system between Srinagar and Gilgit so that supplies for the troops might be easily obtained. A military road was hurriedly constructed.[41] Transport on the Gilgit road was maintained by forced labour and thousands of people from Kashmir were pressed into service to carry provisions over the dreary passes to the Gilgit Agency.[42] Lord Lansdowne was very much satisfied with the work of the Gilgit Agency.[43]

Indian opinion was deadly against the establishment of the British Agency at Gilgit. They were of the view that Kashmir was put to an indirect control of the Government of India through a Resident Governor, as the former was gripped with a fear psychosis of an invasion on India, and therefore it wanted to plug every passage which might lead an enemy to India and it was with that view that Kashmir was taken in indirect possession through a Resident Governor. The Government of India, it was alleged, was squandering away its resources in fruitless fortifications. In spite of the heavy expenditure the scientific frontier was still untraceable. It shifted from one place to another. At first the place of danger was Baluchistan, afterwards it centred around Gilgit. It did not matter with the Indian officials if a work of enormous cost was found useless and then abandoned forever.[44]

The Government of India in fact had no desire to have sovereign authority over these frontier tribes, but they only wanted to watch the foreign relations of these tribes. For this they offered a psychological justification. Lord Lansdowne thought that in political geography, nature abhors a vacuum. Therefore, if any space was left vacant on the Indian frontiers, it would be filled by others. It would be utter foolishness on their part to be indifferent towards that 'No Man's Land.'[45]

The re-establishment of the Gilgit Agency was not an end in itself; it was a means to an end.[46] With the establishment of the Gilgit Agency detailed information was received about the neighbouring principalities, and constant relations were kept up between Chitral and Gilgit. The tribal politics, Russian expansion, Hunza and Nagar expedition, and the Amir of Afghanistan's covetous eyes on the tribal states involved the Government of India in every direction. The result was that the staff of the Gilgit Agency was increased by two political officers, one for Hunza and Nagar, and the other for Chitral, and by four military officers.[47]

Lord Lansdowne thought that the Gilgit outpost ought to be made "a centre of British influence" on the northern frontiers, of Kashmir.[48] In reality Gilgit was the watch tower to the defence of the Indian sub-continent.

SECTION 1: PRATAP SINGH—A VICTIM OF MISCHIEVOUS MACHINATIONS

Maharaja Pratap Singh had an ill-starred life. As a prince he was always ignored, snubbed, and even openly insulted by his father, Ranbir Singh.[49] He had only a faint hope that he would be allowed to succeed to the throne, as Ranbir Singh twice had made representations in 1881 and 1884 that his youngest son Amar Singh ought to be recognised as his successor, as he was 'wiser' than his two elder brothers Pratap Singh and Ram Singh.[50] Prof. Hassanain says that Pratap Singh's younger brother had a misconception that their father, Ranbir Singh had secretly exchanged his baby daughter with the son of a Brahmin on the same day, when Pratap Singh was born. It was due to this that Pratap Singh was maltreated by his brothers especially by Amar Singh, the favourite of his father.[51]

Perhaps this was the reason that he suffered from a fear psychosis and fell in the company of astrologers and wicked persons, prominent among them was Sawal Singh.[52] Plowden called them 'Sawal Singh & Co.', and alleged that they were at the bottom of much mischief. Financially they were 'eating, up the State'. He alleged that the Maharaja paid ₹25,000/-to one of them for the transfer of St. John. It was a fact that the Maharaja was under their thumb. Even Maharani Bishen Devi, Pratap Singh's wife, complained against Sawal Singh to Dufferin.[53] Nilambar Mukherjee, the Finance Minister, felt the influence of Sawal Singh on the administration most revolting.[54]

Pratap Singh was regarded as a weak man. This opinion was held by the successive Viceroys and Residents,[55] and even Lady Dufferin, who saw him only once, formed a very unfavourable opinion about him.[56] He was perhaps chosen by the Government of India to succeed Ranbir Singh because of his weakness, as a man of Ranbir Singh's calibre would not have allowed the stationing of a Resident in the State. In spite of his weaknesses, Pratap Singh was an honest ruler and sincerely wished to ameliorate the condition of his people.[57] He was from the very beginning interested in revamping the administration. He earnestly requested the Viceroy that, as he had in his mind projects and plans to improve the administration, the imposition of a Resident should be deferred. His prayer was not granted. The Kashmir State, since its creation in 1846 A.D., had ties with the Punjab Government, and both had a reciprocity. The recent fiat of the Government of India to the Maharaja to communicate through the medium of the Resident, instead of the Punjab Government, was not liked by the Maharaja, who wanted the restoration of old connections. He despite of the Viceroy's instructions communicated directly through the Punjab Government which was interpreted as his deliberate move to play one against the other.[58] The Punjab Governor in compliance with the request of the Maharaja wrote about that to Dufferin,[59] who referred the matter to his Foreign Secretary, Mortimer Durand. But Durand was dead against any "restoration of the old order of things".[60] This rigid attitude of Durand resulted in great harassment to the Maharaja by the Residents as the Maharaja had no channel to communicate with the Viceroy except through the Resident. St. John and Plowden both were hostile to the Maharaja, and the third, Colonel Nisbet, had him deposed. Digby has given a poetic and pathetic touch to his narration: "The Resident arrives. He is not to interfere, he is merely to advise; and then he does interfere; and, finally—as is now the case—he becomes the virtual ruler of the country".[61] Both Dufferin[62] and Durand[63] were at their tether's end by the imperious and dictatorial demeanour of the Residents. Dufferin was so much disillusioned with Plowden that he cancelled his visit to Kashmir. Plowden even complained against the Maharaja to the Government of India for his not returning the official visits to him.[64] The Residents dabbled freely in the internecine intrigues and ambitions of the Royal House. Maharaja's younger brothers Ram Singh and Amar Singh were fierce enemies of the Maharaja, and Amar Singh aspired for the throne by ousting the Maharaja.[65] Plowden turned them into his informers[66] and Nisbet got the Maharaja sacked on getting a bunch of thirty-four letters, in Dogri character, allegedly written by the Maharaja.[67] The letters disclosed that the

Maharaja was intriguing against the Government of India in alliance with Russia and Dalip Singh; he also was said to have engineered to take the lives of Plowden and his two brothers. Later on these letters were proved to be forged and, as a result, Nisbet was transferred.[68] But he already had inflicted a great injury to Pratap Singh morally and materially.

Likewise the charge that the Maharaja was not interested in reforms holds no water. The Maharaja was anxious that his subjects should receive a liberal education. But it was Plowden who was against it, and he did not rest until he had secured possession of the Education Rules which the Darbar had framed.[69] Similarly, the Maharaja was interested in land reforms. It is the testimony of Wingate the man brought by Plowden, against the wishes of the Maharaja, who wanted a Panjabi Muslim Settlement Officer, "...the ruler is averse to raising the price of *shali* lest the poor should suffer..."[70] Even Dufferin admitted that considerable progress had been made in the Revenue Administration, and the Public Works and Medical Departments had been reorganised.[71] Still if there was any shortcoming it was due to Raja Amar Singh, his minister and brother, who opposed and checked his sincere measures, "as he (Amar Singh) had an evil desire to enjoy the sole authority of the State."[72]

Similarly, the charge that the Maharaja was prodigal and spendthrift does not hold water. During his early regime much was spent upon building of the roads,[73] donations[74], loans[75] and contribution to the defence of the empire.[76] All this expenditure was incurred upon the Government of India by the Darbar. Lansdowne himself absolves him of the charge, "I am much more favourably impressed by His Highness than I had expected. His habits are simple and he has no expensive tastes."[77] He appeared to him sensible and intelligent.[78]

Pratap Singh's *sub-rosa* dealings with Dalip Singh were a figment of imagination of the Russophobists. Even Ranbir Singh had been suspected of secret manoeuverings with Russia, which were never proved. Forging signatures was a common practice in Kashmir.[79] Even Pratap Singh complained to Plowden that lakhs of rupees were withdrawn from the State treasury by some of his officials, who submitted fake vouchers in his name for flying kites."[80] Thus, all the charges against him fall fiat.[81]

Maharaja was a victim of circumstances and international situation—in the revival of the forward policy. Planting of the Resident on the plea of humanity, but in reality to plunder the State revenues to meet the expenses of the forward policy was the trick of the trade of the Government of India.[82]

References

1. PSD1/7, pp. 331-37.
2. PSLEI, 33, pp. 949-52, GOI to SOS, August 25, 1882.
3. MINWF, June 1885, PSLEI, 44, p. 1112; PCD, June 16, 1886, pp. 1070-71.
4. For. Sec. F., Nos. 175-186 (K.W.), Progs., April 1885.
5. For. Sec. F., July 1888, Nos. 63-86.
6. MINWF, June 1887, PSLEI, 50, pp. 1229-45.
7. PFP, 2700, June 1886, Frontier B, Cons. 7-11.
8. PSDOC, 1, First Series, pp. 1121-23, Letter from a correspondent in St. Petersburg, April 1886.
9. PCD, October 12, 1886, PSLEI, 48, pp. 823-31, MINWF, October 1886, pp. 895-98; Lansdell, H., *Through Central Asia,* pp. 633-34; Dobson, G., *Russian Railway Advance,* p. 413.
10. PCD, October 12, 1876, PSLEI, 48, pp. 823-31; *Ibid.*, MINWF, October 1886, pp. 985-93.
11. For. Sec. F., Nos. 175-186 (K.W.), Progs., April 1885.
12. Lansdowne Papers, IB (*f*), pp. 547-610, GOI to SOS, May 6, 1889; PSDOC, 3, First Series.

12A. For. Sec. F, Nos. 175-186 (K.W.), Progs., April 1885. The Government of India received the information that two years ago, "Russians were at Chitral trying to persuade Aman-ul-Mulk (ruler of Chitral) to lease or sell the Ludkho Valley, that they had failed, but were now offering to lease the Darkot Valley for two lakhs a year with better prospect of success".

On this, the Deputy Foreign Secretary remarked: "If there is any truth in the rumour, it cannot be lightly regarded..........A Russian force holding a lease of Darkot would exercise the same effect on our North-West Frontier as a Russian Army at Herat would on lower Punjab. From the Oxus three passes cross the Hindu Kush. The easternmost is the best, but is temporarily blocked. It is the Karambar or Ishkaman. The head of Ishkaman Valley is only three marches from Gilgit, whence a well-known route leads to Srinagar on to Fabela. The second pass is the Darkot, one day's journey from the same starting point, Sarhad, in the Valley of the Oxus. From Darkot the invader should proceed either south or east to Gilgit, or to Mastuj and the Chitral valley. The third pass .... is the Baroghil .... If then Russians were established at Darkot they would be on the Indian side of Sarhad, the terminus of the three practicable passes from India to the Oxus."............"Any movement (of the Russians) to Darkot could only mean a declaration of war at no distant time. We must therefore, inquire if the report is correct".

13. For. Sec. F., Nos. 175-186 (K.W.), Progs, April 1885.
14. For. Dept., Sec, F., May 1889, Nos. 544-559.
15. For. Dept., Sec. F., January 1888, Nos. 115-118.
16. Lockhart and Woodthorpe, *Gilgit Mission,* pp. 109, 209-80, 348.
17. Dardistan included Hunza, Nagar, Chitral, Dir, Swat, Bajaur, Darel, Tangir and Chilas.
18. Cross Papers, 24, No. 82, Dufferin to Cross, January 26, 1888.
19. For. Dept., Sec. F., July 1888, Nos. 63-86.
20. For. Dept., Progs, Sec. C, October 1888, Nos. 102-121.
21. *Ibid.*
22. *Ibid.*
23. *Ibid.,* He wrote, "There is no Native State (with the recent exception of, Gwalior) or group of Native States of anything like similar importance to Jammu and Kashmir and in which a representative of the Imperial Government resides which has not a British force condoned at some place within its limits".
24. *Ibid.*
25. Gadru, S.N., *op. cit.*, p. 166; *Amrit Bazar Patrika,* October 6, 1889.
26. *Ibid.,* "It will be seen that His Highness was deposed, not because he resigned, or oppressed his people, but because Gilgit was wanted for the strategical purposes by the British Government."; *Statesman,* October 6, 1889.
27. D.P., Reel 526, encl. in No. 64, Maitland the Mackenzie Wallace, March 18, 1887; *Ibid.,* Reel 525, p. 9, Dufferin to Northbrook, January 10, 1886.
28. PSLEI, 50, pp. 1505-1509, Summary of Correspondence in case of Dalip Singh by Col. P.D. Henderson, June 13, 1887.
29. *Ibid.,* 54, pp. 663-67, Note by Henderson, July 1, 1888.
30. D.P. Reel 518, p. 158, Dufferin to Cross, June 24, 1887.
31. For. Dept., Sec. F, January 1888, Nos. 115-118.

32. For. Dept., Sec. F., May 1889, Nos. 544-559.
33. Lansdowne Papers, SB (*i*), pp. 547-610, Durand's Report, December 5, 1888, encl. in GOI to SOS, May 6, 1889.
34. PSDOC, 3, First Series, pp. 205-8, Younghusband to Nisbet, October 24, 1889.
35. Lansdowne Papers, IB (*i*), pp. 547-610, Durand's Report, December 5, 1888, encl. in GOI to SOS, May 6, 1889; For. Dept., Progs, Front. B, October 1889, Nos. 104-151.
36. Durand, A.G., *Making of a Frontier,* p. 119.
37. Knight, E.F., *Where Three Empires Meet,* p. 290; For. Sec. F., Progs., May 1889, Nos. 544-48; For. Sec. F.; Progs, October 1889, No. 104.
38. For. Sec. F., Progs., May 1889, No. 544.
39. Lansdowne Papers, IB (*i*), pp. 1169-80, ends. 6, 9, and 10 in GOI to SOS, December 3, 1889; *Ibid.,* IB (*ii*), pp. 302-9.
40. Durand, A.G., *op. cit.*, p. 227.
41. IFP, 3962, January 1891, Cons. 157-62, p. 83; Durand, A.G., *op. cit.*, p. 227.
42. Docosta, *"Our Indian Feudatories and the Administration of Justice in India"*. Reprinted from the *Law Magazine and Review*, November 1893.
43. He wrote to the S.O.S., "Since the re-establishment of the Gilgit Agency, much has been done to strength influence and control among the petty states lying between Kashmir and the Hindu Kush.", PSLEI, 61, pp. 455-58, October 7, 1890.
44. *The Imperial and Asiatic Quarterly Review* and *Oriental and Colonial Record,* July and October 1893. *The Afghan Dilemma* by Historicus; *Amrit Bazar Patrika,* Kashmir under the British Administration, January 30, 1890; *Statesman,* October 6, 1889; *Ibid.,* October 24, 1889, October 29, 1889.
45. The Viceroy termed the place as a "sphere of influence" and defined it as follows:

    "A sphere that is within which we shall attempt to administer the country ourselves, but within which we shall not allow any aggression from outside" Speeches of Lord Lansdowne, (*ii*), p. 6878; Forrest, G.W., *Administration of Lord Lansdowne,* pp. 52-53; Yasin Madhvi, *Indian Administration,* p. 51.
46. Ghose, D.K., *op. cit.*, p. 177.
47. Lansdowne Papers, IX (*d*) pp. 124-27, Lansdowne to Kimberley, October 19, 1892, "The near approach of the Russians renders it necessary for us to keep Political Officers in both Chitral and Hunza, to obtain early information and to counteract Russian activity".
48. *Ibid.*, pp. 139-43, Lansdowne to Kimberley, November 3, 1892; Robert Papers, 96/2, pp. 1113-15.

49. For. Dept., Sec. E., March 1889, Nos. 107-200, April 19, 1888.
50. For. Dept., Sec., No. 353 (K.W.), Progs, May 1884, Henvey to C. Grant, December 14, 1882.
51. Hassnain, F.M., *Gilgit the Northern Frontier of India*, p. 78.
52. For. Dept., Sec. E., March 1889, Nos. 107-200, M.R. Kashmir in his latter on May 11, 1888, names them as Kaka Joo, Wazir Shib Ram, Sawal Singh, and Fakira Joo; For. Dept., Sec. E., Progs., October 1886, Nos. 235-300, No. 287, Plowden to Durand, August 15, 1886; "These are Sawal Singh, Miran Bux, Mahanand Ju, Pitambar and Jotshi".
53. PSDOC, 3, First Series, p. 816, Bishen Devi to Dufferin, November 20, 1886.
54. For. Dept., Sec. E., October 1886, Nos. 235-300.
55. Ghose, D.K., *Kashmir in Transition,* p. 44.
56. Dufferin & Ava, Hariot Georgina Blackwood, *Marchioness of Our Viceregal Life in India*: Selections from *My Journal*, 1884-1888, Vol. I, p. 220.
57. *The Statesman and Friends of India*, August 2, 1889.
58. For. Dept., Sec. E., Progs, October 1886, Nos. 235-300, No. 268.
59. D.P., Reel 529, pp. 460 (a)—62, Aitchison to Dufferin, December 30, 1885.
60. *Ibid,* pp. 22 (c)—(d) Durand to Wallace, January 6, 1886.
61. Gadru, S.N., *op. cit.*, p. 130.
62. Cross Papers, 24, No. 89, Dufferin to Cross, April 16, 1888.
63. For. Dept., Sec. F., July 1888, Nos. 63-86; For., Sec. E., Progs., March 1888, Nos. 107-200 Durand wrote "If Mr. Plowden will sink his own views and do his utmost to help the Maharaja. I hope there may be a chance of things going straight. It is unfortunate that he was hitherto taken so strong a line in the opposite direction and made the Maharaja afraid of him".
64. *Ibid,* Sec. E., March 1889, Nos. 107-200.
65. Gadru, S.N., *op. cit.*, p. 132; Lansdowne Papers, Durand to Wallace, No. 228, March 3, 1889.
66. Durand wrote: "Amar Singh always wanted to oust the Maharaja of Kashmir". *Ibid.,* Lansdowne to Cross, No. 10, February 25, 1890. Lansdowne admitted that the Maharaja's brothers, "were at different times in the habit of supplying the Resident with secret information".
67. For. Sec., E., No. 80, Progs, April 1889, Col. Nisbet to H.M. Durand, February 27, 1887.
68. Lansdowne Papers, Lansdowne to Cross No. 38, September 1, 1890.
69. Gadru, S.N., *op. cit.*, p. 134.
70. *Ibid.,* p. 145.

71. *Ibid.,* pp. 140-141; For. Dept., Sec. E., March 1889, Nos. 107-200, Alexander Atkinson wrote to Durand, "The wickedness, misrule, and oppression attributed to Kashmir is wholly false".; For. Dept., Sec. E., Cons., October 1856, Nos. 235-300; *Ibid.,* Ext. A., June 1886, Nos. 42-48.
72. Yasin, Madhvi, *Indian Administration,* p. 94.
73. For. Dept., Sec. E., Cons., October 1886, Nos. 235-300, For. Dept. Letter No. 494 E, March 16, 1886.
74. Gadru, S.N., *op. cit.*, p. 156, 'The Lady Dufferin Medical Fund Committee received ₹50,000/- from Kashmir, while ₹25,000 was accepted as a contribution to the Aitchison College at Lahore".
75. Bose, J.C., *Cashmere Prince,* p. 69.
76. Cross Papers, 24, No. 82, Dufferin to Cross, January 26, 1888. Maharaja offers a sum of one million rupees in addition to all the troops and war materials of the State.
77. Lansdowne Papers, to the S.O.S., No. 55, October 31, 1891.
78. *Ibid.*
79. For. Sec., No. 42, Progs, March 1876, Major H.W. Bellow to Foreign Secretary, October 13, 1874. In 1870, the Government of India had found that the letter which implicated Ranbir Singh in the murder of Hayward in Yasin was a forged one.
80. For., Sec. E., Nos. 46-48, Progs, March 1887, Plowden to Cunningham, February 14, 1887.
81. *Statesman and Friend of India*, August 2, 1889.
82. Dacosta, J., *Our Indian Feudatories and the Administration of Justice in India,* Reprinted from *The Law Magazine and Review*, November 1893.

7
Partial Restoration of the Maharaja

Pratap Singh ceaselessly presented representations for restoration of his powers to the Viceroy and to those, who could influence the Viceroy. He appealed to Lord Roberts[1] and Ardagh,[2] and requested the Viceroy that he should be restored on the occasion of Prince Albert's visit to India. But his wish was not complied with.[3] At this time Nisbet had changed his mind towards Pratap Singh and proposed to the Viceroy that, in the context of the improved situation in Kashmir, Pratap Singh might be appointed President of the Council in place of Amar Singh.[4] In fact, Nisbet had already moved in that direction having sent Amar Singh to Jammu to induce the Maharaja to go to Srinagar to take over the charge as President.[5] The Viceroy was exasperated as Nisbet had not taken the permission of the Foreign Office before opening negotiations. Lansdowne directed the Resident that he should not move further without instructions.[6] To Lord Cross the Viceroy gave vent to his hurt feelings,[7] "Nisbet has done a number of foolish things, and has quarrelled with half the people, with whom he has been concerned. Altogether he is a gentleman, who rather keeps me on the tenter-hooks."

Pratap Singh expressed his wish in 1891 to the newly-appointed Resident Prideaux, for an interview with the Viceroy.[8] The latter appreciated the move, as the proposed meeting would boost the morale of the Maharaja.[9] The Viceroy was not averse to it, but before the meeting certain things were to be thrashed out. First, the progress of reforms and financial condition of the State were to be ascertained. He directed the Resident to report about them. Second, was the influence of the private servants upon the Maharaja and, third, his lavishness. Prideaux was instructed that the Maharaja should be told that he should in all seriousness try to reform himself.[10]

In the meantime, Pratap Singh extended several invitations to the Viceroy to come to Srinagar.[11] Prideaux,[12] under instructions from the Governor-General, informed the Maharaja that his restoration would not be a sequel to the proposed meeting with the Viceroy, but would exclusively depend upon his capacity to assure the continued good government of the state.

The Viceroy had made up his mind that in no case the Maharaja, if restored, would be given full powers, as he had no faith in his administrative capability.[13] Lansdowne arrived in Kashmir on October 23, 1891. He was very much satisfied with the affairs in Kashmir. He had several meetings with Prideaux, Chamberlain, Logan, Pratap Singh and his brothers. At the state banquet speech the Viceroy scrupulously avoided any mention of the restoration of the Maharaja,[14] but he was convinced that he was perfectly loyal to the British Government. The Viceroy also realised that the edict of abdication must have been forced upon him. He was very much impressed with Pratap Singh's simplicity and chastity.[15] He also found that in spite of his deposition, the Maharaja was still a power.[16] It was now clear to the Viceroy that the episode of the letters was a trumped up affair. Prideaux played a very important and helpful role in the partial restoration of the Maharaja.

Accordingly, the Viceroy had an interview with the Maharaja, and laid down certain conditions to his re-instatement.[17] Pratap Singh accepted all of them but pleaded that his civil list should be increased. The Viceroy raised his civil list by another ₹50,000/- and Pratap Singh was restored with limited powers.[18] During the Viceroyalty of Lord Curzon some other powers were restored in 1905,[19] but full powers were restored on February 4, 1921.[20]

In spite of the innocence of the Maharaja, it was surprising that the Maharaja was not restored to full powers immediately. His rival, Amar Singh was still a favourite with the Government. As he was relegated to the position of the Vice-President, the Resident recommended that some honours must be bestowed upon him to compensate the loss of power.[21]

The Government of Britain honoured Amar Singh with a knighthood, and shortly afterwards the Maharaja was made a G.C.S.I.,[22] who in 1888 was also granted the title of the Colonel.[23]

The press presented a mixed reaction. *The Civil and Military Gazette* wrote, "intrigues are going on in the Cashmere State, and that the friction is visible."[24] *The Statesman* opined that, if there was any conflict in the state nobody but Raja Amar Singh was to be blamed.[25] It hailed the restoration of the Maharaja. The present Maharaja of Cashmere and Jammu is very much loved by his subjects. ...Lord Lansdowne by restoring the Maharaja to power has not only revived and strengthened the confidence of all the Indian princes and the chiefs in the good and just intentions of Her Majesty's Government, but has also won the sincere thanks of the people of Jammu and Cashmere.[26] Some papers questioned the overall authority of the Resident and said that so long the Maharaja would abide by the orders of the Government to spend the state exchequer on strengthening the frontier, he would be regarded as a friendly ally.[27] *The Amrit Bazar Patrika* said that it was gratifying that the Viceroy had contradicted the allegation against the Maharaja of being a 'drunken imbecile'![28] His speech produced a very good effect upon the people. The paper cautioned that this euphoria was not going to last long, as the Maharaja was being restored to limited powers.[29]

The official circles were happy at the new arrangement. Lord Roberts, a friend of Pratap Singh, was pleased.[30] The Secretary of State, Lord Cross, was very much satisfied.[31] Lansdowne has rectified a wrong, but in fact the credit would go to *Savoir-faire* of Prideaux, who masterminded the whole show.

SECTION 1: OFFICIAL SECRETS ACT

The maxim that 'all is well that ends well', could not be applied in this case. The scape-goats were to be found out. The wide publicity of the case had incurred the wrath of the Viceroy, especially against the *Amrit Bazar Patrika*[32] and the *Indian Mirror*.[33] The Viceroy discussed the matter with A.R.

Scoble, Law member of his council, as to what steps could be taken to punish the *Amrit Bazar Patrika*. The Viceroy desired that the Government, "should hold a weapon in its hand which can, if necessary, be used with exemplary effect against those who are guilty."[34]

When the Official Secrets Act was being introduced, Indians thought that it was for frustrating traitors from helping the Russians, French, and other enemies of the empire by supplying them military secrets. But the surprise of the Indians, knew no bounds when they came to know that the act was a provision to prevent journalists from making use of official secrets for the purpose of commenting upon administrative measures.[35]

The Official Secrets Act was passed in October 1889. It aimed at checking unauthorised acquirement and publication of information which was detrimental to the interests of the Government of India. The law authorised stringent punishment to the erring newspapers, which published any official document without the permission of the Government or attempted to acquire any secret information from responsible public servants. The deterrent penalties fixed for defying the law ranged from transportation for life to imprisonment or fine.[36]

The passing of this act proclaimed that the Government was autocratic.[37] The Indian press opined that freedom of expression was curtailed.[38] The *Patrika* called it as 'something like the gagging Act in another shape.'[39] The public was very much alarmed and legal advice was sought as to the real scope of the provisions of the act. Rash Behari Ghosh, an eminent lawyer, gave his opinion that the "secrets" contemplated by the Government did not mean those relating to the administration of the country, but only to those which could be made use of by the enemy of the State for the purpose of doing it injury. They also sought the opinion of Charles Bradlaugh on the subject. His contention was that Lord Lansdowne had entirely misunderstood the scope and object of the measure. The Act was the outcome of the wrath of the Government on account of the publication of the Gilgit document by the *Patrika*.[40]

References

1. Roberts Papers, Box File 100/6, Roberts to Maharaja, June 21, 1889; *Ibid.,* 100/7, p. 103, Roberts to Maharaja, February 8, 1890.
2. Ardagh Papers, Box 2, Pratap Singh to Ardagh, February 2, 1891.
3. Lansdowne Papers, VII (*b*) p. 224, Lansdowne to Maharaja, October 21, 1889,
4. *Ibid.,* VII (*d*) p. 18, Resident to Viceroy, July 5, 1890.
5. *Ibid.,* p. 23, Cunningham to Ardagh, July 7, 1890.
6. *Ibid.,* pp. 11-12, Lansdowne to Nisbet, July 8, 1890.
7. Cross Papers, 29, No. 90, Lansdowne to Cross, September 1, 1890.
8. Ghose, D.K., *op. cit.,* p. 138.
9. Lansdowne Papers, VII (*e*), pp. 381-82, Prideaux to Ardagh, April 27, 1891.
10. *Ibid.,* Lansdowne to Prideaux, May 12, 1891, pp. 230-32.
11. *Ibid.,* VIII (*f*) pp. 57, 86, Maharaja to Lansdowne, August 2, 1891, and August 15, 1891.
12. *Ibid.,* VII (*f*), pp. 74-75, Lansdowne to Prideaux, September 2, 1891.
13. Cross Papers, 31, No. 151, Lansdowne to Cross, October 25, 1891.
14. *Ibid.,* No. 152, encl. in Lansdowne to Cross, October 3, 1891.
15. Lansdowne Papers, to the S.O.S., No. 55, October 31,1891.
16. *Ibid., The Amrit Bazar Patrika,* October 29, 1891.
17. Lansdowne Papers, IB (*iv*), pp. 1045-47, Lansdowne to Pratap Singh, November 6, 1891, encl. 2, to the S.O.S., December 9, 1891.
18. KGR, File No. 15; 1905; KGR, H.H.P.R., File No. 9, 1896; KGR, Maharaja Pratap Singh's Private Records, File No. 13 of 1898, Jammu Archives.
    (*i*) The Maharaja was to exercise his powers on the advice of the Resident and follow the advice whenever it was afforded to him by the Resident.
    (*ii*) The Annual Budget of the State was to be prepared and passed in consultation with the Resident and any expenditure, not provided for in the Budget, was not to be incurred without the approval of the Resident.
    (*iii*) No reappropriation of funds exceeding ten thousand rupees was to be made without the sanction of the Resident;
    (*iv*) Each department budget estimate was to be submitted to the Minister-in-Charge of the Department, who, after consultation with the Maharaja and the Resident, was to submit it to the Maharaja for its final approval.
    (*v*) The Ministers were to be appointed after the approval of the Government of India had been secured.

(*vi*) The appointment of the Minister-in-Charge of the Foreign Department of the State was to be made subject to the condition that the person appointed the Minister-in-Charge of the Department was acceptable to both the Maharaja and his Prime Minister.

(*vii*) The business of the different departments was to be allocated by the Government of India.

(*viii*) The Maharaja was to have the power to veto or alter any orders passed by the Heads of the Departments and was empowered to call for and revise any proceedings of any Department through the Minister concerned.

(*ix*) The Ministers were to have general control of the departments put in their charge and were to be the channel of communications between the departments, the Resident and Maharaja.

(*x*) The Chief Revenue Officer, the Chief Judicial Officer, the Chief Engineer Public Works, the Engineer-in-Chief Railways, the Settlement Commissioner, the Accountant General, the Superintendent of Customs and Excise and the Director of Sericulture were to be appointed or removed with the concurrence of the Government of India.

(*xi*) The appointments and removals of Gazetted Officers of the State-were to be made by the Maharaja on due cause shown.

(*xii*) The rules of business and the "standing orders" in force were to be adhered to until any necessity for their modification was shown, with the exception that all matters hitherto referred to Council were to be referred to the Maharaja through the Prime Minister.

(*xiii*) An English translation of the proceedings of the Council, orders of the Maharaja or the Ministers, was to be sent to the Resident in the following matters.

(*a*) Orders which modified the budget finally passed by the Maharaja.

(*b*) Orders which involved alienation of revenue or remission of taxation.

(*c*) Orders which involved the appointment and removal of the Gazetted Officers.

(*d*) Orders affecting the Railway Department and the Engineering Department.

(*e*) Orders passed in regard to the Settlement Department.

(*f*) Orders passed on the proposals made by the Sericulture Department.

(g) Orders pertaining to the Administration of the frontier; and,

(*h*) The orders issued in regard to annual or periodical contracts given by the State.

(*xiv*) The existing arrangements in regard to the allowance enjoyed by the Maharaja from the State revenue was to continue unchanged.

(*xv*) No existing resolution of the State Council was to be cancelled or modified until final orders to that effect were passed by the Maharaja in consultation with the Resident; and,

(*xvi*) The powers of the Minister and the Heads of the Departments and the regulation of the work between the various departments, defined by the State Council resolutions, were not to be changed until the necessity for such change had been established.

19. Teng, Kaul Bhatt, Koul, *Kashmir Constitutional History and Documents,* pp. 43-45., KGR, Jammu Archives, File No. 13 of 1898, Maharaja Pratap Singh's Private Records.
20. *Ibid.,* p. 51.
21. Lansdowne Papers, VII (*f*), pp. 248-53, Prideaux to Lansdowne, October 26, 1891.
22. *Ibid.,* (IX) (*d*), encl. in, to the SOS, April 20, 1892.
23. For. Pol. Progs, Sec. E., August 1889, Nos. 162-203, K.W.
24. *Civil and Military Gazette,* December 12, 1889.
25. *Statesman,* December 12, 1891.
26. *Ibid.*
27. *The India Nation,* a weekly magazine, Dec. 14, 1891. "So long as the Maharaja guards his frontiers with his men and money, and in the way desired by the Government of India, and lays down the military roads at the cost of the State, and thus willingly bears a heavy strain on the resources of his country, he ought to be looked upon as a friendly ally in whom confidence may be well placed".
28. *The Amrit Bazar Patrika,* October 29, 1891. "We are deeply obliged to His Excellency for having thus given the lie to the cowardly and brutal attacks levelled against His Highness by Sir Lepel Griffin, Mr. Rudyard Kipling, and a host of other mean-minded writers, who had found in the fall of Maharaja Pratap Singh an opportunity for satisfying a propensity, which leads a certain class of people to trample under foot a man already overtaken by serious calamity".
29. *Ibid.*
30. Lansdowne Papers, VII (*f*), p. 294, Roberts to Lansdowne November 15, 1891.
31. PSDI, 18, pp. 3-6, From the SOS, January 8, 1892.
32. Issue of October 3, 1889.
33. Issue of September 28, 1889.
34. *Speeches of Lord Lansdowne,* i, p. 75.
35. *The Amrit Bazar Patrika*, May 24, 1893.
36. Misra, J.P., *The Administration of India under Lord Lansdowne,* p. 162.
37. *The Statesman,* November 22, 1889.
38. *The Hindoo Patriot,* October 21, 1889.
39. *The Amrit Bazar Patrika*, October 24, 1889.
40. *Ibid.,* May 24, 1893.

8

Hunza and Nagar Campaign and Chitral Affair

The Gilgit Agency brought in its sequel the Hunza and Nagar expedition. The allied states of Hunza and Nagar, comprised the valleys-stretching into upper portions of Kanjut or Hunza river, which flows into Gilgit river two miles below the Gilgit fort.[1] The region is extremely inaccessible[2] and the inhabitants understood the advantages thereof. They lived upon the plunder of the surrounding countries.[3] They followed the manners and customs of their forefathers of the 14th century.[4]

On the right bank of Hunza is Chalt, which is twenty-five miles from Hunza. The Hindukush mountain surrounds it on the north and east, and separates it from the Pamir and the Yarkand river. In the west it is separated by a range from Iskuman valley, and in the south the Hunza river divides it from Nagar. The country is racially separated into two divisions, Gujhal and Kanjut. Gujhal is at about eighteen miles above Hunza. Kanjut or Hunza comprises the rest of the country it is inhabited by the Dard race of Yeshkun caste speaking Burishki.[5]

The only means of communication between Hunza and Nagar was a weak rope bridge which could be cut off in a minute. Between the two the importance of Hunza is greater, because it possessed an extremely difficult caravan route leading to the Pamirs, and to the Valley of the Yarkand river.[6] The people of Hunza was of Maulai sect, and those of Nagar were Shias. But both the tribes were of the same stock.[7] Hunza men were more morose and sedate.[8] The Kings of Hunza and Nagar were called Thums. Patricide and fratricide were the hereditary characteristics of the royal family. The ruler of Hunza, Safdar Ali Khan, murdered his father in 1886 and usurped the throne. Raja of Nagar killed his two brothers in 1891. These states were tributary to the Kashmir Government, but its hold was very slight. They considered China as the greatest Empire in the world, and Russia the second. Great Britain, according to their conception, was the third.[9]

The Chinese considered Kanjut as their vassal state. They received annually a tribute from the Raja of Hunza in the month of September, when he used to send a deputation of three or four persons to Kashghar. The tribute consisted of two nuggets of gold worth about two hundred rupees. It was presented with a petition addressed to the Taotai of Kashghar. The Chinese, considering Hunza as their vassal state, thought that only they had the right of issuing orders; but the Raja of Hunza cared little for their orders. The Chinese called Hunza 'Kanjut Indian' meaning thereby, that Kanjut was beyond doubt a Chinese territory.[10]

On the other hand, the states of Hunza and Nagar had definite treaties with the Kashmir Government, which clearly signified that Hunza owed allegiance to the Kashmir Darbar. Russian activities in Pamirs and its future consequences led the Chinese Government to send Chang Tajen to the Pamirs to watch the Russians on Alai, and to prevent them from entering Chinese territory as well as Kanjut.[11]

In 1889, the Nagar chief entered into a treaty with Colonel Durand. They undertook to put an end to the raiding on the Yarkand road and promised to allow properly accredited British officers to travel through their territories though after some time the treaty was violated.[12]

In 1891, Colonel A. Durand visited both the countries. He was satisfied with the behaviour of the Nagar chief and was dissatisfied with the chief of Hunza. Tracing his descent from Alexander the Great, the Hunza chief behaved arrogantly with Captain Younghusband, and refused to pay a visit to India, saying that it was not proper for great Kings like himself and his ancestor Alexander the Great to leave their own, dominions.[13]

Troubles again began to brew in Hunza and Nagar. Towards the middle of the year 1891, Uzr Khan, the Thum of Nagar murdered his two brothers, Gouri Thum and one younger brother, partly because they were favourites of their father and their subjects alike, and partly because the Government of India looked upon them with favour. The Hunza chief was unsympathetic towards the Government of India. He called A. Durand and his party as camels straying into his country without nose-rings and uncontrolled, and the English as an unwarlike woman. He broke the terms of agreement, and raided the northern passes. Some of his people, kidnapped a Kashmiri subject at Nomal, and sold him in northern passes.[14]

The Kashmir troops had in their charge the small fort at Chalt, close to it was Chaprot fort, in which also there was a detachment of Kashmir forces. Uzr Khan collected his forces to attack Chalt and Chaprot. He was in active correspondence with the Hunza chief. Hearing about these preparations A. Durand thought of making a bold dash for Chalt. As luck was in his favour, Major Gokul and his party had built a new road up to Gomal. He collected two hundred men of Kashmir bodyguard Regiment and some Gurkhas and Dogras with their ammunitions. With great difficulty they managed to carry the guns over the rope bridge on the Gilgit river. The British advance unnerved the Hunza and Nagar chiefs, and they sent their agents for truce. Colonel A. Durand did not want to give up the fort of Chalt, whereas the envoys informed him that the tribes prized the fort of Chalt as "on the strings of their wives' pyjamas." A. Durand, with obvious diplomacy, carefully averted a rupture, as he had not enough resources at hand. He warned the tribes that any attempt to occupy the Kashmir posts or hold the road between them and Nomal would be considered as an unfriendly act.[15]

In the meanwhile the tribes informed the Chinese authorities that an English officer forcibly demanded passage through their territories. Raja Zafar Khan wrote arrogant letters to Colonel Durand that he and his sister's son were friendly, and were loyal to the Government of India. They were respectable personalities still they were looked down with contempt. It was the English officials who were considered aggressors. They had brought forces from Gilgit and entered Gilgit on the pretext of obtaining passage. They would not allow them to pass through their territory, nor would they allow the Chinese, Russians and Afghans to do so. He refused Colonel A. Durand's offer to supply them with bullets and powder, if they had none. From ancient times, he informed Durand, they had been strengthened with the wealth of China, and they possessed bullets of gold. He threatened A. Durand that he would report to the Government of India about his behaviour and the head of the Colonel would be put upon a pole. His territory belonged to the Chinese Emperor and the Russian Czar. The war would be among the Government of India, China and Russia. They should not be jolly in taking over the fort of Nilt. It was repeatedly seized many times before, but it never remained for long in their hands.[16]

The Government of India called Colonel A. Durand to Simla. The question was seriously examined. The Government of India ordered for the mobilization of troops to Chalt in October 1891, to build a small fort there, and to improve the road to Gilgit. A detachment of two hundred men belonging to the 5th Gurkha regiments and two guns were despatched to Gilgit Agency.[17] Captain A. Durand on moving his forces to Chalt informed Thums of Hunza and Nagar that it was necessary for their safety, and for that of Kashmir, that he should have free access to their territory.[18] They replied that they were ready for war, and said that Muhammad Safdar Ali Khan's minister Daud with Hunza troops was at Nilt. The minister of Raja Zafar Khan Shah Murad was at Mayeur with Nagar troops. They obviously depended on the strength of their defiles.[19]

After fruitless negotiations, A. Durand made preparations, for an offensive.[20] In the fight which ensued, Hunza and Nagar troops struggled desperately. After two days' fighting the Nagaris gave way. Their attitude became submissive. Hunza Chief Safdar Ali and Nagar Chief Uzr Khan fled northwards across the frontier. The Hunza people were also forced to submit.[21]

Safdar Ali and Uzr Khan took shelter in Chinese territory. The Taotai of Kashghar wrote a letter to the Zandari of the British Empire complaining of their behaviour towards Hunza Chief. They wrote that Kanjut was a dependency of the Chinese Empire, and so it was wrong on the part of the Government of India to send troops without informing them (The Chinese Government). If the Kanjutis had done any act of disrespectful behaviour towards them their duty was to intimate them and they would have managed everything. Finally, he wanted to know the cause of their fight with the Kanjutis and asked that the English troops should withdraw to their own frontiers, so that the fugitives might go to their land and live there with safety.[82]

Durand replied in a polite and diplomatic manner. He touched on every enquiry of Taotai. Kanjutis were a sore trouble to their neighbours. Most obnoxious were their raids and slave trade. They had depopulated Rashken Valley and rendered the trade route between Kashmir and Yarkand unsafe. Sardar Ali Khan in a treaty had promised to put an end to these depredations. Not only had he defied the treaty, but also had made encroachments on Kashmir and sold its people. These were the reasons that compelled the Government of India to punish them. The Government had no desire to cross the Chinese territory or cause annoyance or injury to them. Being afraid of his misdeeds, Safdar Ali Khan fled to the Chinese territories on his own accord. Some misguided persons also followed him, but the greater number of population stayed behind. No harm was done to those who submitted. The Government of India fully agreed with the Chinese Government that the fugitives should be sent back to their homes. The troops would be ordered to stay in Kanjut until the British Agent at Gilgit was assured of order in Kanjut, and the ruler would conduct his administration in due subjection to Kashmir and without committing depredations upon his neighbours. On the satisfaction of the British Agent, the troops would be withdrawn to their former position, *i.e.*, thirty miles distant from Hunza. The Government of India was empowered to send troops and to prevent disorders in future, if necessary.[23]

Many letters were intercepted from the fort of Hunza, although the Raja took with him many of them when he had fled. Some of them (Nos. 1-5) were from Gromochevsky, the Russian Officer. No. 5 was unsigned, but evidently it was from the Russian Consul at Kashghar. It referred to a Hunza deputation to meet some Russian officers. It also asked the Raja of Hunza to intercept letters passing between Gilgit and Kashghar *i.e.*, between Captain Younghusband and the British Agent at Gilgit. The letter was dated 13th September, 1891.[24]

The Government of India thought that the claim of Hunza to Tughdumbush Pamir might not be abandoned.[25] But, if the Chinese wanted to hold Tughdumbush Pamir the English would not extend their control. The reason was that, if the Chinese and the Government of India would abandon their control on Tughdumbush Pamir, the Russians would take advantage of it, and would occupy it. That would be more advantageous to the Russians on ethnological grounds, which would be contrary to the English interests.[26] Later on the Government of India realised that making China strong was a short-sighted policy.[26A] By then it was too late, as the Chinese had established their control over the region.

The Raja of Nagar, Zafar Khan, was granted a sanad. Although he had revolted against Kashmir State, yet on account of his submission and as an act of expediency he was appointed the Thum of Nagar.[27] The ruler of Hunza was deposed and the Kingship was granted to Muhammad Nazim Khan, a member of the ruling state of Hunza.[28] The situation in Hunza and Nagar gradually improved.

SECTION 1: THE CHITRAL AFFAIR

The Government of India was interested in the affairs of Kashmir, therefore, it also came in contact with Chitral. The Indian Government wanted to establish its agency there. The State of Chitral recognised the suzerainty of Kashmir in the year 1846,[29] With the establishment of Gilgit Agency Chitral came into prominence. Russian activities in Central Asia forced the Government of India to look upon Chitral with interest.[30] Chitral had some of the lowest and easiest passes across the Hindukush, and afforded a convenient way to India from Bokhara *via* Badakshan. The capital of Chitral was also situated at the junction of several valleys, which led as well as commanded these passes.

By the engagement of 1878 Aman-ul-Mulk, the Mehtar or Chief of Chitral, got an annual subsidy of ₹12,000 from the ruler of Kashmir. The Mehtar was to present the latter annually three horses, five hawks and five Tezi dogs.[31] Further a treaty was signed between the Amir of Afghanistan and Mortimer Durand that the former would not interfere in Bajaur, Dir, Swat and Chitral.[82] But the disagreements increased after settlement.[33]

Aman-ul-Mulk was a sagacious and wise ruler. He ruled over Upper and Lower Chitral extending from the borders of Punjab on one side to the borders of Kafiristan and Dir on the other. The northern boundary of his dominions was the water-shed of Hindukush. Colonel Durand often visited Chitral during his regime. He was shrewd enough to realise that the safety of Chitral lay in alliance with the Government of India. He wished that not only Chitral but Asmar, Bajaur, and Dir should know that he was a protege of the British Government.[34]

Aman-ul-Mulk had several wives and eighty sons. The principal sons were Nizam-ul-Mulk and Afzul-ul-Mulk. They were by the same mother. Nizam-ul-Mulk had the title—Sardar—in consideration of his being heir apparent, and Afzul-ul-Mulk was called *Taik Mehtar* or Little *Mehtar.* He had a magnetic personality and created a spell on those whom he knew. He understood the power of the British Government better than his father.[35] No love was lost between the two brothers. The throne was the bone of contention. The animosity strengthened so much that even their followers were the deadliest enemies of each other.[36]

With the death of the old Mehtar in 1892, Chitral entered a period in its history marked by fratricidal wars, murders and anarchy.[37] On the September 10, 1892, the Gilgit Agency sent the news to the Government of India that a sudden change had occurred in Chitral. Details of the news were wanting, because the road beyond Yasin was completely blocked by the rival brothers. Nizam-ul-Mulk was afraid that his brother might influence the British Agent by his letters, while Afzal's men were careful to prevent any of the Sardar's emissaries from entering Chitral. The whole of the Chitral proper and Mastuj were in the hands of his son Afzul-ul-Mulk. Shah-i-Mulk, Bahram and Wazir-ul-Mulk were murdered in cold blood.[38]

Nizam-ul-Mulk was powerless to overthrow his more powerful and obstinate brother Rahmat-ul-llah, Nizam-ul-Mulk's deputy and "Hakim" of Ghizr went over to Afzul's side taking with him one hundred men. He was appointed Governor of Mastuj. A marriage with Afzul-ul-Mulk's little daughter was to cement the union between Rahmat-ul-llah and his new master. Thus, Nizam-ul-Mulk could only command a hundred fighting men in Yasin and sixty more came to him from Turikho and another sixty were expected from the latter place. That was the sum total of his resources.[39]

It was quite evident that relations of Afzul-ul-Mulk and his late father were strained for some time past. The latter was determined to remove Afzul from Mastuj. There was a rumour that Afzul-ul-Mulk had poisoned his father.[40] Shah-i-Mulk, who was at Chitral at the time of his father's death was immediately put to death. A big treasure belonging to Shah-i-Mulk came into the hands of Afzul. He also got murdered Murid-i-Dastgir, one of the most precious adherents of Shah-i-Mulk.

Nizam-ul-Mulk wrote two letters to the British Agent. He complained bitterly against Afzul, for killing his three half brothers and turning the unhappy mother out of Chitral fort with her three little sons. Further that Afzul had completely blockaded Turkho.[41]

Nizam's position was indeed desperate. He collected his men in the fort of Yasin. Even including his Turikho adherents, they were but few in number. His own people detested him for his brutal views, tyranny and especially for his parsimony.

Afzul-ul-Mulk wrote to the Viceroy announcing his succession which he described as having taken place "with the unanimous consent of his rival brothers" and of the "leading men and all the people".

The Viceroy acknowledged Afzul-ul-Mulk as the Mehtar of Chitral. He congratulated him on his accession with the consent of his people and of his brothers. He delivered his felicitations that he would live long to enjoy the Chiefship. He would prove himself by his action a loyal friend of the Kashmir Darbar and the Government of India.[42]

Afzul-ul-Mulk requested the Viceroy to favour him. The India Government should render aid in enabling him to strengthen his own position. As Nizam-ul-Mulk was not in Chitral, it was known and evident that according to the usage and custom of the country the Government and its Mehtarship had no concern and connection with the eldest brother. The rule of primogeniture did not apply to the Mehtarship. On the contrary any of the brothers who would be elected by the unanimous consent of the people could assume the Government. Consequently, Afzul-ul-Mulk would maintain enmity with him, he was not going to surrender the throne and territory, and would oppose him till the end.[43]

The Viceroy in a letter to the Secretary of State gave out the reasons why he considered the accession of Afzul-ul-Mulk as the most appropriate. Primarily, it was an unopposed succession. It put an end to the fratricidal wars, which otherwise could have disturbed the whole agency. Moreover, Afzul-ul-Mulk was always loyal to the British. His first act after his succession was to send for a British officer to Chitral. If he proved a trustworthy and friendly ruler as the Viceroy surmised, the position of Gilgit agency might be greatly strengthened.[44]

Nizam-ul-Mulk was regularly corresponding with the British agency to remove his own grievances. The British agent desired to establish amicable relations between the two brothers and Robertson was told that, if he passed through Yasin, he must see and advice Nizam-ul-Mulk who was going to Chitral. Now, finding himself utterly weak, Nizam-ul-Mulk came to Gilgit, and there he lived as a refugee.[45]

Every succession in the North-West Frontier signalled bloodshed and murder before and afterwards. Afzul-ul-Mulk was no exception. The murder of three brothers and their adherents was not enough. He added fuel to the fire by announcing a list of head men, who were to be killed. A general discontent prevailed in Chitral as to whose death was awaited next. As a result his own adherents turned traitors, and a plot was hatched in Afghanistan to overthrow Afzul-ul-Mulk and he was subsequently killed.[46] As soon as Afzul-ul-Mulk died, all his men gave up arms and surrendered themselves. The territory from Darosh to Mastuj came under the suzerainty of Sher Afzul. Mehtar Ju Ghulam Dastgir, Kohkhan Beg, and Yedgar Beg fled towards Dir with some companions.

It was evident that the attack of Sher Afzul was with the connivance of the Amir of Afghanistan. He ordered that all the Chitralis, whether sold or in the district of Badakshan, should be set free and placed under the command of Sher-Afzul, so that he might be able to seize Chitral. Sher Afzul acted according to the orders of the Amir. The Sawars, who accompanied Sher Afzul, were all Chitrali slaves except eight persons, who were the servants of the Amir. The war materials as, for instance, horses, supplies, *Khillats* etc., were supplied by the Amir of Afghanistan. It was surprising that while Sher Afzul was endeavouring to capture the fort of Chitral, no one gave any inkling to Nizam-ul-Mulk or to any other person about the matter.[47]

The British Agent enquired from the Amir of Afghanistan, whether the attack of Sher Afzul on Chitral was due to his orders. The Amir showed his ignorance about that. But he said that if Sher Afzul had asked for his permission, he would have gladly given it. It is interesting to note that Sher Afzul informed the British Agent about his succession. He wrote that the interests of the Amir and the British Government were one and the same and therefore, he was a friend and a well-wisher of the latter.[48] Sher Afzul was a loyal and intimate friend of the Amir of Afghanistan. The communication between the Amir and Sher Afzul was carried on through the

Governor of Badakshan and the Sipah Salar at Asmar.[49] Sher Afzul later on called and warned the British news-writer that no letter without his permission and perusal could be sent to anyone. He placed a guard over the house of Khan Bahadur Rub Nawaz Khan, the British news-agent at Chitral.[50]

Nizam-ul-Mulk on being aware of the change at Chitral wrote to the British Agent at Gilgit. The letter stated that if he became the Mehtar of Chitral, he would accept the English mission as well as the establishment of the telegraph lines. He would also willingly submit to the orders of the Government of India. He further said that Sher Afzul, his uncle, had no real following in Chitral and as soon as he would enter Chitral the nobles would come to his side. Nizam-ul-Mulk came to Gilgit of his own volition. He was treated as a guest and not as a prisoner. With the British Agency behind him Nizam-ul-Mulk crossed the frontier. He was joined by the people of Turikho and Murikho. Sher Afzul sent an army of 1,200 people to oppose Nizam-ul-Mulk. That army went over to him. Nizam immediately marched to Mastuj, which he occupied without difficulty and Drason also came into his hands. Shortly afterwards Sher Afzul fled to the Afghan Commander-in-Chief at Asmar. Nizam-ul-Mulk being afraid of treachery and the possible return of Sher Afzul with Afghan force was afraid of advancing beyond Drason. He wrote to the British Agent to send a British officer to help him and to occupy Yasin. Colonel Durand recommended the case of Nizam-ul-Mulk to the Government of India. The latter sanctioned both the proposals on the understanding that Nizam-ul-Mulk was actually in possession of Chitral. Captain Younghusband marched with a small escort. The troops were again posted at Gupies to keep Yasin quiet.[51]

Nizam-ul-Mulk became the Mehtar of Chitral. Colonel Durand sent Robertson's mission to Chitral as originally intended by Afzul-ul-Mulk. Robertson took Captain Younghusband and an escort of fifty Sikhs.[52]

The Chitral mission withdrew to Gilgit on June 6, 1893. Mr. Robertson reported that the country was extremely quiet and peaceful. During the advance headmen proved uniformly friendly. Villagers were very amicable in their dealings with British Officers. Muhammad Wali and Raja Akbar Khan of Puniyal were intriguing in Yasin. Their policy was to discredit the Mehtar's authority. Yasinis wanted that their country should be taken under the control of the Government of India. Yasinis were much afraid of Muhammad Wali. They presumed that he might not be restored in Yasin, like Nizam-ul-Mulk, as he was treated there with honour. If it happened, he would take full vengeance against them.[53]

There was again a report current in Chitral of a combination of Afghan and all tribes between Chitral and Peshawar to drive the English from Chitral. The report was supposed to have been circulated by Muhammad Afzul Beg, a son of Mehtar Joo Kohkan Beg, governor of Drash. Muhammad Afzul Beg recently paid a visit to the Baba Sahib of Dir. He was strongly influenced by that fanatical priest.[54]

The Mehtar of Chitral wanted to send an army to Drash, because he thought that Umra Khan on the pretense of waging a religious war against the Kafirs, was planning to seize the fort of Drash. Captain Younghusband rejected the proposal of the Mehtar. It was clear that the massing of Chitral troops on Dir frontier would probably precipitate a conflict between Bajaur and Chitral. It could only be justified by the imminent danger of an invasion of Drash district by Umra Khan. The Assistant British Agent acted judiciously in restraining the Mehtar from needlessly irritating Umra Khan.[55]

The Mehtar of Chitral also wanted to retain his lost territory at Nursut. He also wished to help his friend and relative, Muhammad Sharif Khan, ex-Khan of Dir. He also wanted to take revenge on the Khan of Jandol. These purposes could only be realised by stopping the more or less friendly relations which had existed between Umra Khan and the Government of India. Neither the Mehtar nor his advisers could be credited with much political wisdom. They would probably all have been pleased at the prospect of a war between Chitral and Bajaur, especially, if the latter power could be incited to become the aggressor. They believed that under the existing circumstances Chitral would be actively supported by the Government of India. As a matter of policy, the Government of India was not inclined to get entangled in the rivalries and intrigues which were always rife in that part of the country.

Towards the end of 1893, Lord Lansdowne intended to remove the political agent from Chitral. But due to two reasons he could not do so. First, the Pamirs boundary dispute was still unsettled. If the British Agent was recalled from Chitral, Russian might have further resorted to aggression. Second, Umra Khan had become a most intriguing personality of the North-West Frontier.[56]

The Government of India guaranteed the independence of Chitral under the suzerainty of Kashmir State. The Assistant British Agent resided there. To keep an eye on the North-West Frontier, it established its agency at Gilgit. That was most obnoxious to the tribes. There were constant reports and rumours that the tribes between Chitral and Peshawar had combined together to drive English from the former place.

The most interesting figure was that of the Amir of Afghanistan. He had by the Agreement of 1892 promised not to interfere in Chitral, Swat and Bajaur. But his best efforts were to create troubles in Chitral. He employed Sher Afzul as a fit instrument for it. He wanted to win over Umra Khan of Jandol, who had in turn also an instrument (Amir-ul-Mulk) in harassing Chitral. The Government of India constantly had to encounter difficulties due to the Amir and Umra Khan.

References

1. The region is also called Kanjut, and its inhabitants Kanjuties. The region is on the side of the Indian mountain ranges, which separates India from the Chinese mountains. For. Dept., Sec. F., January 1888, Nos. 115-118.
2. For. Dept., 1892, Sec. F., April 1892, Nos. 1-92, No. 83. Letter from H.M. Durand, K.C.I.E.C.S.I. Secretary to Government of India Foreign Department. To-Taotai in civil and military charge of Kashghar.
3. Knight, *Where Three Empires Meet*, p. 345.

4. These valleys are buried in a gigantic mountain system containing some of the highest peaks in the Himalayas, Mount Raka Poshi, which towers above the sea level, while several other summits exceed 24,000 feet. Hunza and Nagar are famous for its glaciers and ravines. Above Nagar is a wild tangle of ground, where three huge glaciers fought out for mastery. Thus, the states of Hunza and Nagar present a peculiar spectacle. No part of the world is so rugged and inaccessible as this country is. This inaccessibility has been their salvation.
5. Biddulph said—"They probably present the spectacle of a race living under almost the same conditions now as their forefathers did fourteen centuries ago." Durand, A., *Making of a Frontier,* p. 155.
6. The rich caravans from India to Central Asia were always waylaid and pillaged in the neighbourhood of Shahdulah. The Thums had their information agents at Yarkand, who sent the news of expected caravans. *Ibid,* p. 147.
7. Originally Hunza and Nagar were ruled by the same Chief when once the ruler divided his kingdoms between his sons. Though they were Muslims, but they were bye word on the frontier for their laxity in morals. The men considered themselves honourable, if his wife attracted the notice of the Thum, and the hospitality enjoined to offer his wife to the guest, *Ibid.,* pp. 141, 140.
8. The reason for this is the winter, when the sun is in the south, the great mountains backing their Valley shut out all the light and warmth, ...Thus devoid of the blessings of sun for months makes them-morose and sad, also it has influenced their national character. Nevertheless the land of Hunza is more fertile, when it enjoys the full benefit of summer. Nagar as call their country "the land of gold and apricots," because gold can be washed out of every stream, and the earth yields apricots in rich abundance. *Ibid.*, p. 143.
9. It was the custom of the Kanjuties court that the Wazir would ask in the presence of the Thum "who is the great King of the East," and some other person was to reply "Surely the Thum of Hunza, unless perhaps the Khan of China, for these two without any doubt are the two greatest." Compare Knight, *Where Three Empires Meet,* pp. 348-556.
10. For. Dept., 1892, Sec. F., April 1892, Nos. 1-92, No. 1, Yangi Hisar, the 24th October 1891. From—G. Macartney Esq. on special duty to—The Assistant Secretary to the Government of India, For. Dept.
11. *Ibid.*
12. Knight, *Where Three Empires Meet,* p. 352.
13. Durand, A., *op. cit.*, p. 252.
14. *Ibid.,* pp. 238, 103, 231, 248, Knight, E.F., *Where Three Empires Meet,* p. 382.
15. Durand, A., *op. cit.*, pp. 238-242.

16. For. Dept., 1892, Sec. F., April 1892, Nos. 1-9, No. 83, 17th March, 1892. From—Sir H.M. Durand, Secretary to the Government of India, For. Dept., To—Taotai in Civil and Military Charge of Kashmir.
17. Blue Book, Corres., relating to the operations in Hunza and Nagar 1892; IFP, 3962, December 1891, Cons. 53 and 55, pp. 52-53.
18. Sykes, P., Sri Mortimer Durand, p. 184; Knight, E.F., *op. cit.*, p. 336.
19. Durand, A., *op. cit.*, pp. 254-255.
20. The Hunza Nagar field force comprised 188 men of the 5th Gurkhas, 28 men of the 20th Panjab infantry; 76 men of Hazara mountain battery; 7 Bengal sappers and miners and 661 Imperial Service Troops, 257 from the Rgt, Pertab on 1st Kashmir Infantry Regiment, and 404 from the Bodyguard or 2nd Kashmir officials. In addition to these were irregulars, the Punialis and Speeding's Pathans. Two thousand Balti coolies performed the bulk of the transport service. Sixteen British officers accompanied the Field Force.
21. Durand, A., *op. cit.*, p. 256.
22. For. Dept., 1892, Sec. F., April 1892, Nos. 1-92, No. 1, Dated Yangai Hissar, the 24th October, 1891; From—G. Macartney Esq. on special duty. To—Assistant Secretary to the Government of India For. Dept.; Lansdowne Papers, IB (V), pp. 357-58, George-Macartney to Mortimer Durand, January 31, 1892, encl. 2 in GOI to SOS, April 1892.
23. *Ibid.,* Lansdowne Papers, IB (V), p. 265, encls. in GOI to SOS, March 23, 1892.
24. For. Dept., Sect. F., September 1892, No. 396-472.
25. For. Dept., Progs., August 1892, Nos. 156-198, No. 162, No. 906/214, Dated Gilgit, the 13th May, 1892. From Lieutenant Colonel A.G. Durand, British Agency at Gilgit. To—The Resident in Kashmir.
26. *Ibid.,* No. 164, No. 1250 F., Dated Simla, the 27th June, 1892 (Confidential) From W.J. Cunningham Esq. Deputy Secretary to Government of India, For. Dept. To—The Resident in Kashmir.

26A. Lansdowne's Note, September 28, 1889, For. Sec. F., Progs, October 1889, Nos. 160-169.

27. Lansdowne Papers, IB (V), pp. 231-33, Durand to Kashmir Resident, January 20, 1892, Sub. encl. in GOI to SOS, March 16, 1892.
28. Lansdowne Papers, IB (V), pp. 557-78, 601-04, "To the SOS May 31, 1892, encl. 9.
29. Vide, Davies, *The Problem of North-West Frontier*.; F.O. 65, 1062.
30. For. Dept., Sec. F., January 1888, Nos. 115-118. The boundaries of Chitral: North—Hindukush, South—Indus, Kohistan Laspur Range, and Kunar. East—Hunza, Gilgit, and Punjab, West—Kafiristan. Chitral

is the most important country to be dealt with, and our interest there is strategical rather than political. Chitral commands one or more passes of the Hindukush which military authorities regard, or used to regard, as valuable or vulnerable points. It was with special reference to these passes that Lord Lytton's Government determined at the end of the year 1876 to establish a Political Agency at Gilgit; Quarter-Master-General's Gazetteer of Afghanistan on Chitral.

31. Aitchinson, XI, No. XCIV.
32. For. and Pol. Dept., Sec. F., 1894, No. 193-217, No. 195.
33. F.O. 65, 1062, No. 49 of 1879.
34. Durand A., *op. cit.*, pp. 74, 82.
35. *Ibid.*, p. 76.
36. For. Pol. Dept., 1890, Sec. F., Progs., August 1890, Nos. 196-206, No. 197.
37. A. Durand, *op. cit.*, p. 182.
38. For. Pol. Dept., 1892 Sec. F, October 1892, Nos, 400-440, No. 437, Extract from the Diary of the British Agency, Gilgit, for the week ending 10th September, 1892.
39. The legitimate son of Mirwali, the infamous Mehtar of Yasin.
40. It ran so that the old Mehtar was suffering from a pain in the chest. Afzul told him that he had some good medicine, which the old man agreed to take. On taking it, he at once fell back dead.
41. *Ibid.*, No. 439, No. 193 of 1892. Letter to the SOS.
42. *Ibid.*, No. 418, from H.M. Durand K.C.I.E. to Sardar Afzul-ul-Mulk, Mehtar of Chitral.
43. *Ibid.*
44. *Ibid.*
45. *Ibid.*
46. Rub Nawaz Khan, the News-writer at Chitral wrote that Sher Afzul came to Laktu with one hundred men from Badakshan via Dura Kotal road. He attacked the fort at Laktu at 1 O'clock in the night. Mehtar Ju Murid Dastgir was sleeping soundly. He was seized and killed. The people of Laktu were enemical with Afzul-ul-Mulk for the last few years, took advantage of the situation. They followed Sher Afzul. On the following night, they attacked the fort of Showghat, and occupied in the night at 12 O'clock. From these Sher Afzul took with him Mehtar Ju a boy of fourteen years of age. On the 3rd Night *i.e.*, 6th November, 1892, he managed to open the gate of Chitral fort through the confidential servant of the Mehtar Afzul-ul-Mulk at 2 O'clock in the night, and entered the fort with his troops. Sleeping Afzul-ul-Mulk was stirred aback to receive the news. He ran towards the tower of the fort in panic. A bullet passed through his hand causing his death. For. Dept., Sec. F., Progs., January 1893, Nos. 1-161. No. 60—Translation of a letter from Jamadar Rub

Nawaz Khan, News—writer at Chitral, to the address of the Secretary, Dated the 9th November, 1892.

47. *Ibid.*
48. For. Dept, 1893, Sec. F., January 1893, Nos. 292-295, No. 292.
49. For. Dept, 1893, Sec. F., Progs., January 1893, Nos. 1-161, No. 60.
50. *Ibid,* No. 160, No. 233, Dated 28th December, 1892, from the Government of India, to —The SOS. *Ibid.,* No. 152 (9A) Chitral.
51. *Ibid.,* No. 160 and No. 233, Dated 28th December, 1892, from the GOI to the SOS.
52. For. Dept., 1893, Sec. F., January 1893, Nos. 292-295, No. 292.
53. For. Dept., Sec. F., Nos. 636-655, No. 639; British Agency Political Diary for the week ending 10th June, 1893.
54. *Ibid.,* No. 641, British Agency Gilgit Official Diary for week ending the 17th June, 1893.
55. *Ibid.,* No. 645, British Agency *Gilgit* Official Diary for week ending 1st July, 1893.
56. P.P., 1895, LXII (C-7864), 29.

Epilogue

The British considered India as 'the brightest jewel in the British Crown',[1] hence were very much solicitous for its safety. Many a crimes were committed for this. The two Afghan wars and the occupation of Quetta are some of the illuminating examples of it. The Government of India, until 1886, was intent only on guarding the western frontier, as it was apprehensive of a Russian attack on India through Afghanistan, but the Russian advance towards the Pamirs and Chinese interests in Hunza and Nagar made the Government alert on the northern frontier also. The northern frontier meant the small states lying on the frontiers of Kashmir which enjoyed a nominal suzerainty over them. The Government of India geared itself to intensify its defence. It meant that the limited independence enjoyed by the Kashmir State was to be liquidated, as the Russian and British Empires, "here on the northern frontier were closer together than anywhere else in the world," .... and as they drew closer "increasingly on each side did suspicion beget suspicion and activity beget activity."[2] The Government of India under Lansdowne envisaged a bold frontier policy both towards the western and northern frontiers and, as a result, the British frontier advanced up to the Hindukush.[3]

The first step was the re-establishment of the Gilgit Agency. Its prelude was the posting of the Resident in Kashmir, which was decided ironically enough during the viceroyalty of Lord Ripon, the most liberal Viceroy of India. The time for posting was selected after the death of Ranbir Singh. After the death of Ranbir Singh, his eldest son, Pratap Singh's first encounter with St. John, the Officer on Special Duty, was in intimating him that the Government of India had recognised Pratap Singh as the Maharaja of Kashmir, and that his own designation was changed into the Resident. He would act as an adviser to the Maharaja in reforming the administration. As months rolled by the Resident became more assertive of his authority, like the Story in the Arabian Nights of the camel and the householder. St. John's tenure was a short one, but before going he left a very damaging report about the administration and character of Pratap Singh.[4] The second Resident Plowden was more masterful. His ambition was to act as the real ruler of Kashmir. He encouraged and favoured the anti-Maharaja faction, whose leader was Amar Singh. The Maharaja was overruled in every way. He could not have the councillors of his choice. The classic example is that of the controversy over the appointment of Nilambar Mukherjee whom the Maharaja wanted to retain in his council while the Resident wanted to throw him out of Kashmir on account of his loyalty to the Maharaja and sharpness of intellect. The Maharaja even could not communicate directly with the Viceroy, —every communication was routed through the Resident. The Foreign Office, which was considered a synonym for progressive diehard authoritarianism, traditions, and ideals, was also fed up with Plowden.[5] The Foreign Secretary, Mortimer Durand apprised Dufferin, that the turn of affairs in Kashmir could still be straightened, if Nisbet moderated his preconceived prejudices against the Maharaja. That the Maharaja was afraid of Plowden was admitted by Durand. Thus, it was clear that Plowden wanted to set aside the Maharaja to fit in Kashmir in the Imperial chess-board. For his autocratic demeanour Lord Dufferin, as Viceroy of India, removed him from office.[6]

The appointment of the Parry Nisbet was made by Dufferin with very high expectations to set the things right 'in the most important corner of the world'.[7] But his euphoria was not shared by the Foreign Secretary, who did not like the Punjab Government official to be posted as the Resident.[8]

Nisbet overacted in his zeal for promoting Imperial interests in Kashmir. The discovery of a batch of 34 letters alleged to have been written by Pratap Singh in Dogri script to the Russian Government were a windfall to him to carry out the Imperial mission. Though the Viceroy advised restraint and a thorough inquiry into the matter Nisbet ignored all.[9] Durand, who suspected this sort of trouble from Nisbet, cautioned Lansdowne, the Viceroy of India:

"His sense of right and wrong is often too acute and his energy explosive. Colonel Nisbet should, I think, be restrained."[10]

A slight restraint on the part of Nisbet would have saved the muddle. With the passage of time he would have come to know that this was a common characteristic of the Kashmir politics. Even such a domineering personality as that of Ranbir Singh was allegedly suspected to be in the contact of the Russians.[11] Lansdowne from the start doubted the authenticity of the forged letters and after an interview with the Maharaja his doubts became a certainty.[12] Similarly, the Viceroy got convinced that the abdication of the Maharaja was not voluntary but had been forced upon him. He wrote, "Whether the Maharaja ever meant to abdicate or not, we certainly 'jumped down his throat' very sharply, and the opportunity of setting the affairs of the State right was no doubt too good a one to be lost."[13] The Viceroy also realised that the Maharaja wielded a considerable influence and without his co-operation the council could not work smoothly.[14] Between the highhanded and arbitrary Residents, Plowden and Nisbet, Prideaux's appearance on the Kashmir politics was like a warm sun in an overcast sky.

Lansdowne restored the Maharaja to limited powers. Between the deposition "and restoration, the Government of India achieved its objectives, *i.e.,* the re-establishment of the Gilgit Agency, and the stalling of Russian expansion. The Gilgit Agency proved a mirage. Very soon Chitral was more vital for its interests. An Agent was established there under the control of the Gilgit Agency.[15] The Government of India got involved in tribal politics. In 1895 the British Resident was suddenly attacked while on a visit to the capital, resulting in the counter-offensive by the Government of India.[16]

For the first time under Lord Lansdowne the northern frontier of Kashmir was delimited.[17] The Karakoram and Hindukush mountains were fixed as the northern frontier of

Kashmir. The Government of India committed a blunder in encouraging China, against Russia to extend her influence in the region of Shahidulla.[18] Actually Shahidullah belonged to the Maharaja of Kashmir. Scare of Russia made the Government of India short-sighted, and it unwillingly helped China to extend her frontiers up to the Pamirs.[19] When further explorations were made it was discovered in 1898 that the demarcation of the Kashmir frontier up to the Karakoram mountains, following the watershed, was defective, and a demand was made to extend the limits up to the Kuenlun mountains. It was like weeping over the spilled milk, as the Chinese had by this time established their hold over the region.[20] This legacy of the British Government of India is taking its toll in the present times, when a powerful China is progressively nibbling at the outlying regions in the Jammu and Kashmir State of India. The Amir of Afghanistan also fished in the troubled waters in Chitral using Sher Afzul as his instrument. The short war with Hunza and Nagar was the aftermath of the establishment of the Gilgit Agency.[21] The defeat of the Hunza and Nagar by the Kashmir State troops of the Imperial Service Corps, a part of the Imperial defence scheme, proved its calibre as a fighting force. It showed that the Kashmir Service Corps was quite capable of fighting side by side with the Indian troops.[22] One member of the Viceroy's Executive Council remarked "the Gilgit officers were, to say the least, not reluctant to fight."[23]

Thus, the whole episode of the Maharaja's misery hinged upon Gilgit. If the Government would have been scrupulous enough to tell the Maharaja that it wanted Gilgit for the defence of India, and in return would have compensated it with some territories of equal value adjoining the boundaries of Kashmir, the Maharaja would have been saved from the mental torture and the Government of India of calumny.[24] The story of the forged letters reveals also the weakness of the Maharaja to check intrigues and his inability to rise above party politics.[25]

The Government after the victory over Hunza, Nagar got more concerned with Chitral. Its agency at Chitral became the target of attacks. The plight of the Government became rather like that of a man caught in a marsh, the harder it struggled to get out the deeper it sank in the morass.

The Indian Press deserves Kudos, for taking up the cause of the Maharaja, and in publishing the most sensational documents.[26] The editors, not so rich, contributed money from their own pockets to highlight the case of the Maharaja in the British Parliament. This speaks of the high standard of journalism in those times. The press had to pay a heavy penalty when the Official Secrets Act was passed in 1889.[27]

Lord Lansdowne, in a speech during his visit to Kashmir, spoke that Kashmir owed its existence, to a 'grant'.[28] In other words, according to *The Amrit Bazar Patrika,* it was sold to Gulab Singh in perpetuity.[29] Hence the British 'Government had no moral or legal right for interference.[30] This question has plagued the historians, since then. Dr. Kapoor calls the Treaty of Amritsar a 'sale of Kashmir', and imposition of the Resident as 'Kashmir snatched'. But Dr. Ghosh says that the British . had every right of interference in Kashmir. "A state, avowedly created in British interest and maintained for the safety of the Indian Empire, could hardly be conceived of as belonging outside the Indian political system."[31] He further says that, when the Resident was stationed in Kashmir, there was a scare that it was a prelude to the annexation of Kashmir,[32] but no annexation was ever made.[33]

Thus all the ado was due to the fact that Kashmir, the "Happy Valley" of India, held the key to the northern frontier of the Indian Empire. The Government of India was in search of a scientific frontier to ward off the Russian move. The territories which it wanted were under the suzerainty of Kashmir over which it exercised a loose control. "Hence, the Government of India decided to gain a hold over Kashmir so as to get the command over the outlying territories as well as the internal resources of Kashmir beef."[34]

References

1. Lansdowne Papers, Letters from Persons in India, P. Roberts to Lansdowne, No. 454, April 20,1891.
2. Alder, J.A., *British India's Northern Frontier*, p. 309.

3. Lansdowne Papers, Correspondence with the SOS, Lansdowne to Kimberley, No. 48, October 5, 1892.
4. For. Dept., Progs., Sec. E., March 1889, Cons 108, Memo of January 8, 1886.
5. For. Dept., Sec. E., March 1889, Nos. 107-200.
6. Cross Papers, 24, No. 96, Dufferin to Cross, June 1, 1888.
7. *Ibid,* 25, No. 121, Dufferin to Cross, December 3, 1888.
8. D.P., Reel 533, pp. 174-75, Durand to Wallace, September 5, 1888.
9. Lansdowne Papers, IB (*i*), G.O.I. to Resident, March 4, 1889, encl. 2 in GOI to SOS, April 3, 1889.
10. For. Dept., Sec. E., April 1889, Cons. 90-98, K.W.I., Durand's note, March 16, 1889, on Nisbet's Report on Kashmir.
11. Kapoor, *Kashmir Sold and Snatched*, p. 150.
12. Lansdowne to Cross, No. 18, March 20, 1889, Lansdowne Papers, Correspondence with the SOS; Cross Papers, 31, No. 152, Lansdowne to Cross, October 31, 1891.
13. Lansdowne Papers, VII, (*f*), pp. 176-77, Lansdowne to Hutchins, member of the Viceroy's Council, November 9, 1891.
14. "In spite of his abdication, the Maharaja is still a power in the State and able to some extent to thwart the action of the Council." Lansdowne Papers, Lansdowne to Cross, No. 55, October 31, 1891; Cross Papers, 31, No. 152, Lansdowne to Cross, October 31, 1891; *The Amrit Bazar Patrika*, October 29, 1891.
15. Lansdowne Papers, Correspondence with the SOS, Lansdowne to Kimberley, No. 35, June 6, 1893.
16. Misra, J.P., *The Administration of India—under Lord Lansdowne,* p. 30.
17. For. Sec. F., Progs., October 1890, Nos. 141-170, K.W. 2, August 21, 1890.
18. For. Sec. F., Progs., October 1890, No. 168, No. 87, July 14, 1890.
19. For. Sec. F., Progs, October 1889, Nos. 182-87, Lansdowne's Note, September 28, 1889.
20. For. Sec. F., Progs., January 1198, Nos, 160-169, W.J. Cunningham's Note, January 7, 1898.
21. Lansdowne Papers, IB (*iv*), pp. 985-86, To the SOS, October 25, 1891; Yasin, Madhavi, *Indian Administration,* p. 52.
22. *Ibid.,* IB (*v*), pp. 37-45, to the SOS, January 6, 1892.
23. For. Sec. F., Progs., June 1892, Nos. 243-273, Brackenbury's Note, April 17, 1892.
24. *The Amrit Bazar Patrika,* October 29, 1891.
25. Cross Papers, 26, No. 16, Lansdowne to Cross, March 20, 1889.

26. Among the various newspapers espousing the case of Pratap Singh the name of *The Amrit Bazar Patrika* stands unparalleled. It published the letters alleged to be written by the Maharaja to Meeran Bux in its issue dated June 27, 1889. Earlier in its issue dated March 27, 1889, the Paper wrote, "We have explained our own conviction that somebody wants Cashmere. It is not the view of this man or this Paper, but we believe of whole of India." In the same issue *Patrika* continued "To convict the Maharaja of treason the government will not do. They will find him an idiot, a fool and all that and then take the administration of the State in their own hands. Probability is they will not depose him, they will give a Dewan as they gave a Dewan and a Council to Dewas Senior Branch. The Maharaja will get the salute but the Resident will rule the kingdom." The foreboding proved prophetic.
27. Misra, J.P., *op. cit.*, p. 162.
28. *The Amrit Bazar Patrika*, October 29, 1891.
29. *Ibid.*
30. Kapoor, M.L., *Kashmir Sold and Snatched.*
31. Ghose, D.K., *Kashmir in Transition,* pp. 217-218.
32. *The Statesman and Friend of India* (Weekly), October 3, 1885, Letter to the Editor by A.W.H., September 27, 1885.
33. Ghose, D.K., *op. cit.*, p. 217; Pannikar, K.M., *Gulab Singh*, p. 126.
34. Yasin, Madhavi, *op. cit.*, p. 79.

APPENDICES

Appendix I

Relevant Portions of the Treaty of Amritsar March 16, 1846

Art. 1. The British Government transfers and makes over forever, in independent possession to Maharaja Gulab Singh and the heirs male of his body, all the hilly or mountainous country, with its dependencies, situated to the eastward of the river Indus and westward of the river Ravee, including Chumba, and excluding Lahul, being part of the territories ceded to the British Government by the Lahore State, according to the provisions of Article IV, of the Treaty of Lahore dated 9th March 1846.

Art. 3. In consideration of the transfer made to him and his heirs...Maharaja Gulab Singh will pay to the British Government the sum of seventy-five lakhs of rupees... .

Art. 4. The limits of the territories of Maharaja Gulab Singh shall not be at any time changed without the concurrence of the British Government.

Art. 5. Maharaja Gulab Singh will refer to the arbitration of the British Government any disputes or questions that may arise between himself and the Government of Lahore or any other neighbouring State, and will abide by the decision of the British Government.

Art. 6. Maharaja Gulab Singh engages for himself and heirs to join, with the whole of his Military Force, the British troops, when employed within the hills, or in the territories adjoining his possessions.

Art. 7. Maharaja Gulab Singh engages never to take or retain in his service, any British subject, nor the subject of any European or American State, without the consent of the British Government.

Art. 9. The British Government will give its aid to Maharaja Gulab Singh in protecting his territories from external enemies.

Art. 10. Maharaja Gulab Singh acknowledges the supremacy of the British Government, and will in token of such supremacy present annually to the British Government one horse, twelve perfect shawl goats of approved breed (six male and six female), and three pairs of Cashmere shawls.

Appendix II

From

Colonel R. PARRY NISBET, C.I.E.

Resident in Kashmir,

To

Sir U. MORTIMER DURAND, K.C.I.E., C.S.I.,

Secretary to the Government of India,

Foreign Department, Calcutta,

Fort William, *the 16th March 1889.*

Sir,

1. In continuation of my telegram of the 5th instant informing you how certain papers, the originals of which have been shown to you and translations of which are annexed, written by His Highness Maharaja Pratap Singh of Kashmir came into my possession, I think it is necessary to elaborate the matter in an official report which I have now the honour to submit.

2. My chief object in this report will be to satisfy you that no pains have been spared to establish completely the authenticity of these letters of which I have myself never had any doubt.

3. The letters were handed to me by Munshi Hursukh Rai, proprietor of the *Kohinoor* newspaper and press, a man of leading social position at Lahore. Now, I have known Hursukh Rai for upwards of 20 years, and for the five years during which I was the chief Magistrate at Lahore—my private and official acquaintance with him was frequent and intimate, and his character as a safe man is well-known to me. As a friend of mine Munshi Hursukh Rai could not, I believe, have been induced by any improper motive to lay before or hand over to me, unsolicited, documents that were not authentic.

4. The narrative he gave and which is set out in my previous telegram as to how the papers came into his possession, and that he was acting in the matter only as a commission agent of Sardar Dyal Singh or Mrs. Spitta, appears to me natural and credible. He did not conceal from me that endeavours had been made to get the Maharaja of the Kashmir State to buy back these letters. In support of this statement he handed to me two letters written to him by Shiv Sarn, Wazir of the State and an intimate courtier of the Maharaja, negotiating for the purchase of the documents. These negotiating letters are dated in October 1888, or before I ever assumed the office of Resident. Wazir Shiv Sarn's letters in accordance with native parlance speak of the purchase of jewels which the seller valued too high, but for which he was directed to offer ₹20,000 to 30,000—for Munshi Hursukh Rai is not a jeweller, and all he had for disposal were these documents to the purchase of which the negotiating letters clearly therefore relate.

5. Munshi Hursukh Rai further stated that these documents were obtained by Dewan Luchman Das on his search of the premises of Meeran Bux and Seth Ramanund on their sudden apprehension by him and how he, Luchman Das, kept the documents himself for future use. He produced them only when in great extremities, after being turned out in disgrace from the office of Dewan of the Kashmir State—he sought restoration to that position by any means possible, and wished to use these compromising documents with the Maharaja as an unanswerable argument in his own favour seeing that they placed the Maharaja in his power.

6. The story that he entrusted the documents to the Counsel he engaged to plead his case with the Maharaja is natural, and as to the rest it is a well-known fact that his Counsel fell ill during the conduct of the case and died. The statement that the papers were given by Mr. Spitta to Sardar Dyal Singh to keep till he returned from England, or to dispose of for the benefit of his widow in case of his death which unfortunately occurred does not appear to me incredible. In support of this part of the story I have shown you two letters from Munshi

Hursukh Rai, in which the widow's interest in the disposal of the documents is distinctly mentioned.

7. Munshi Hursukh Rai strongly urged me to purchase for the Maharaja these compromising letters for which ₹50,000 had been asked and ₹30,000 had been offered, but for which he was authorised to accept as the lowest sum ₹40,000. After a long interview Munshi Hursukh Rai agreed, as he said out of old friendship, to let me keep the papers for a month' on a promise to pay ₹40,000 for the letters or to return them.

8. Having received the documents I believed that the whole arrangement was an intrigue on the part of the brothers of His Highness the Maharaja to reveal to me the incapacity and imbecility of their brother and their utter hopelessness of his ability to reform or maintain the State and family, I therefore arranged at once a meeting with Raja Amar Singh, the brother and Prime Minister of the Maharaja, and as I thought best to do to show him the letters and question him about them. This meeting took place at Sialkot in the presence of Major Massy of Kapurthala, Political Superintendent of that State, who happened to be on a visit to me at the time, and who being intimately acquainted with the Jammu family and their affairs I had been glad to associate with myself in my previous interviews with Munshi Hursukh Rai and as long as he was with me throughout this enquiry.

9. Major Massy possesses skill and experience in political matters connected with Native States, superior perhaps to any other officer of his standing in Northern India, and as he is an intimate and valued friend of the Maharaja and all his family and knows all that has been going on of late years in the State, I valued his advice and opinion on this important occasion. Raja Amar Singh, while expressing real or feigned surprise at the compromising nature of some of these documents, readily admitted with some emotion, being nearly in tears, that the letters were certainly in the handwriting of his brother, the Maharaja, of that he had no doubt at all.

10. As to the signatures on the letters he did not speak so positively, but said it was the usual form of the Maharaja's

common and informal signature. Raja Amar Singh admitted that negotiations for the purchase of letters of the Maharaja from Munshi Hursukh Rai had proceeded in October last but had fallen through. He expressed his sense of the foolish weakness of his brother, the Maharaja, saying that he was totally in the hands of low and designing persons, who could induce him at any time to write such letters. Raja Amar Singh expressed himself aware that the Maharaja wrote such crazy correspondence both before and since his accession, and again that both he and his brother had given letters of the kind to Dewan Lachman Das, who also he knew had seized a number of such papers on the arrest and search of Sheikh Meeran Bux and Seth Ramanund.

11. Raja Amar Singh, when asked for proof of the authenticity of the letters, said that comparison of the handwriting as that of his brother the Maharaja with undoubted and harmless documents in the records of the State would entirely clear up any doubt on the point.

12. Raja Amar Singh expressed himself not at all displeased that the documents had come into my possession only begging me to save the family and State from the disgrace and ruin the Maharaja was by this and other acts and his general incapacity certain to bring on them.

13. Raja Amar Singh solemnly pledged himself that he had been no party to the misconduct of the Maharaja and was personally free from blame. I and Major Massy had several interviews with Raja Amar Singh and long discussions on the subject of the letters, the authenticity of which he frequently affirmed.

As far as he could do so Raja Amar Singh confirmed many details of the narrative of how the letters came to Luchman Das and of the subsequent traffic in them with Munshi Hursukh Rai through Wazir Shiv Sarn before I became Resident, thus thoroughly convincing Major Massy and me of the authenticity of the letters and the truth of the whole circumstances, and that the present denouncement was by no means a clumsy or fraudulent plot.

14. I also on or about the same date saw Raja Ram Singh, the elder of the two brothers of the Maharaja, but who is not nearly so interested in or mixed up in State business as Raja Amar Singh. I told Raja Ram Singh of my having the letters, at which he did not seem at all surprised, thereby convincing me that their production to me was an arrangement he had been privy to. He said that he had himself given several such foolish letters of the Maharaja to Dewan Luchman Das, and that Luchman Das had told him of finding a whole bundle of such letters on the apprehension and search of Meeran Bux and Seth Ramanund. Raja Ram Singh also begged me to use the letters, as well as every endeavour to save the family and State from ruin.

15. I then sent for a man named Inayat Ulla, brother to Sheikh Meeran Bux, to whom most of the letters now under discussion are addressed, and asked him if he or his brother had any letters of the Maharaja to show me. He said his brother had plenty of such letters, and that he would go and see Meeran Bux about them. On his return a second time, later in the day, he was more on his guard and said Meeran Bux had now got on letters, they having been taken from him by Dewan Luchman Das, but that he would himself come and see me. He also added that he and Meeran Bux could procure for me from the Maharaja any sort of letter or writing I might wish for, but to this I made no answer but dismissed him.

16. I then sent for Meeran Bux, but he was very guarded and all this man would say was, that his correspondence had been seized by Dewan Luchman Das.

Meeran Bux was, as you are well aware, once all powerful at Jammu, and though in banishment is still one of the greatest favourites of the Maharaja, and I understand in the receipt of allowances from him.

He was imprisoned by Dewan Luchman Das, but the proceedings which formed the case against Meeran Bux, reported to you in my predecessor's No. 25C., dated 16th August, 1887, include an order of His Highness the Maharaja acquitting Meeran Bux from any blame and highly eulogising the way in which he bore his persecution by Dewan Luchman Das and maintained discreet silence and complete confidence with regard to many delicate affairs of the Maharaja of which he was the repository. Still this man's admission to me that Luchman Das seized his correspondence is confirmatory of the genuineness of the letters addressed to Meeran Bux among those now submitted to you.

17. For the sake of comparison of the Maharaja's handwriting I sent for ordinary State records which I examined with Pundit Suraj Koul, now an official of Kashmir, a man of the highest character whose long experience in political matters and the intrigues of native courts on less than his probity and caution is well-known to you.

18. He assured me that the letters in question are certainly genuine and written by the Maharaja, is his own and the general opinion at Jammu—and that the comparison with harmless papers is complete and satisfactory. Pundit Suraj Koul was himself acquainted with the widow, residing at Lahore, of an old servant of the Maharaja and as a very reliable and certain way of attesting the Maharaja's signature he wrote off and obtained from her certain old papers which would bear the Maharaja's signature and these again readily compared with that on the papers under reference.

19. Though I did not show him the letters or consult him much about them, Pundit Bhag Ram, who likes Pundit Suraj Koul, is a Member of the Council of the Maharaja said he cordially approved my action in the matter and did not doubt the letters being really written by the Maharaja, so generally is that fact now known.

20. I also obtained from one Ram Labya, who is mentioned in the letters in question as an intimate favourite of the Maharaja and who had no knowledge of why I required them, samples of the Maharaja's handwriting and signature and both fully support the genuineness of the signature and handwriting of the Maharaja in the documents under discussion.

21. I have so far stated the steps taken by me to obtain the best positive evidence of the authenticity of the letters, but

I will now as shortly as possible remark on the negative evidence which even more strongly in my opinion completely supports the genuineness of the documents. While it has not been possible to keep secret the fact of the letters being in my hands or what has passed regarding them no single person in or out of the State has come to me or ventured to express any doubt of their authenticity, and yet I suppose no officer in India is more accessible to native visitors who come and discuss all kinds of subjects with me at any time.

22. If the case is not a true one than both Raja Amar Singh, the brother and first Minister of the Maharaja and his elder brother Raja Ram Singh have, by vouching the authenticity of the letters entered into a conspiracy, the discovery of which must involve them both in irretrievable ruin and disgrace, and this it is beyond reasonable belief they would bring on themselves.

23. Except from a sincere wish to relieve the State of the misrule and folly of the Maharaja no plot to supplant him could primarily benefit Raja Amar Singh. His elder brother Raja Ram Singh and that brother's son are before him in the line of succession to power in the State. Nor again is there any such cordiality between Raja Amar Singh and his brother Raja Ram Singh which would induce the latter to join any plot to supplant the Maharaja to assist the ambition of his brother. Further Raja Amar Singh himself has for a long time past hoped that the Maharaja would adopt him as his heir and abdicate in his favour, but the Maharaja would certainly never do this now if Amar Singh was in this instance plotting against him. In no aspect therefore is Raja Amar Singh likely immediately to benefit by a plot for the removal of the Maharaja, and I therefore do not doubt that only the patriotism of the brothers has led them on an isolated occasion to make common cause for the benefit of themselves and the State.

24. I will now mention what occurred at my first interview with the Maharaja after he knew I had the letters in my possession.

I went to Jammu and was received by the Maharaja on the 7th instant. He took me aside into his private drawing room and enquiring if all was well. I replied that such was not the case. The Maharaja himself then said I know all about the papers, my brother tells me, you have got. He denied utterly that they were written by him, and added that the whole thing was a plot against him by Dewan Luchman Das. I replied but Maharaja I have not asked you anything about the papers or to deny their authenticity though I have frequently asked you to trust and confide in me. His manner was excited, and he made many appeals to me to help him and to save him from disgrace, saying I was such an old friend I was altogether in place of his own father. The only answer I could make was that you deny that you have any disgrace to fear so far as these papers are concerned, why are you so anxious to-day to do well? The Maharaja then went on to say that you have always been urging me to pay attention to State affairs and give powers to my Council. I will give them full powers, and they shall manage everything, I will have no more to do with affairs. I spoke kindly and smoothingly to the Maharaja, but said I had lost confidence in his possessing any steadfastness of purpose or any real wish to reform the affairs of his State, and that though in the impulse of the moment he now appeared to wish to do something he would change his mind immediately after.

25. He said will you and the Council manage the State then all will be well? I said I thought this would not be practicable. He pressed me to say what he could do. I told him he must know by this time that he had no trustworthy old officials of any grade in the State, but that they were forever-intriguing one against the other, and that the constant changes due to such intrigues and his own weakness and vacillation left them free to plunder the State and the people for their own benefit, and that there was no discipline or fear of wrong doing among them. The Maharaja replied no one ever spoke so openly and kindly to me of the condition of the State as you have done—if you manage the State for me all this will come to an end. The Maharaja again expressed his wish to give, as I had frequently suggested, at once full powers to his Council and not himself interfere with their legitimate work.

26. It seemed to me the Maharaja was not only frightened, but that he was thoroughly tired of the worry and trouble his officials had given him as he frequently repeated his intention to abandon the management of the State altogether.

The discussion on this occasion was long and earnest. The Maharaja said several times that he would rather go away and live in peace privately. I told the Maharaja his proposal that I and the Council should manage the State did not appear altogether feasible, and that the Government of India did not contemplate any such arrangement, but that the presence of an English officer on his Council might undoubtedly offer the required guarantee for freedom from intrigue and insure continuity of administration.

27. The Maharaja then mentioned who the other Members of the Council should be, *viz.*, his two brothers with Pundit Suraj Kaul, and Pundit Bhag Ram, thus excluding any of the Kashmir old official element.

28. The interview with the Maharaja lasted an hour or more till dark. I would have particularly remark that what struck me as most convincing of the falsehood of the Maharaja's denial of the authenticity of the letters was that he merely charged the late Dewan Luchman Das with contriving a plot against him. He did not for a moment mention or alleges any intrigue or plot on the part of his brother and Minister Raja Amar Singh who had told him all about the letters in my hands and charged him with their authorship.

At other times the Maharaja is most jealous and suspicious of his brothers Raja Amar Singh and Raja Ram Singh, and bears no real affection for either of them and yet he did not, instead of Dewan Luchman Das who is no longer in the State or powerful for evil, charge them, as he much rather might have done, if the letters were false, with being in cabal against him. Then again there was the Maharaja's extraordinary anxiety on this occasion to give guarantees for future good Government of the State. These connected circumstances clearly convinced me that the Maharaja intended by his acts to belie his words as to his feeling himself the victim of any false or libelous charge with reference to the letters.

29. At parting the Maharaja said I will send down my brother and Prime Minister Raja Amar Singh at once to discuss the matter further with you. I received Raja Amar Singh later in the evening and held a long and anxious discussion with him. He declared that the presence of an English officer with the other Members mentioned was undoubtedly the best and only hope for the suppression of intrigue and the restoration of order and good government in the State, but that the Council should be allowed the services of some more English and several native officials trained under the English system for some years to come in the various minor offices in the State.

30. The next morning at 8 a.m. Raja Amar Singh again came to see me and said the Maharaja would certainly give up any interference with the public affairs for five years, and intended to approve and issue orders for the formation of the Council including an English Member who ought to be an officer of very special selection to be kind to them and to the State.

31. I clearly explained to Raja Amar Singh what the actual effect of a Council so constituted would mean, but the Raja who is, I think, fond of Europeans and possesses unusual intelligence himself admires the English system. I also at that time sent by Raja Amar Singh a few lines to the Maharaja telling him that it was entirely at his own option to do anything or nothing, as I did not wish him to feel that he was under any pressure at all to form a new Council or give them control over the State which was in the first existence entirely his own proposal, but I added I would not recommend for the approval of the Government of India anything but what was really a complete and workable scheme.

32. At 10 a.m. that day I again went to the palace and saw the Maharaja who took me aside privately as he did the evening before. He struck me as still in great anxiety which indeed he assured me had filled him all night. He said I wish to have the new Council and again urged me to join it, but said if that was impossible he would leave the selection of an English officer to the Government of India, but hoped I would

secure a friend for them, though the only person he mentioned, besides myself was Major Massy, Superintendent of Kapurthala State, who, as I have before said, he knows very well. I again said that it was optional with him to make any change. He replied no, I wish it—only the Council must not interfere with my private affairs. The interview ended and I received an hour or two afterwards your order to come to Calcutta.

33. At 3.30 p.m. that day Raja Amar Singh brought me the Maharaja's edict constituting a fresh Council of State including an English member also an official letter requesting Government to nominate an English officer to the post, both of which edict and letter I have laid before you and copy of which is herewith annexed for the orders of the Government.

34. I would here repeat that so far as the bearing of the Maharaja and his anxiety to himself abandon the cares of State and to have some workable scheme of future administration, both his manner and acts on the occasion entirely belied his previous denial of any misconduct or fear of consequences with reference to the letters which he knew to be in my possession and which he had been openly charged by his brother with writing.

35. Before concluding this discussion regarding these letters I would only add that though generally bearing no date their contents clearly refer to events subsequent to the succession of the Maharaja. Mr. Plowden was only Resident very lately and the visit of the Maharaja to Calcutta as well as the matter regarding Maharaja Dalip Singh are events that have occurred since the death of late Maharaja. Again both Sheikh Meeran Bux and Seth Ramanund to whom most of the letters are addressed only secured their greater influence over the Maharaja since his succession to the throne.

36. It is hardly necessary for me to supplement the narrative I have now given you by referring to the mass of correspondence in your office which details in clearest terms the entire failure of the present Maharaja to organize anything like even decent administration of public affairs in the Kashmir State.

37. The result of such misrule is that, notwithstanding the ample resources and revenues of the State, the Treasury is quite empty. Corruption and disorder are rampant in every department and every office of every grade in the State.

38. I have long known the members of the ruling family of Kashmir, but the friendship and kindness I desire to bear them cannot blind me to the incurable faults of the present Maharaja or his total incapacity to govern or control the affairs of the State.

39. So far as the letters which form the subject of the present discussion are concerned, highly compromising and dangerous as some, and still more foolish as many of them are, I earnestly trust that the most serious construction will never be placed upon them.

I submit that these letters cannot be taken in their most literal sense, but may rather be regarded as the foolish and mischievous invention of a weak and ill-balanced mind. Their author is a man possessing no strength of character or intellect—addicted to opium under the influence of which he could, especially in the hands of low and designing persons as the Maharaja is, be induced to commit acts of folly and unwisdom which a sober or even moderately-wise person would be able to avoid.

40. The Maharaja is not at times without intervals of good sense and propriety but these do not last long, and at other times he gives way to uncontrolled passion is suspicious and vindictive. Thus under the influence of opium or instigated by low and unworthy favourites in whose power he has placed himself by giving them written promises of ruinous rewards or writing to them compromising letters such as are now in point, the Maharaja shows himself a man utterly void of reason.

41. Those remarks regarding the Maharaja for whom and his brothers I have much real affection are not stronger than those already made to you on the subject by other officers who have not failed to assure the Government of India of the incapacity of the Maharaja to govern his country. Still after all I feel very strongly that the Maharaja himself is not entirely bad but rather an object for compassion and leniency.

Whatever faults he commits are the result of being placed in a position for which he is disqualified by natural character, education and intellect.

42. The continued misgovernment of so important a State as Kashmir immediately on the North-Western Frontier of India, is a matter fraught with extreme danger and consequences of the utmost seriousness to the Government of India.

An incapable and foolish ruler in such a situation may by his acts plunge the Government of India at any moment into difficulties which he neither contemplates nor appreciates.

43. The correspondence in your office regarding Kashmir ever since the succession of the present Maharaja more than three years ago will show that His Excellency the Viceroy in Council both at personal interviews and in writing has never ceased to reiterate admonitions and advice to the Maharaja to introduce a decent system of Government and necessary reforms in the Kashmir State. No good result has however followed, the country is steadily declining in prosperity, its revenue capable of large expansion and improvement does not find its way into the State Treasury which is empty, but into the pockets of corrupt officials of every grade and the cry of the millions of the poor industrious population for just, impartial, or even moderately good administration falls on no regardful of sympathetic ear in the State.

44. If as I hope I shall have satisfied you that the general condition of the Kashmir State has now reached a climax which the Government of India can no longer ignore or permit without interference then the question arises how such interference can best be applied so as to secure the necessary relief without permanently departing from the general policy of the Government in its relation with Native States.

Such policy can be I apprehend only general and must be modified to suit the special circumstances as they arise in each case. With much difference and anxiety therefore I venture to offer the following remarks on what in my humble opinion are the remedies that suggest themselves to relieve the present deplorable condition of mismanagement into which the affairs of the Kashmir State have fallen, and to secure the building up of future administration and the restoration of order and discipline in the State.

45. If there were any old officials of the State who were either capable or trustworthy or who had by keeping themselves even fairly aloof from intrigues and corruption shown any capacity for honest work, then I would say certainly let a selection be made from them and give them at least a trial in the future management of State affairs without the assistance of strangers at all. You are well aware that in the last few years it has from time to time, for sufficient reason, been necessary to interdict the employment of many of the old official's altogether, whose misconduct has proved them quite untrustworthy or has forfeited for them the Maharaja's confidence. It is a singular and the same time deplorable state of things that I suppose there is no other State in India—certainly none of the importance of Kashmir—which is so entirely at this moment without any decent native officials. I except of course Pundits Suraj Koul and Bhag Ram, but I do not call them old officials as they have only lately come to the State—they are quite trustworthy and will I feel confident be a great support to any future administration, but they are not enough themselves to form the Council or work alone. I cannot after diligent search mention another native official of any character on the spot who could be associated with these two men in the State Council or trusted with any powers in the State affairs. All the Kashmir officials of any standing have of late years, by the bitterest and most pernicious intrigues done their utmost to expose the weakness and faults of the Maharaja, and by their dishonesty, tyranny and idleness ruined the State and themselves in public reputation. What hope for the future could there be in the continued employment of such men? It is the incompetence of his own officials which led the Maharaja several times lately to place his confidence in clever Bengalis who he has brought up from Calcutta, but these men even more than the indigenous official have shown themselves corrupt, idle, and unsuited to the task of Government and are loathed by the people at large, and ought to be utterly discouraged as quite incapable

to understand, much less to govern an alien race especially one like the Muhammadans of Kashmir. This attempt of the Maharaja to rid himself of his old official by the importation of Bengali foreigners has been as disastrous to the prosperity of Kashmir as any move that could possibly have been taken. The Maharaja and his brothers are so fully sensible of the utter dearth of officials and of the mistake they have made in their own selection of outsiders that this feeling more than any other I believe induces their present extreme anxiety that the Government of India should come to the rescue and by aiding them with the loan of an English officer of high character and position on the Council, and such subordinate officials, a few European, but mostly natives trained in the English system, as may from time to time be required, endeavour to form a government in the country.

46. The Maharaja and his clever brother and Prime Minister Raja Amar Singh and their thoughtful and intelligent relative, Raja Ram Singh, are not at all insensible to the necessity for reform, good order and discipline in the State, but they lack the instruments with which to work and have lost confidence in the ability of native officials alone to do what is required. I myself agree that in the present miserable state of things and broken up as all the State officials of every rank are into cliques and parties combined to intrigue and destroy one another as in turn they may obtain any power, position on influence, it is hopeless to expect an entirely native administration to work long or stand alone. The presence of even a single English officer with the necessary special qualifications on the Council Board of the State in association with two such men as Pundits Suraj Koul and Bhag Ram would offer I hope a barrier unassailable to intrigue and corruption and secure decency and continuity of administration in every Department which more than anything else is required to restore peace, justice, and good order in this distressful country.

47. Of course there is the alternative, for which there is good precedent of appointing the Resident in Kashmir also Superintendent of the State, but I am myself somewhat opposed

to any such arrangement, I think the Resident ought to maintain his present special character and position as an adviser of the Maharaja, but the representative and mouthpiece of Government who is not supposed to mix himself up in the actual duties of the State administration. It is well to have an independent officer of this character and more strength would be given to the future Government and to the Maharaja by leaving the Resident as he is, and appointing if thought desirable a separate English officer to the Council or as Manager of the State.

48. Under these circumstances and keenly anxious as Rajas Ram Singh and Amar Singh, the leading Members of the ruling family are for reform, good order and discipline in the Kashmir State, it did not seem possible for me to refuse to submit to you the application made, no doubt through their instigation, by His Highness the Maharaja for the formation of a fresh Council of State constituted as mentioned in the edict and official application referred to in paragraph 33 of this report.

49. It is impossible at present or perhaps ever again to trust the Maharaja after his writing and disseminating letters of the character of some of those I have placed before you, with uncontrolled power in the Kashmir State. There is no saying how many of such letters he has written or may in future write or into whose hands they may come. The fact of the recipients not knowing the weakness and incapacity of the Maharaja as we do makes the letters none the less harmful and till his power of performance is stopped the alarming danger to the Government of India will continue. I may repeat the opinion already stated that the Maharaja did not appreciate or intend the mischief which some of the letters portray or suppose that the contraction they bear and would deserve should be placed upon them. At the same time if the authenticity of the letters is as I believe fully established, it will be highly impolitic to take the gravest measures against the Maharaja or by giving more publicity to the matter than absolutely necessary to publish to the world the incapacity and misconduct of so important a feudatory of the English Government as the Ruler

of Kashmir. It is however manifestly of great concern to put a stop to any similar acts, or it may be worse, in future.

50. On the whole therefore I would recommend that nothing but absolutely complete measure be now adopted, and this I think will only be found by appointing the Resident in Kashmir also Superintendent of the State—or by sanctioning the proposal made by the Maharaja himself in his edict and letter of the 8th instant, under which he asks that a specially selected English officer may be appointed to assist the native Members of the Council and I myself much prefer this last plan. If this is done, and no subsequent recantation of the Maharaja within five years listened to, I see the fairest prospect for the early and complete redress of that neglect of State affairs which presents itself now so prominently in Kashmir. No half measures will do any good at all, and I am satisfied that rigorous action on the part of Government of India will be fully endorsed with the approval of the best Native as well as English public opinion in India in any steps for the amelioration of the condition of the Kashmir State which without removing the present Maharaja or alienating the State from its present possessors provides security for the future proper administration of State affairs.

51. The earnest and unselfish desire of the Government of India to give early assistance when so urgently demanded without proceeding to the extremities which the present crisis in Kashmir might as may appear to many have justified should be fully appreciated and understood. His Excellency the Viceroy in Council will I feel sure never have reason to regret the extension of clemency and forbearance to the Maharaja of Kashmir on this occasion and if this be done the same should act as a great encouragement, no less than a warning to the Chiefs of India not to neglect the frequent admonition of the paramount power to the Ruler of this and every Native State to perform the duties of his high position and establish just, impartial, and good administration within his jurisdictions.

52. I will add nothing more, the case is one beset with difficulty and anxiety and I can only ask favourable consideration upon it, and that the circumstances under which this

report has been written may excuse anything that may appear wanting in it.

I have the honour to be,

Sir,

Your most obedient servant,

(Signed) R. Parry Nisbet, Col.,

Resident in Kashmir

Telegram, No. 647 E., dated the 24th March 1889.

From—The Foreign Secretary, Calcutta,

To—Colonel R. Parry Nisbet, C.I.E., Sialkot.

Do not go to Jammu till you get my telegram—which will reach you to-day or to-morrow.

Telegram, dated the 26th March 1889.

From—The Foreign Secretary, Calcutta,

To—The Resident in Kashmir, Sialkot.

No. 663 E. Your letter sixteenth. Government of India have decided that for a time at least the Maharaja should hand overpowers of Government to his Council, and refrain from all interference with the administration, keeping however his rank and dignity as Chief of the State. It is not thought desirable that an English officer should be appointed Member of Council, but you should submit proposals for appointment of any native member or members whom you may think actually necessary, and for removal of any inefficient members. Raja Amar Singh will be President. Council will have full powers subject to provision that they must consult you before taking any important step, and that they must follow your advice whenever you may offer it. You should also ascertain requirements of State in regard to trained subordinate officials, and suggest precise conditions to which Maharaja will be expected to conform. He must have adequate, but not extravagant allowance, and must resign all power of alienating State Revenues. Letter follows. Affair should be managed as quietly as possible, the Maharaja simply retiring from conduct of affairs. There should be no ceremonial and no unnecessary change in externals. Government wishes this matter to attract as little attention as possible. Your proposals for loan of officers, &c., should be moderate, indigenous agency being utilised as much as possible. You can pay for letters and should, without formal enquiry, endeavour to make certain whether they are genuine.

If you find that you must go to Jammu, and that it is very desirable to inform the Maharaja and those about him of the decision of Government, you may do so confidentially, basing our action not solely upon letters, nor upon Maharaja's offer, but upon a consideration of all circumstances of case, these included. But formal announcement should be deferred until you receive Viceroy's letter, and unless there is strong reason, you had better say nothing at present.

Telegram, dated the 25th March 1889.

From—The Resident in Kashmir, Sialkot,

To—The Foreign Secretary, Calcutta.

In compliance with yours, shall not proceed to Jammu till I hear from you. But unless Viceroy's letter reaches me tomorrow, think I must postpone delivery till I meet Maharaja at Srinagar. The Maharaja has already postponed his departure once till 29th. I wish to avoid asking him to do so again unless you wish him told to await orders of Government at Jammu.

Telegram, No. 8C., dated the 27th March 1889.

From—The Resident in Kashmir, Sialkot,
To—The Foreign Secretary, Calcutta.

Your telegram of 26th. I quite agree that until receipt of Viceroy's letter and until action can be taken upon it, silence is best, and will defer further action until I meet Maharaja and Council at Srinagar. You say Amar Singh will be President of Council. Why pass over his elder brother? I would put both on leave council to make rules of business one being senior Member of Council present to be President at each meeting namely Ram Singh, Amar Singh, & c., (*sic.*)

I have written to Lyall to give generous assistance in the way of best natives trust well pleased, (*sic.*) also I shall be much guided by his opinion of men. I wish to add a Muhammadan member to the Council, so that he should join if possible when work begins at Srinagar, and will offer the appointment, if you agree, to Extra Assistant Commissioner, Khan Bahadur Ghulam Mohi-ud-din Khan, if Lyall agrees in my opinion of him. Proposal as to other officials can follow, but to avoid inevitable delay of referring, I ask permission to appoint first, six men applied for by Council for superior offices at once, subject to your subsequent confirmation.

Telegram, dated the 28th March 1889.

From—The Foreign Secretary, Calcutta,
To—The Resident in Kashmir, Sialkot.

No objection to Mohi-ud-din and six others, but go quietly to work. I cannot make out your proposal about Presidency.

Surely one man must be President, and as Amar Singh is Minister and Vice President now, he seems natural man.

No. 707E., dated Fort William, the 1st April 1889

From— The Secretary to the Government of India, Foreign Department,
To—The Resident in Kashmir.

I am directed to acknowledge the receipt of your letter No. 6C, of the 16th March, reporting upon certain recent occurrences in Kashmir.

2. It appears from this letter and your previous telegrams, as well as from the personal explanations which you were able to make during your recent visit to Calcutta, that you lately obtained possession of some letters alleged to have been written by the Maharaja of Kashmir, which presented his character and conduct in a very unfavourable light. You made enquiries regarding the authenticity of these letters, and came to the conclusion that they were in fact written and signed by the Maharaja.

3. In the course of your enquiries you went to Jammu and saw the Maharaja, who denied that he had written the letters, but showed much excitement and alarm on the subject, and announced his desire to resign the management of the State. Shortly afterwards, he issued an Irshad or edict, which conferred full powers of administration, for a period of five years, upon a Council of State composed of the Maharaja's brothers, an English officer to be hereafter nominated, and the two native members whose services have lately been lent to the Kashmir Darbar. The arrangement was made subject to certain reservations which need not be enumerated here.

4. In your letter of the 16th March you discuss at some length the situation of affairs in Kashmir and make proposals for the future administration of the State, Having regard to

the incapacity of the Maharaja, the corruption and inefficiency of the executive services, the want of trustworthy Kashmiri officials, and other considerations, you express the opinion that no half measures will do any good, and that vigorous action is necessary. You therefore recommend the Government of India either to appoint you Superintendent of the State, or to accept the Maharaja's proposal for the transfer of power to a Council, one of whose members shall be a selected English officer. You much prefer the latter plan.

5. My telegram of the 26th March explained to you the views and wishes of the Government of India with regard to this important matter. It has always been known that the Maharaja was a man of weak character, and much under the influence of unworthy favourites, who took advantage of his timidity and superstition. It was also known that he was capable at times of very mischievous inclinations, and that he believed himself to have brought about the death of his father, Maharaja Ranbir Singh, by means of sorcery. The letters which you have submitted did not therefore strike the Government of India with any great surprise, or throw much fresh light upon His Highness's proceedings and disposition especially as a very similar batch of letters had been submitted by Mr. Plowden a year ago. Nevertheless, if they are authentic, which you have apparently no good reason to doubt, they afford additional evidence of His Highness's unfitness for his position; and taking into consideration all the circumstances of the case,—the Maharaja's voluntary resignation of power, the disorganised condition of the State, and improbability of any satisfactory reformation under existing conditions,—the Governor-General in Council has come to the conclusion that the opportunity of establishing a stable and efficient Government in Kashmir should not again be allowed to pass by.

6. I am now to request you to inform the Maharaja that for a time at least he will be expected to retrain from all interference in the administration. He will retain his rank and dignity as Chief of the State; but full powers of government will be vested in a Council consisting of the Maharaja's brothers and three or four officials selected by the Government

of India. It is not thought desirable that one of these officials should be an Englishman. The President of the Council will be Raja Amar Singh. Besides retaining his rank and dignity the Maharaja will receive from the revenues of the State an annual sum sufficient to maintain his household in due comfort, and to defray any expenditure which may rightly devolve upon him, but he will have no power of alienating the State revenues and the sum placed at his disposal, though adequate, must not be extravagantly large.

7. I am further to request you to make the Maharaja and the Members of Council thoroughly understand that although the Council will have full powers of administration, they will be expected to exercise those powers under the guidance of the Resident. They will take no step of importance without consulting him, and they will follow his advice whenever it may be offered.

8. In communicating to the Maharaja and others concerned the decision of the Government of India, you should be careful to avoid basing that decision exclusively either upon the letters or upon the Maharaja's resignation. The letters are repudiated by the Maharaja, and as I have said before they are not of a very noble character; while on the other hand, the Government of India are by no means prepared to make the present settlement a matter of compact with the Maharaja, and to accept all the conditions laid down by his edict of the 8th March, for example the five years' limit. You should therefore base the decision of the Government upon a full consideration of all the circumstances, the letters and the Maharaja's wish to retire from the control of affairs being considered amongst other things, but only as portions of a difficult and complicated case, which it has been necessary to settle on broader grounds of general policy.

9. You should now proceed to work out fresh proposals upon the lines I have indicated. It will be necessary in the first place to define exactly the future position of the Maharaja, the amount of his annual allowance, the expenses which it is intended to cover, the extent of his powers over his own household, and generally the conditions to which he will have to conform. It will also be necessary to show the proposed

constitution of the Council, the duties falling upon each of its members, and the method of transacting business. You should also ascertain the requirements of the State in the matter of subordinate officials, and should submit for the approval of the Government your view as to the steps to be taken for reorganising the administrative services. In forming those views you should remember that the Government of India has no desire to turn Kashmir into the semblance of a British district, or to place all administrative posts in the hands of Punjabi foreigners. The want of good native officials makes it necessary to import some trained men from the outside, but the number so imported should be kept as low as possible, and your object should be to form with their help a class of Kashmiri officials who will be capable hereafter of administering the State themselves. It is altogether against the wishes and policy of the Government to interfere unnecessarily with the customs and traditions of a Native State, or to force upon it the precise methods of administration obtaining in British territory. Administrative efficiency is not the only object to be attained in such cases, nor indeed the principal object.

10. The Government of India will be glad to know, as soon as possible, the true facts as to the financial position of Kashmir. A separate report should be submitted on this point, and in submitting it you should enquire into the question of the *jagirs* and allowances given by the Maharaja, and should make proposals as to the manner in which such grants should be treated.

11. Finally, I am to request that the new arrangements may be introduced as quietly as possible. There should be no ceremonial, and nothing that can be regarded as the public degradation of the Maharaja, who should simply retire from the conduct of affairs. It is desirable that the change should attract no more attention than necessary, and above all, that it should not be regarded as the punishment of a great native Chief for proved disloyalty to the Crown. Rumours to the effect that the Maharaja has been convicted of treasonable practices have already been in circulation, and such rumours, do harm both in India and elsewhere.

No. 50 of 1889
GOVERNMENT OF INDIA
FOREIGN DEPARTMENT
SECRET
External

To

The Right Hon'ble Viscount Cross, G.C.B.,
Her Majesty's Secretary of State for India.
Fort William, *the 3rd April 1889.*

My Lord,

1. With our Despatch No. 142, of the 18th August 1888, we forwarded for Your Lordship's information certain papers regarding the affairs of the Kashmir State.

2. The condition of Kashmir was then by no means satisfactory; and the Resident, Mr. Plowden, had come to the conclusion that so long as the present Maharaja was maintained in power there could be no hope of better things. He, therefore, urged the Government of India to interfere and exclude His Highness from all concern with the administration. There was much to support Mr. Plowden's view, and we were by no means confident as to the result of any further abstention from interference; but on the whole we decided that the Maharaja should have another opportunity of showing, under favourable circumstances, whether he was capable of ruling the State. He was accordingly continued in power; and Mr. Plowden, who soon afterwards left Kashmir on promotion, was succeeded by Colonel Parry Nisbet, C.I.E., a personal friend of the Maharaja, and an officer of large administrative experience. It was hoped that Colonel Nisbet might succeed in establishing a strong influence over His Highness's mind, in freeing him from the domination of certain unprincipled persons about him, who took advantage of his timidity and superstition, and in gradually bringing him to a proper sense of his position and its responsibilities.

3. The papers now enclosed will show Your Lordship that this hope was disappointed, and that after four months in the Kashmir Residency, Colonel Nisbet has come to the same conclusion as his predecessor. The immediate cause which led him to resubmit the matter for our orders was the discovery of some letters, said to have been written by the Maharaja, which were of such a nature as to present his character and conduct in a very unfavourable light. We were not disposed to attach any excessive importance to these letters, because we had received a number of very similar documents a year before, and were not ignorant of the Maharaja's failings. But in this instance the discovery of the letters was immediately followed by a voluntary resignation of power on the part of the Maharaja; and taking into consideration this and all the other circumstances of the case we felt that the time had come when some measure of interferences could be no longer deferred. We have therefore determined that the Maharaja's resignation shall be accepted, and that we should avail ourselves of the opportunity in order to effect a thorough reorganisation of the Kashmir Government.

4. The form in which our interference is to be exercised will be seen from the terms of our instructions to Colonel Nisbet. To sum these up in a few words, the administration of the State will be handed over to a Council, consisting of the Maharaja's brothers and certain selected officials in the British service. This Council will have full powers, subject to the condition that they will take no important step without consulting the Resident, and that they will act upon the Resident's advice whenever it may be offered. This is the arrangement established in Gwalior, where it is working well. The Maharaja will be excluded from all interference with public affairs, but will retain his rank and dignity as Chief of the State, and will receive from the State revenues an adequate but not extravagant allowance for the maintenance of his household and any other necessary expenditure.

5. These arrangements will not be exclusively based upon the Maharaja's edict of resignation, which was an attempt to save his dignity and secure better terms than he could otherwise

expect. This edict contains some inconvenient stipulations, and it would be embarrassing to agree to it as it stands. We prefer to treat it as a confession of incapacity for the rule of the State, and to base our further proceedings upon general grounds.

6. Your Lordship will observe that our instructions to Colonel Nisbet deprecate any interference in the affairs of the State beyond what is necessary for the reform of the administration. We greatly regret the necessity for any interference at all. But we are now convinced that in the interests of the people of Kashmir, and of the ruling family itself, it is no longer right or possible to leave the control of affairs in the hands of the Maharaja; and we trust that Her Majesty's Government will concur in this opinion.

We have the honour to be My Lord,

Your Lordship's most obedient, humble servants,

(Signed) Lansdowne

" A.R. Scoble

" C.A. Elliott

" P.P. Hutchins

" D.M. Barbour

Bibliography

I. UNPUBLISHED SOURCES

(A) Private Papers

(1) Ardagh Papers: Correspondence and papers of Sir John Ardagh, Private Secretary to Lords Lansdowne and Elgin, 1888-94. The Public Record Office, London (PRO 30/40).

(2) Cross Papers: Correspondence of 1st Viscount Cross, Secretary of State for India, 1886-92, National Archives of India.

(3) *Papers of the Marquis of Dufferin and Ava.*

The Dufferin Papers, originating from Hans Crescent, London (3rd March 1958), were miscrofilmed by "Recordak" Miscrofilm Service, London by permission of Marchioness of Dufferin and are now available at the National Archives of India, New Delhi. Volume I contains 689 letters and telegrams in all written or sent to Lord Dufferin. These are mostly hand-written; typed letters are available from No. 532 onwards. Vol. II contains 592 letters and telegrams to persons in India from Lord Dufferin.

(4) *Lansdowne Papers* (*1888-1894*).

The following volumes are available in the National Archives of India, New Delhi:—

(*i*) Correspondence with Secretary of State (Series IX of India Office Library)...5 volumes

(*ii*) Letters from Persons in India
(*iii*) Letters to Persons in India } 10 volumes

(*iv*) Notes and Minutes...I volume (Series XIII of India Office Library).

These papers are helpful in assessing the policy and administration of Lord Dufferin in India.

(5) Lytton Papers: Correspondence and papers of the 1st Earl of Lytton, Viceroy of India, 1876-80. National Archives of India.

516. Secretary of State's Letters, 1876-80, 13 vols.

518. Letters Despatched, 1876-80, 6 vols.

539. Correspondence in India, 1876-80, 13 vols.

520. Minutes and Notes, 1876-80, 3 vols.

(6) Mayo Papers: Correspondence and papers of the 6th Earl of Mayo, Viceroy of India, 1869-72. University Library, Cambridge.

(7) Northbrook Papers: Correspondence of the 1st Earl of Northbrook, Viceroy of India, 1872-76. National Archives of India.

(8) Roberts Papers: Correspondence and papers of Sir (afterwards Lord) Frederick Roberts, Commander-in-Chief of India, 1885-93.

(9) Ripon Papers (Second series). Special correspondence relating to India. British Museum. Additional Manuscripts 43565-43619 (RP). Another set of the correspondence relating to India, privately printed by Ripon, is in British Museum, Indian State Papers 290/5, 290/7, 290/8 (B.M.I.S.).

These Papers are important as they provide to some extent, the perspective for the policy which Dufferin followed in India.

(B) Official Papers

The National Archives of India, New Delhi.

Considerable use has been made in the preparation of this work of the Secret E, F, I, General A, Pol. A, series of the Foreign Department Proceedings in the National Archives of India, New Delhi—Papers which were not sent to the Home Department, Government from India.

India Office Library, London.

Papers on the Indian States which were sent by the Government of India and were received in the Political and Secret Department of the India Office, such as Political and Secret Letters and Enclosures from India, Political and Secret Home Correspondence etc.

Other Political and/or Secret Department papers consulted at the India Office Library are:

(*i*) Secret Letters and Enclosures from India and Madras, 1866-68, Vols. 1-3. Continued as—

(*ii*) Secret Letters and Enclosures from India 1869-74, Vols. 4-19. Continued as—

(*iii*) Political and Secret Letters and Enclosures from India, 1875-95, Vols. 1-83.

(*iv*) Collections to India Political Despatches.

(*v*) Political and Secret Home Correspondence, 1885-95, Vols. 69-162. Mainly correspondence between the IO and FO relative to Indian affairs.

(*vi*) Political and Secret Demi-official Correspondence: First Series: Vols. 1-7.

These volumes contain D.O. letters received in the Political and Secret Department with Minutes, Memoranda, Drafts and copies of letters sent.

Second Series: Vols. 1-4.

These volumes contain copies of D.O. letters sent out by the Political and Secret Department and copies of Minutes and Memoranda.

(*vii*) Political and Secret Despatches to India, 1875-95, Vols. 1-21. This series contains minutes and notes written at the India Office on letters received from the Government of India, and trace the preparation of despatches to India in their different stages including the final drafts which were ultimately sent.

(*viii*) Political and Miscellaneous Correspondence, 1846-74, Vols. 1-5.

India-Foreign Proceedings.

Of this series all the volumes of the following categories for the period between 1885-96 have been consulted.

(*a*) Political

(*b*) General

(*c*) Frontier

(*d*) External, and

(*e*) Internal.

India Public Works Proceedings, only select volumes.

Punjab Foreign Proceedings, 1871-95, select volumes.

Some material from the B series has also been used.

Foreign Office, (P.R.O., London) FO 65, only select volumes.

War Office, London.

W.O.32/

(*a*) 218. Mobilisation arrangements in India.

(*b*) 263. North-western Frontier Defences, Committee on, 1885.

(*c*) 264. Defence of Afghanistan against Russia, 1889.

W.O. 32/

(*a*) 46. Defences of North-west Frontier, Committee Report on, 1886.

(*b*) 49. Central Asia, Report of Indian Mobilisation Committee on strategical situation in, 1889.

II. PUBLISHED SOURCES

(A) Parliamentary Papers:

Year	*Command No.*	*Description*
1846	C. 705	Treaties with Lahore Darbar and Gulab Singh.
1849	C. 1071	Punjab : Papers relating to
	C. 1075	the Second Sikh War, 1847-49.
1856	(245)	Minute dated 28th February 1856 reviewing Dalhousie's administration, 1848-56.
1867-68	147(H.C.)	Appointment of a Commercial Agent at Ladakh.
1871	60	Mission of Douglas Forsyth to Yarkand.
1873	C. 699	Central Asia: Correspondence with Russia (1872-73) re: boundaries of Afghanistan.

Year	Command No.	Description
	C. 704	Central Asia: Correspondence, 1869-73.
1874	217	Kashgar: Treaty of Commerce.
1878	C. 2164	Central Asia: Correspondence.
1878-79	C. 2190	Afghanistan: Correspondence (1863-78) respecting the relations between the British Govt., and the Amir Shere Ali.
	C. 2191	Afghanistan—Further Papers.
	C. 2250	Afghanistan—Further Papers.
	C. 2401	Further Correspondence, Afghanistan, 1878-79.
1878-79	C. 2402	Despatch from SS. 7 August 1879.
1881	C. 2844	Correspondence, 1879-81 re: Russia's military operations.
	C. 3032	Occupation of Tekke Turcoman country by Russia.
1884	C. 3930	Central Asia: Correspondence, in continuation of C. 3032.
1884-85	C. 4387	Further Correspondence:
	C. 4389	Central Asia, Afghan Boundary Commission, Panjdeh Affairs etc.
	C. 4418	
1887	C. 5114	Central Asia, Further Correspondence re: Afghan boundary and its further delimitation.
1890	C. 6072	Kashmir: Papers relating to.
1892	C. 6621	Hunza Expedition: Correspondence.

(B) Parliamentary Debates

Third and Fourth Series: Select volumes such as have been referred to in footnotes.

(C) India Government Records

(*i*) Report of a Mission to Yarkand in 1873, Calcutta 1875.

(*ii*) Sir-i-Kol, Chilas, and the North-eastern Boundary of Afghanistan, Calcutta 1879.

(*iii*) The Famine in Kashmir during 1877-80 (by F. Henvey), Kashmir 1880.

(*iv*) The Kashmir Army (by Major J. Biddulph) Calcutta 1880.

(*v*) Gilgit Diary (by Major J. Biddulph), Calcutta 1881.

(*vi*) Memo, by Major J. Biddulph on the present condition of affairs in Gilgit 1881.

(*vii*) Routes of the hill country about Gilgit (by Major J. Biddulph), Calcutta 1881.

(*viii*) Account of Dardistan, Dehra Dun 1884.

(*ix*) Confidential Gazetteer of Kashmir and Ladakh, Calcutta 1890.

(*x*) Correspondence relating to the operations in Hunza and Nagar, Calcutta 1892.

(D) Punjab Administration Reports.

Select volumes.

(E) Other Published Sources of an Official Character: Treaties, Reports, Memoranda etc.

Aitchison, C.U., *A Collection of Treaties, Engagements and Sanads Relating to India and Neighbouring Countries*, Fifth Edition, Calcutta 1929-33.

Baird, J.G. (ed.), *Private Letters of Lord Dalhousie*, Edinburgh 1910.

Barrow, E.G., *Confidential Gazetteer of Dardistan and Kafiristan*, Calcutta 1885.

.........., *Memo, on the Strategical Aspect of Chitral and the Hindu Kush Regions*, Simla 1886.

Bates, C., *A Gazetteer of Kashmir,* Calcutta 1873.

Benson, A.C. and Brett, R.B. (ed.), *The Letters of Queen Victoria*, 3 Vols., London 1907.

Bower, H., *Confidential Report of a Journey in Chinese Turkistan*, 1889-90, Calcutta 1891.

Buckle, G.E., *The Letters of Queen Victoria*, 2nd Series, 3 Vols., London 1928.

Campbell, F., *Catalogue of Official Reports Relating to India,* London 1893.

Crawford, J., *Cashmere Precis,* Calcutta 1884.

Douglas, J.A., *Report on Gor,* Simla 1884.

Dufferin, Marquis of., *Summary of the Principal Measures of the Viceroyalty*, Calcutta 1888.

Elias, N., *Confidential Report of a Mission to Chinese Turkistan and Badakshan in 1885-86*, Calcutta 1886.

Forsyth, T.D., *Memo, on Trade with Central Asia*, Calcutta 1879. *Imperial Gazetteer of India, New Series*, Oxford 1908.

Lansdowne, Marquis of, *Summary of the Principal Measures of the Viceroyalty*, December, 1888-January, 1894.

Lockhart, W.S.A. and Woodthorpe, R.G., *Confidential Report of the Gilgit Mission, 1885-86,* London 1889.

Macgregor, C.M., *The Defence of India Confidential Report on the Explorations in Part of Eastern Afghanistan and in Kafiristan during 1883*, Dehra Dun 1885.

Meyendorff, A.F., *Correspondence Diplomatique de M. de Staal, 1884-1900, 2 Vols.*, Paris 1929.

Plowden, T.C., *Confidential Precis of Correspondence Relating to Affairs on Central Asia, 1875-77*, Calcutta 1878.

Robertson, G.S., *Confidential Report of a Journey to Kafiristan,* London 1894.

Roberson, W.R., *An Official Account of the Chitral Expedition,* Calcutta 1898.

St. John, O.B.C., *Confidential Notes on Afghanistan as a Theatre of War*, Simla 1885.

Singh, G., *Private Correspondence Relating to the Anglo-Sikh Wars*, Amritsar, 1955.

Temple, R., *Journals Kept in Hyderabad, Cashmir, Sikkim and Nepal, 2 Vols.*, London 1887.

Trotter, H., *Secret and Confidential Report on the Trans-Himalayan Explorations by the Great Trigonometrical Survey of India during 1873-75*, Calcutta 1876.

Wallace, D.M. (ed.), *Dufferin's Speeches in India, 1884-88,* London 1890.

Younghusband, F.E., *Confidential Report of a Mission to the Northern Frontier of Kashmir in 1889*, Calcutta 1890.

III. NEWSPAPERS & PERIODICALS

(*a*) Newspapers

The Amrita Bazar Patrika,
The Bengalee,
The Civil and Military Gazette,
The Englishman,
The Friend of India,
The Hindoo Patriot,
The Indian Mirror,
The Pioneer,
The Statesman,
The Times, London.
Selections from the Vernacular Newspapers.

(*b*) Periodicals

Asiatic Quarterly Review,
Asiatic Researches,
Bulletin of the School of Oriental and African Studies,
Central Asian Review,
Central Asiatic Journal,
Indian Historical Quarterly,
Journal of Asian Studies,
Journal of the Royal Asiatic Society,
Journal of the Royal Central Asian Society,
Proceedings of the Royal Geographical Society.

IV. SELECT SECONDARY WORKS

Aitchison, C.U., *Lord Lawrence and the Reconstruction of India under the Crown*, Oxford 1897.

Alder, G.J., *British India's Northern Frontier, 1865-95*, London 1963.

Anon., *Letters from India and Kashmir, written 1870*, London 1874.

Anon., *The Foreign Policy of Lord Rosebery*, London 1901.

Argyll, Duchess of, *Autobiography and Memoirs of George Douglas, 8th Duke of Argyll, 2 Vols.*, London 1906.

Argyll, Duke of, *India under Dalhousie and Canning*, London 1865.

..........., *The Eastern Question*, 2 Vols., London 1879.

Arnold, E., *The Marquis of Dalhousie's Administration of British India*, 2 Vols., London 1862.

Balfour, B., *The History of Lord Lytton's Indian Administration*, London 1899.

Bamzai, P.N.K., *A History of Kashmir*, Delhi 1962.

Barton, W., The *Princes of India,* London 1934.

Bau, M.J., *The Foreign Relations of China*, London 1922.

Bell, E., *The Annexation of the Punjab and Maharaja Daleep Singh*, London 1882.

Bell, M.S., *China: Reconnaissance Journey through the Central and Western Provinces.........to Ladakh and India*, 2 Vols., *Confidential*, Calcutta 1888.

Bellew, H.W., *Kashmir and Kashgar,* London 1875.

Biddulph, J., *The Tribes of the Hindoo Koosh,* London 1880.

Birdwood, Lord, *A Continent Decides*, London 1953.

Black, C.E.D., *The Marquess of Dufferin and Ava,* London, 1903.

Blacker, L.V.S., *On Secret Patrol in High Asia,* London 1922.

Blunt, W.S., *India under Ripon,* London 1909.

Boggs, S.W., *International Boundaries*, New York 1940.

Bonvalot, G., *Through the Heart of Asia, Over the Pamir to India*, 2 Vols., London 1889.

Bose, J.C., *Cashmere and Its Prince,* Calcutta 1889.

Boulger, D.C., *The Life of Sir Halliday Macartney*, London 1908.

Bourbel, R. de, *Routes in Jammu and Kashmir,* Calcutta 1897.

Brinckman, A., *The Rifle in Cashmere,* London 1862.

Bruce, C.D., *Chinese Turkistan,* London 1907.

Bruce, C.G. (Mrs.), *Kashmir,* London 1911.

Bruce, C.G., *Twenty Years in the Himalaya*, London 1910.

..........., *Himalayan Wanderer*, London 1934.

Burne, O.T., *Memories,* London 1907.

Cable, A.M., *The Challenge of Central Asia,* London 1929.

Cecil, Lady G., *Life of Marquis of Salisbury,* 4 Vols., London 1921-32.

Churchill, W.S., *Lord Randolph Churchill,* 2 Vols., London 1951.

Charak, Sukhdev Singh, *History and Culture of Himalayan States, II.*

Clark, J., *Hunza: Lost Kingdom of the Himalayas*, London 1957.

Clarke, M., *From Simla Through Ladac and Cashmere*, Calcutta 1862.

Coates, T.F.G., *Lord Rosebery, His Life and Speeches,* 2 Vols., London 1900.

Cobbold, R., *Innermost Asia,* London 1900.

Crewe, Marquess of, *Lord Rosebery,* 2 Vols., London 1931.

Cunningham, A., *Ladak Physical, Statistical and Historical,* London 1854.

Curtis, W.E., *Turkistan: The Heart of Asia*, London 1911.

Curzos, G.N., *Russia in Central Asia in 1889 and the Anglo-Russian Question*, London 1889.

............, *The Pamirs and the Source of the Oxus*, London 1897.

Danvers, F.C., *An Index to Events Relating to India and the East Referred to in The Times, 1850-89*, London 1897.

Davies, C.C., *The Problem of the North-West Frontier*, 1809-1908, Cambridge 1932.

Digby, W., *The Queen Empress's Promises: How they are Broken. A Letter to the Members of the House of Commons*, London 1889.

.... *Condemned Unheard: The Government of India and H.H. The Maharaja of Kashmir*, London 1890.

Dilke, C.W., *The Present Position of European Politics,* London, 1887.

Dilke, C.W. & Wilkinson, S., *Imperial Defence,* London 1892.

Dobson, G., *Russia's Railway Advance into Central Asia,* London 1890.

Dodwell, H.H. (ed.), *The Cambridge History of India,* Vol. VI, Cambridge 1932.

Doughty, M., *A Foot Through the Kashmir Valleys*, London 1902.

Douglas, W.O., *Beyond the High Himalayas,* London 1953.

Douie, J.M, *The Punjab, North-West Frontier Province and Kashmir*, Cambridge 1916.

Drew, F., *The Northern Barrier of India, A Popular Account of the Jammoo and Kashmir Territories*, London 1877.

............, *The Jammoo and Kashmir Territories: A Geographical Account*, London 1875.

Dufferin and Ava, Marchioness of, *Our Vice regal Life in India*, 2 Vols., London 1889.

Dummore, The Earl of, *The Pamirs*, 2 Vols., London 1893.

Durand, A.G.A., *The Making of a Frontier*, London 1899.

Durand, H.M., *The Amir Abdul Rahman Khan*, London 1907.

............., *Life of Sir Alfred Comyn Lyall*, London 1913.

Dutt, P., *Memoir of Motilal Ghose*, Calcutta 1935.

Eastwick, E.G., *Handbook of the Punjab, Cashmere and Upper Sindh*, London 1883.

Eckenstein, C., *The Karakorams and Kashmir*, London 1896.

The Editor, The People's Journal, *The Kashmir Conspiracy or The Truth of the Maharaja's Case—Being a Reproduction of a Series of Articles from the People's Journal*, Lahore 1890.

Edwardes, H.B. and Merivale, H., *Life of Sir Henry Lawrence*, 2 Vols., London 1872.

Edwards, L., *Reminiscences of Forty-three Years in India*, London 1874.

Elsmie, G.R., *Thirty-five Years in the Punjab*, Edinburgh 1908.

Etherton, P.T., *Across the Roof of the World*, London 1911.

..........., *In the Heart of Asia*, London 1925.

Featherstone, B.K., *An Unexplored Pass*, London 1926.

Ferguson, J.P., *Kashmir*, London 1961.

Fillipi, F. de, *Karakoram and the Western Himalaya*, London 1909.

Forrest, G.W., *The Administration of the Marquis of Lansdowne, 1888-94*, Calcutta 1894.

................, *The Life of Lord Roberts*, London 1914.

Forsyth, E. (ed.), *Autobiography and Reminiscences of Sir Douglas Forsyth*, London 1887.

Fraser, D., *The Strategic Position of Russia in Central Asia*, London 1904.

Gadru, S.N., *Kashmir Papers*, Srinagar 1973.

Gathorne-Hardy, A.E. (ed.), *Gathorne-Hardy, First Earl of Cranbrook, A Memoir*, 2 Vols., London 1910.

Ghose, D.K., England and Afghanistan, A Phase in Their Relations, Calcutta 1960.

..............., *Kashmir in Transition*, Calcutta 1975.

Gibbon, F.P., *The Lawrences of the Punjab*, London 1908.

Gleason, J.H., *The Genesis of Russophoia in Great Britain*, Harvard 1950.

Gopal, S., *The Viceroyalty of Lord Ripon, 1880-84*, London 1953.

Gordon, H., *The War Office*, London 1935.

Gordon, T.E., *The Roof of the World*, Edinburg 1876.

Graham, S., *Through Central Asia*, New York 1916.

Greaves, R., *Persia and the Defence of India, 1884-92*, London 1959.

Grulef, M., *The Rivalry of Russia and England in Central Asia*, St. Petersburg, 1909.

Hamley, E.B., *The Strategical Conditions of Our North-West Frontier*, London 1878.

Hanna, H.B., *Indian Problems*, 3 Vols., London 1869.

Harcourt, A.F.P., *Our Northern Frontier*, London 1869.

Harding, H.I., *Diary of a Journey from Srinagar to Kashgar, via Gilgit* (for private circulation only), London 1922.

Hassnain, F.M., *British Policy Towards Kashmir*, 1974.

.........., *Gilgit, The Northern Gate of India*, 1978.

Hasrat, Bikramajit, *Punjab Papers*, 1974.

Hervey, Mrs., *Adventures of a Lady in Tartary, Tibet, China and Kashmir, 3 Vols*., London 1853.

Holdich, T.H., *Political Frontiers and Boundary Making*, London 1916.

Hunter, W.W., *A Life of the Earl of Mayo*, 2 Vols., London 1876.

India, Standing Committee of the Chamber of Princes, *The British Crown and the Indian States*, London 1929.

Indian Officer, *Russia's March Towards India*, London 1894.

Innes, J.J., *Sir Henry Lawrence*, London 1898.

James, D., *Lord Roberts*, London 1954.

James, L., *With the Chitral Relief Force*, Calcutta 1895.

Jeyes, S.H., *The Life and Times of Marquis of Salisbury*, 4 Vols., London 1895-96.

Kapoor, M.L., *Kashmir Sold and Snatched*, Jammu, 1968.

Kaul, G.L., *Kashmir Through the Ages*, Srinagar 1960.

Kaye, J., *Lives of Indian Officers,* 2 Vols., London 1904.
Khan, S.M. (ed.), *Autobiography of Abdur Rahman Khan,* 2 Vols., London 1900.
Khilnani, N.M., *The Punjab under the Lawrences,* Simla 1951.
Knight, E.F., *Where Three Empires Meet,* London 1893.
Knight, W.H., *Diary of a Pedestrian in Cashmere and Tibet,* London 1863.
Korkell Joseph, *Danger in Kashmir*, 1954.
Lamb, A., *Britain and Chinese Central Asia*, London 1960.
Lambert, C., *A Trip to Cashmere and Ladak*, London 1877.
Langer, W., *European Alliances and Alignments*, New York 1950.
Lansdell, H., *Through Central Asia*, London 1887.
..........., *Chinese Central Asia,* 2 Vols., London 1893.
Lattimore, O., *Inner Asian Frontiers of China,* New York 1951.
Lawrence, W., *The Valley of Kashmir,* London 1895.
..........., *The India We Served*, London 1928.
Layard, A., *Autobiography and Letters,* 2 Vols., London 1903.
Lee-Warner, W., *The Life of the Marquis of Dalhousie,* 2 Vols., London 1904.
.............., *The Native States of India*, London 1910.
Leitner, G.W., *Results of a Tour in Dardistan, Kashmir, Little Thibet, Ladak etc.*, London 1969-78.
.............., *The Languages and Races of Dardistan*, Lahore 1877.
.............., *The Hunza and Nagar Handbook*, Woking 1893.
.............., *Dardistan in 1895,* Woking 1895.
Low, C.R., *Major-General Sir Frederick Roberts*, London 1883.
Lyall, A., *The Life of the Marquis of Dufferin and Ava*, 2 Vols., London 1905.
Macgregor, Lady C., *Life and Opinions of Sir C.M. Macgregor*, 2 Vols., London 1888.
Mac Intyre, D., *Hindu Koh: Wanderings, and Wild Sport on and Beyond the Himalayas*, London 1889.
Maisey, F., *The Typography, Ethnology, Resources and History of Ladak*, Calcutta 1878.
Mallet, B., *Thomas George, Earl of Northbrook*, London 1908.
Malmesbury, S., *The Life of the Major General Sir John Ardagh*, London 1909.

Marden, W., *Across Asia's Snows and Deserts*, New York 1927.

Mason, K., *Routes in the Western Himalaya, Kashmir etc.* Calcutta 1929.

Mersey, Viscount, *The Viceroys and Governor-General of India, 1857-1947*, London 1949.

Milne, J., *The Road to Kashmir,* London 1929.

Misra, J.P., *The Indian Administration of India under Lord Lansdowne*, 1975.

Mons, B.H., *High Road to Hunza,* London 1958.

Montgomerie, T.G., *Routes in the Western Himalayas, Kashmir etc.*, London 1874.

Morison, J.L., *From Alexander Burnes to Frederick Roberts—A Survey of Imperial Frontier Policy*, Raleigh Lecture, 1936.

Murray-Aynsley, J.C., *Our Visit to Hindostan, Kashmir and Ladakh*, London 1879.

Nazaroff, P.S., *Moved On ! From Kashgar to Kashmir*, London, 1935.

Neve, A., *Picturesque Kashmir,* London 1900.

.............., *Thirty Years in Kashmir*, London 1913.

Newall, D.J.F., *The Highlands of India Strategically Considered,* 2 Vols., London 1882.

Newby, E., *A Short Walk in the Hindu Kush,* London 1958.

Newman, E., *Umra Khan and the Chitral Campaign of 1895,* Lahore 1897.

Nicholson, A.P., *Scraps of Paper: India's Broken Treaties, Her Princes, and Their Problem*, London 1930.

Norins, M.R., *Gateway to Asia,* New York 1944.

Olufsen, O., *Through the Unknown Pamirs*, London 1904.

Pal, D., *The Administration of Sir John Lawrence in India, 1864-69*, Simla 1952.

Panikkar, K.M., *Introduction to the Study of the Relations of Indian States with the Government of India*, London 1927.

.............., *Indian States and the Government of India*, London 1932.

.............., *Gulab Singh, or the Founding of the Kashmir State,* London 1953.

Pavlovsky, M.N., *Chinese-Russian Relations*, New York 1949.

Pithawala, M.B., *An Introduction to Kashmir, its Geology and Geography*, Muzaffarbad 1953.

Pritchard, I.T., *The Administration of India, 1859-1868*, 2 Vols., London 1869.

Rawlinson, G., *A Memoir of Major-General Sir H. Rawlinson,* London 1898.

Ripon, The First Marquess of, *The Native States of India,* London 1886.

Roberts, F., *Forty-one Years in India,* 2 Vols., London 1917.

Roberts, P.E., *A Historical Geography of India,* 2 Vols., Oxford 1916.

Robertson, G.S., *Chitral*, London 1898 *Kafirs of the Hindu Kush*, London 1896.

Ronaldshay, The Earl of, *The Life of Lord Curzon*, 2 Vols., London 1928.

Sapru, A.N., *Building of the Jammu and Kashmir State*, Punjab Record Office No. 12, n.d.

Saraf, Mohammad Yusuf, *Kashmiris Fight for Freedom,* Volume I, Lahore 1977.

Schomberg, R.C., *Between the Oxus and the Indus*, London, 1935.

.............., *Unknown Karakoram*, London 1936.

Schuyler, E., *Turkistan,* 2 Vols., London 1882.

Seaver, G., *Francis Younghusband, 1863-1942*, London 1952.

Showers, C.L., *The Cossack at the Gate of India*, London 1885.

Sinclair, G., *Khyber Caravan, Through Kashmir, Waziristan etc.*, London 1936.

Skrede, W., *Across the Roof of the World,* (Transl.) London, 1954.

Skrine, C.P., *Chinese Central Asia,* London 1926.

Smith, B., *Life of Lord Lawrence,* 2 Vols., London 1885.

Stein, M.A., *Mountain Panoramas from the Pamirs and Kwen Lun*, London 1908.

.............., *An Archaeological Tour in Upper Swat and Adjacent Hill Tracks*, Calcutta 1930.

Strong, A.L., *The Road to the Grey Pamir*, Boston 1931.

Sufi, G.M.D., *Kashmir: Being the History of Kashmir from the Earliest Times to Our Own*, Lahore 1949.

Sykes, P.M., *The Right Honourable Sir Mortimer Durand,* London 1926.

Taylor, A.J.P., *The Struggle for Mastery in Europe, 1848-1918,* Oxford 1954.

Taylor, B., *Travels in Cashmere, Little Thibet and Central Asia,* New York 1874.

Teng, Kaul Bhatt, Kashmir: Constitutional History of Documents, New Delhi 1977.

Thompson, H.C., *The Chitral Campaign,* London 1895.

Thorp, R., *Cashmere Misgovernment,* London 1870.

Tilman, H.W., *China to Chitral,* Cambridge 1951.

Torrens, H.D., *Travels in Ladak, Tartary and Kashmir*, London 1862.

Trinkler, E., *The Storm Swept Roof of Asia,* Philadelphia 1931.

Vigne, G.T., *Travels in Kashmir, Ladak, Iskardo etc.,* 2 Vols., London 1842.

Wakefield, W.W.V., *Happy Valley,* London 1879.

West, A., *Private Diaries,* London 1922.

.............., *Sir Charles Wood's Administration of Indian Affairs,* 1859-66, London 1867.

Wolf, L., *Life of the First Marquess of Ripon*, 2 Vols., London 1921.

Yasin, Madhavi, *Indian Administration,* 1979.

Younghusband, F.E., *The Heart of a Continent. A Narrative of Travels etc., Through the Himalayas, the Pamirs and Hunza, 1884-94*, London 1896.

.............., *Kashmir,* London 1924.

Younghusband, F.E. and G.J., *The Relief of Chitral,* London 1895.

Younghusband, G.J., *Forty Years a Soldier,* London 1923.

Index

Q

R

S

T